W9-AZR-930

Contents

No-Nonsense
COVER
LETTERS

The Essential Guide to
Creating Attention-Grabbing
Cover Letters That Get
Interviews & Job Offers

Wendy S. Enelow
Master Resume Writer

Arnold G. Boldt
Certified Professional Resume Writer

CAREER
PRESS

Franklin Lakes, NJ

No-Nonsense Cover Letters
Edited by Kara Reynolds
Typeset by Eileen Dow Munson
Cover design by Design Concept
Printed in the U.S.A. by Book-mart Press

To order this title, please call toll-free 1-800-CAREER-1 (NJ and Canada: 201-848-0310) to order using VISA or MasterCard, or for further information on books from Career Press.

The Career Press, Inc., 3 Tice Road, PO Box 687,
Franklin Lakes, NJ 07417
www.careerpress.com

Library of Congress Cataloging-in-Publication Data

Enelow, Wendy S.
    No-nonsense cover letters : the essential guide to creating attention-grabbing cover letters that get interviews and job offers / by Wendy S. Enelow and Arnold G. Boldt.
        p. cm.
    Includes bibliographical references and index.
    ISBN-13: 978-1-56414-906-0
    ISBN-10: 1-56414-906-4
    1. Cover letters—Handbooks, manuals, etc. 2. Applications for positions—Handbooks, manuals, etc. I. Boldt, Arnold G. II. Title.

HF5383.E47894 2007
650.14′2--dc22
                                                                    2006022101

Introduction

Cover letters are often considered the plague of the job search. Most job seekers spend a great deal of time and effort preparing a winning resume, and then fail to appreciate just how important cover letters are to their successful efforts. To ensure that you don't fall into this trap, we've written this book to share our insider secrets to cover letter writing, design, formatting, and distribution.

If you're currently in the job market, we've got some great news for you! According to the U.S. Bureau of Labor Statistics, total employment in the United States is expected to increase by 14.7 percent between the years 2004 and 2014 (*www.bls.gov*). As the numbers indicate, it's a great time to be looking for a job, whatever your particular situation (such as graduating college student, skilled tradesperson, mid-level professional, senior-level executive, return-to-work mom, or military veteran). Opportunities are everywhere, and *your* challenge is to position yourself so that you can capture those opportunities and land a great new job.

Developing a powerful cover letter to accompany your resume is key to opening doors and generating interviews. Ultimately, cover letters and resumes do not get jobs; people do. But by creating a set of documents that clearly communicate who you are, what you can do, and how well you do it, you can present yourself as a desirable candidate in the eyes of prospective employers. Equipping yourself with one or more cover letters that complement a powerful resume will instantly give you a distinct and measurable advantage over your competition.

To help you achieve that competitive edge, we've created a one-of-a-kind cover letter book that clearly and concisely guides you through the letter-writing process. To be sure that this book is easy to use, we've cut through all the confusion and gotten right down to brass tacks: our no-nonsense approach. We've given you the information you need, provided you with the worksheets to assemble all of your information, demonstrated how and where to use that information, and included more than 100 sample cover letters addressing a wide array of situations. When you're finished with this book, you should have a cover letter, or perhaps a set of letters, that are powerful and polished—true no-nonsense cover letters that position you to successfully pursue your career goals.

As you read this book, you will note references to *No-Nonsense Resumes*, our companion book (also from Career Press), which provides you with similar insights into the resume-writing process. We encourage you to consult that book in preparing your resume and use the two books together in developing an integrated and powerful approach to your job search documents.

Chapter 1

▶ Simple Truths About Cover Letters

There was a time when cover letters were merely letters of transmittal. They simply alerted the reader that the applicant was enclosing a resume and was available for an interview. Today, however, as the job market has become both more sophisticated and more competitive, the importance of cover letters has changed dramatically.

Covers letters have evolved into a vital part of the "package" a job seeker presents to a prospective employer. Well-constructed cover letters must simultaneously complement your resume, address an employer's job requirements, and communicate your strengths to the hiring manager. In a word, your cover letters must *sell* you as the ideal candidate for the job. As with your resume, cover letters encompass a unique combination of creative language, careful planning and strategy, and effective execution.

As professional resume writers, we follow a very systematic, *no-nonsense* approach to cover letter writing that has helped tens of thousands of job seekers grab the attention of employers, secure interviews, and achieve their career goals. Now, we're going to share that information with you in the first-ever, *no-nonsense* guide to cover letter writing that gives you insider secrets to writing polished, well-positioned, and powerful cover letters. If you follow the steps, activities, and strategies outlined in this book, you'll be able to prepare cover letters that work hand-in-hand with your resume to offer employers sharp, distinctive, on-target presentations that will generate interviews and offers. For more information and advice on writing your resume, be sure to consult our companion book, *No-Nonsense Resumes* (Career Press, 2006).

uths About Cover Letter Writing

your cover letters, there are six key concepts that you
ional resume writers live by these truths and understand
afting cover letters that position applicants as attractive
areer opportunities.

ive cover letters contain 10 key components.

Truth #2: Cover letter writing is sales.

Truth #3: Cover letter writing is all about strategy.

Truth #4: Targeted letters work best.

Truth #5: The cover letter must match the resume.

Truth #6: Each circumstance presents its own challenges.

If you can truly grasp what these concepts mean and how they apply to your particular job search situation, you will be able to write powerful letters that will attract an employer's attention and lead to interviews. Let's explore each of these simple truths in much greater detail.

Truth #1: Effective Cover Letters Contain 10 Key Components

If it's been a while since you have been engaged in an active job search, you may well be asking yourself, "Exactly what goes into a cover letter? What should I say?" Following is a list of the key elements every letter should contain, followed by an example that effectively integrates all 10 components. Chapter 2 (design and formatting) and Chapter 3 (cover letter writing) deal with essential format and content issues in much greater detail, but for now, remember to include each of these items in your letters:

1. **Your contact information:** Name, phone number, and (personal) e-mail address should appear at the top.

2. **Date:** The preferred format: December 12, 2006.

3. **Inside address:** The name and address of the person who will receive the letter.

4. **Reference line:** This line is optional, but when used, should appear directly below the inside address. It states the title of the position for which you are applying and may include a reference code or job number if applicable.

5. **Salutation:** This is the familiar, "Dear Mr. Jones:" or "Dear Ms. Smith:". If you don't know the name of the recipient, it might say, "Dear Hiring Authority:" or "Dear Sir/Madam:".

6. **Opening paragraph:** Who you are and why you are writing. The more compelling this is, the better.

7. **Content/main body of the letter:** Your unique skills and why you are an ideal candidate for the job opening in question.

8. **Closing paragraph/call to action:** Ask for an interview or tell the recipient that you will follow up soon to schedule an interview.

9. **Closing:** "Sincerely," "Respectfully," or another similarly appropriate closing, followed by your signature.

10. **Enclosures:** Reference what other documents are enclosed in the "package" (for example, resume, reference list, job application, and/ or leadership profile). Do not include anything that was not requested. Note that this element—enclosures—is optional and does not necessarily have to be included to make your letter effective.

The example on the following page illustrates the 10 key components of every successful cover letter.

Truth #2: Cover Letter Writing Is Sales

Just as with resumes, cover letter writing is about sales, marketing, and brand positioning. Envision yourself as a unique and special commodity: just the right solution to a problem for employers who need the *features and benefits* you have to offer. Your resume should reflect the best plan for *marketing* yourself to those employers who have a *demand* for the skills and qualifications you offer. If developed properly, your resume should serve you well throughout your job search. In some instances, you may wish to "tweak" your resume to emphasize a particular skillset or highlight an accomplishment especially relevant to a particular job opening, but by and large, it will remain the same.

By contrast, when you write your cover letters, your goal should be to demonstrate to a *particular* employer just how your unique skills and qualifications relate to that firm's *specific* needs. As such, each cover letter you write will be unique, depending on the recipient and the specifics of the situation (job description, your research on the company, or other information you've learned about challenges facing the employer).

Think of the cover letter/resume package that you present to a prospective employer as a piece of direct-mail advertising. Not unlike direct-mail pieces that arrive in our mailboxes, the goal of the cover letter and resume package is to grab the reader's attention and prompt that person to act; namely, by reading the cover letter and resume, and then offering the candidate the opportunity for an interview.

The *no-nonsense* approach to the job search is a bit more subtle than that used by mass advertisers in direct-mail campaigns. However, the underlying strategy is the same: specifically, prompting the recipient to read and respond to the material in a favorable manner. Your cover letter must capture the reader's interest and draw him or her into the resume, ultimately encouraging a decision-maker (HR director or hiring manager) to decide, "I want to speak to this candidate!"

DENNIS GREGORY

1. Contact Information

6 Cranberry Grove • Farmington, New York 14425 • 585-924-9999 • dennis@resumesos.com

April 24, 2007

2. Date

Ms. Rosanna Rodriguez
Managing Partner
Executive Search Partners, LLC
1234 Executive Tower
New York, NY 10199

3. Inside Address

4. Reference Line

Re: Financial Management / Operations Management Opportunities

Dear Ms. Rodriguez:

5. Salutation

6. Introductory Paragraph

Following a rewarding career in the U.S. Air Force, where I gained extensive experience in the areas of financial management, operations management, employee development, and project management, I am seeking a new opportunity that will capitalize on one or more of my skillsets. With this goal in mind, I have enclosed a resume for your consideration that briefly outlines my background.

Some of the ways I can bring unique value to one of your clients include:

✓ Analyzing business operations and developing strategies that optimize the utilization of capital assets and human resources. Often, I have been able to cut costs and reduce headcount while simultaneously expanding operational capabilities and production capacities.

✓ Designing strategic plans for large-scale global organizations to ensure that operational objectives and budgetary requirements are maintained. I served as Director of Operations for headquarters and subordinate operating units encompassing 1,500 people and a $52 million annual budget.

✓ Employing innovative, "out-of-the-box" approaches to solving complex financial, logistical, and operational problems. During my career, I have pursued creative approaches to funding projects and devised innovative solutions to unique problems.

✓ Spearheading IT infrastructure initiatives and addressing a full range of facilities management issues which have included needs assessment, site selection, vendor negotiation, and project management functions.

✓ Demonstrating a consistent pattern of sound independent judgement, and the ability to communicate vision and mission to subordinates, colleagues, and the general public.

7. Content/ Main Body of the Letter

I believe that I can contribute to a dynamic firm in a financial management, operations management, and/or project management role, and would welcome an opportunity to speak with you in detail about how I can address the needs of one of your clients. I will contact you early next week to arrange a convenient time for initiating a dialogue.

8. Closing/ Paragraph Call to Action

Thank you for your time and consideration. I look forward to talking with you soon.

Sincerely,

Dennis Gregory

Dennis Gregory

9. Closing & Signature

Enclosures: Resume; References; Management Philosophy

10. Enclosures

Know Your Audience

The first step in writing your *no-nonsense* cover letter is to know your target audience and understand their needs and desires. Try to put yourself in the employer's shoes and recognize how the unique skills and qualifications you offer will be able to address that employer's specific needs. Your cover letter should focus on your capabilities as they directly relate to the target company's particular requirements.

If you're applying for a specific position, the job posting should give you a great deal of information about what skills, knowledge, competencies, and other qualities are essential. When you're applying to a company in the absence of a specific job advertisement, you can learn a great deal about the organization, its needs, and its challenges by researching the company on the Internet. This will allow you to focus your letter on the skills and experiences you offer that will help the employer meet those challenges.

Position Yourself as "The" Solution

In our companion book, *No-Nonsense Resumes*, we stressed the importance of writing your resume in the first person. When you write your cover letters, you still want the focus to be on you, the candidate, and you may use the first person where appropriate. However, to be optimally effective, your cover letter should position you as the solution to one or more of the *employer's* challenges. The prospective employer should feel that you are writing *to* him or her, that you know what his or her firm needs, and that you can deliver what you promise. For this reason, we recommend that you minimize the use of the personal pronoun, "I," especially at the beginning of a sentence or paragraph. The goal is to highlight your qualifications for the job, while at the same time making the employer believe that you understand the firm's specific needs and can fulfill them. Take a look at these two examples of opening paragraphs to better understand what we mean:

Example #1: Overuse of "I"

Dear Ms. Smith:

I am most interested in the position of Customer Service Representative you advertised in Sunday's newspaper. **I** believe that **I** can perform this job very well, and **I** have enclosed my resume, which highlights my skills and qualifications.

Example #2: Same message, with focus on the employer

Dear Ms. Smith:

Your recent advertisement for a Customer Service Representative appears to be an excellent match for my existing capabilities. My account relations experience, organizational skills, and careful attention to detail are all consistent with **your** requirements for this position, as you'll note on my enclosed resume.

Examples 1 and 2 convey the same information, but notice how Example 2 flows much more smoothly and engages the reader more fully by the strategic use of second-person pronouns (you, your, and so on).

Here are two more examples, from the middle paragraphs of a cover letter, that also demonstrate the concept of focusing your letter on the employer's needs:

Example #3: Poorly placed first-person pronouns

I expedited customer orders at Medco, where I also resolved billing discrepancies and tracked shipments. I also advised customers about new products that were potentially beneficial to their business. I note that these skills are similar to those mentioned in your job posting.

Example #4: Better sentence structure and use of pronouns

Among my duties at Medco, I expedited orders, resolved billing discrepancies, and tracked shipments, as well as promoting new products to existing accounts. All of these functions directly relate to the duties outlined in **your** posting.

The goal is to make the reader feel like the focus is on *him* or *her,* even though your objective is to tout *your own* skills and qualifications.

Taking this concept one step further, your ultimate goal is to *sell* yourself to potential employers. Draw the reader into the resume by referencing one or more of your accomplishments that are clearly relevant to the employer's specific hiring needs. Demonstrate how you can be a solution to a challenge facing the business. Both of these concepts are demonstrated in this example:

Example #5: Selling yourself into your next job

You'll notice on my enclosed resume that while at Automotive Electric, Inc., I was instrumental in reducing scrap and reworks on the armature winding line by 83%, leading to annualized savings approaching $500K. I understand that your firm is aggressively pursuing Lean Manufacturing initiatives driven by cost-reduction programs. My demonstrated success in achieving tangible results in this area will be an asset to your manufacturing operations as you seek to advance these goals.

Also inherent in the previous example is the "Sell It; Don't Tell It" concept, which is a compelling way to communicate your value and the benefits you can bring to a new employer. Rather than simply *telling* your reader what you have done, you want to *sell* what you've accomplished and contributed. Here are some more examples:

Example #6: Sell It; Don't Tell It

➤ **Telling It:**

> I performed customer service and inside sales duties for a firm selling hydraulic valves.

➤ **Selling It:**

> As an Account Manager for Valiant Valves, I maintained a 93% customer satisfaction rating (second highest in the department) and was the leader among a 10-member team in selling additional products and services to my existing account base.

➤ **Telling It:**

> I handled general ledger, accounts payable, and payroll functions for a large company.

➤ **Selling It:**

> In my capacity as a Senior Staff Accountant, I managed general ledger and accounts payable for a $26 million manufacturing operation, plus administering payroll for 120 hourly and 14 salaried employees.

Notice how each of the "Sell It" examples *sells* the candidate's capabilities by offering *quantitative* information about the scope of that individual's responsibilities and measurable results. As you read the later chapters of this book, you will see numerous additional examples of how this sales principle can be powerfully applied to virtually any career field.

Truth #3: Cover Letter Writing Is All About Strategy

When we talk about cover letter strategy, it's really all about understanding *who* your audience is and what *approach* will be most appealing to a particular audience. The tone, content, and format of your cover letters will necessarily change based on what you know about the reader. Is that person a recruiter or does he or she work for the company? In Chapter 3 we discuss in detail how to create letters that are appropriate for each of these different recipients. For now, just know that it's important to understand that the message you communicate and the information you share will differ from one audience to another.

The lion's share of cover letters that you will write over the course of your job search will most likely be directed to companies—the firms that would actually employ you, and many of those will be for specific job openings. These letters should be targeted to the specific opportunity, and you should avoid sending a generic, one-size-fits-all cover letter in such circumstances.

The best way to approach these letters is to carefully read the job posting and identify how your qualifications match what the employer is seeking.

16 ...Ils and accomplishments demonstrate your ability to fulfill ...quirements as stated in the job description. Then write a cover ...s your capabilities to that specific employer for that specific job. Exa... bullet points work best when you want to convey a list of specific th... ...cations, skills, projects, or achievements. Paragraphs, on the other hand, ...w you to tell one or more brief *stories* about how your experiences relate to the employer's needs.

Unique Strategies for Writing to Recruiters

Recruiters are generally in a hurry and, with a few exceptions, they only get paid if they find the ideal candidate for their customer, the *employer* that they represent. Note that we said they represent the *employer,* not the *job seeker.* This is a vitally important concept to remember because the recruiter's motivation lies completely in satisfying the hiring company. For this reason, cover letters directed to recruiters should be succinct and to the point, so bullet-format letters are often your best choice.

You may also want to include information in a letter to a recruiter that many experts would advise against including in a letter written directly to an employer. This might include information about your salary history or salary requirements, geographic preferences, and availability for travel. That type of information will help the recruiter match you to an appropriate position and not waste his or her, your, or the employer's time. However, when writing directly to a prospective employer, offering this information in an initial cover letter can harm your chances of employment.

You'll read more about the differences in company and recruiter letters in Chapter 3. For now, just remember that the recruiter is an agent for an employer, so you should reference "your client" or "your client's firm" instead of "you" and "your company" when writing recruiter letters.

During the course of your job search, there are a number of other audiences you may write to, under a variety of different circumstances. These may include broadcast letters to recruiters or companies and networking letters to friends or professional contacts. You will find these covered in detail when you read about design and format (Chapter 2) and the actual writing of your letters (Chapter 3). Understanding the different types of letters and how to use them when writing to various audiences will help you to prepare letters that hit their target, grab attention, and generate interviews.

Truth #4: Targeted Letters Work Best

Broadcast letters and networking letters are the best examples of cover letters that are *not* targeted. They're more general letters, written and sent to more general audiences that may not have any specific job openings. Think of a radio or TV *broadcast* that reaches thousands (perhaps millions) of people with the same message. Similarly, you might send a *broadcast cover letter* (along with your resume) to dozens (or possibly hundreds) of potential employers.

However, the vast majority of cover letters you will write are likely to be *targeted* toward a *specific* job opening with a *particular* company. For these situations, you'll want to create cover letters that respond directly to the employer's needs and convince the hiring authority that you are a strong candidate for that particular position.

To accomplish this, carefully examine each job posting to identify the specific requirements of the position and, when possible, research the company's mission statement and values, its corporate culture, and any critical challenges they are facing. This information will help you to better understand the employer and how you can deliver value to that company. What's more, in today's Internet-based world, finding that information can be as easy as a few keystrokes!

Once you've identified the key requirements for the job—what the employer sees as most important—you can develop bullet points, or short paragraphs, that tie your experiences to the company's specific needs. Here are two examples:

Example #7: Bullet point (employer's stated requirement in bold)

- **Developing and managing budgets:** As Director of the Erie County (PA) Library System, I was accountable for an $18 million annual operating budget. As Library Director in Meadville, I developed a five-year capital improvement plan and championed a three-year technology plan.

Example #8: Paragraph style (telling a brief story):

While reviewing information on your Website, I noted that you are pursuing an array of fund-raising initiatives. Shortly after assuming the role of Executive Director for the Healing Education & Arts Retreat of Tonawanda (HEART), I established the Assistant Director of Marketing & Community Relations role, recruited a talented professional, and charged her with raising community awareness. Through a series of special events, we boosted membership, increased program participation, and developed a strategy for promoting our spacious facility as a meeting venue, creating an entirely new revenue stream for the organization.

You will find many more examples of bullet points and paragraphs in subsequent chapters, with samples specific to your career field in Chapters 5-16.

Get Contact Information

Ideally, your cover letters should always be directed to a specific individual. Hopefully, that person's name and contact information will be listed in the ad or posting. When it's not, some applicants will take the extra step of doing some detective work to find the name of the appropriate person. Sometimes, this is as simple as visiting the firm's Website and finding the name (and click-through e-mail address) of the director of human resources, the general sales manager, the VP of manufacturing, or any one of a number of other individuals you may want to contact.

There are also directories at the library that list key people at various companies, or you can call the company and ask the receptionist, "Who is the chief marketing person with your company? What is his or her proper job title? How would I best direct a letter to his or her attention?" This works more often than you might think, because the receptionist is there to provide information and be helpful. Should you encounter an automated, menu-driven phone system, with a bit of persistence you can usually navigate the system to acquire the information you need.

However, we don't recommend spending all of your time sleuthing for the right contact at a firm. If you absolutely can't find the name of a specific individual, you'll want to follow the instructions in the job posting or possibly look for a link to career opportunities on the firm's Website. If you're in doubt about what to use for a salutation, we prefer "Dear Hiring Authority," "Dear Recruiter," or "Dear Sir/Madam" as opposed to the outdated "To Whom It May Concern." Of course, the rest of your letter should follow all the principles previously mentioned in addressing specific job requirements and connecting your skills and accomplishments to that employer's needs.

Truth #5: The Cover Letter Must Match the Resume

If you followed our advice in *No-Nonsense Resumes*, you should already have a resume that portrays the *best* you for the type of position(s) you are seeking. Now, your challenge is to write cover letters that complement and support your resume. Specifically, this means that your cover letters must "match" your resume and be targeted to the same types and levels of positions.

Consider this: A senior manager uses different language, tone, and style when writing his or her resume and cover letter than an engineer or technology professional does. Likewise, a skilled tradesperson has a different vocabulary than a school teacher. All must use proper grammar and spelling, while at the same time staying true to their own experiences and the environments in which they work.

Your cover letter should also complement your resume without repeating the exact same information you've already included in your resume. You do want to connect the reader to your resume by highlighting relevant points, but try to avoid using, verbatim, the same words that appear in the resume. Read the examples and you'll see exactly what we mean:

Example #9: Paragraph style—overtly directing reader to the resume:

During the 1990s, I led a creative team with Epstein & Partners, LLP, where I successfully managed PR campaigns supporting the launch of new consumer products, food products, and business-to-business equipment. All of these campaigns delivered exceptional results for my clients as outlined on the attached resume.

Example #10: Bullet style—references to past employers subtly encourages reader to flip the page and read the resume:

Among my experiences directly relevant to your needs are the following:

☆ Full-charge bookkeeping for manufacturing, professional services, and retail sales firms. (Andrews & Arthur, LLC)

☆ Preparation of sales, income, and payroll tax filings, as well as consultation with clients on tax-planning issues. (GMPK)

☆ Implementation of automated accounting applications for a variety of small business clients. (Thomas Williams, CPA)

Keywords Are Critical

Using keywords is one of the best ways to link your resume and your cover letters. In simple terms, keywords are those *buzz words* found in each and every profession. They identify the essential skills, knowledge, and expertise that distinguish someone in a particular field. For example, keywords for a sales professional include **territory management**, **account management**, **sales presentations**, **sales negotiations**, **product management**, and many more. Keywords for a bookkeeper include **accounts payable**, **accounts receivable**, **payroll processing**, **general ledger**, **tax filings**, and more. You probably already know what the keywords are for your current job—you use them every day— but they've become so second nature to your day-to-day activities that you might not recognize their importance.

The use of the proper keywords in your cover letters will not only help match your letters to your resume, but will also increase your chances of landing an interview if your cover letter and resume package gets uploaded into an electronic database. When this happens, both your resume and cover letter will be scanned by specialized software that searches for keywords that are relevant to a particular position. Once the software identifies the *right* keywords in your documents, you will be chosen to move on to the next phase in the candidate selection process.

The Final Presentation

One final word on matching your cover letters to your resume: In order to present prospective employers with an attractive, integrated package, the fonts (typestyles) and overall design of your cover letters should coordinate with your resume. In the example that appears on the following pages, notice how the graphic design used for the candidate's contact information is consistent between the resume and cover letter. Note, also, that the same distinctive font (in this case, Bookman Old Style) has been used for both the letter and the resume, and that bold print and italics have been used to highlight achievements and notable information in each document.

ARCHIBALD GARRISON

630 East Ridge Road   ~   Rochester, New York 14622   ~   (585) 544-9999

October 13, 2006

Mr. Ronald Reynolds
Manufacturing Supervisor
Plastics Manufacturing, LLC
1234 Industrial Park
Rochester, NY 14699

Dear Mr. Reynolds:

Capitalizing on my 20-plus years of experience, I am most interested in **Injection Molding / Set-Up** positions that will advance your production objectives. I have enclosed my resume, which outlines my employment history, skills, and training.

Some of the key qualifications I can bring to your organization include:

❖ *Extensive experience with an ISO-9000 company, including seven years as an **Injection Molding Technician** in charge of setting up, maintaining, monitoring, and ensuring continuous production of 12 automated injection molding machines.*

❖ *Consistent contributor recognized with many Suggestion Awards. I am diligent in identifying ways to make processes run more efficiently, quickly resolving process problems and taking corrective action to minimize down times.*

❖ *Highly recommended by Senior Manufacturing Engineer, Harvey Townes: "His quality of work is exceptional and he always completes his in-process checks on time. Without question, Gary is the fastest and most thorough set-up person in our molding areas."*

❖ *Training that includes Hydraulics, Pneumatics, Blueprint Reading, Hazardous Materials, Confined Space Entry, Set-Up, Preventive Maintenance, Lift Truck Certification, Lockout / Tagout, and ISO-9000 Principles.*

I would appreciate the opportunity to speak with you in person about my background and skills, and am eager to secure a permanent position with a dynamic, growing company. Please telephone me at **(585) 544-9999** to arrange a mutually convenient date and time for an interview. Thank you for your consideration.

Sincerely,

Archibald Garrison

Enclosure

ARCHIBALD GARRISON

630 East Ridge Road   ~   Rochester, New York 14622   ~   (5

SUMMARY OF QUALIFICATIONS

Injection Molding Technician with more than 20 years of experience in an ISO-9 manufacturing environment. Lead Set-Up Operator in a state-of-the-art manufacturing plant producing 29,000 assemblies per day. Self-directed and reliable in troubleshooting process problems and improving quality. Skilled in the use of micrometers, dial indicators and digital calipers; blueprint reading; and the operation of lift trucks, scissor and boom lifts, and overhead cranes.

EMPLOYMENT HISTORY

MONROE PRECISION MANUFACTURING; Rochester, New York   1983 to Present

Injection Molding Operator (7 years)
Line Operator (10 years)
Assembly Line Set-Up (6 years)

Function as area Lead Set-Up Operator. Oversee operation of 12 automated injection molding machines, including Cincinnati, Van Dorn, and Engels molders.

- Perform routine preventive maintenance. Identify and diagnose problems during breakdowns; contact and collaborate with skilled trades, including electricians, plumbers, maintenance mechanics, etc.
- Perform process parameter checks on each machine and adjust where necessary.
- Ensure water and temperature levels meet specifications.
- Collect parts and assemble first-piece samples.
- Perform mold changeovers.
- Relieve other operators as needed.

Achievements:

✓ *Developed improvement proposal that suggested combining B and C shifts, which boosted productivity and enhanced product quality.*
✓ *Reduced scrap 12% by recommending lowering of mold temperature for a particular product.*
✓ *Eliminated an average of 50 rejects per shift by redesigning process.*
✓ *Traveled to Oswego, NY plant to identify and correct quality problem.*

PROFESSIONAL TRAINING

Lift Truck Certified (Walkie, Walkie/Stacker)	*Asbestos Safety*
ISO-14001; ISO-9000	*Blueprint Reading*
Basic Set-Up	*Confined Space Entry*
Hazardous Materials	*Preventive Maintenance*
Pneumatics	*Lockout/Tagout*
Hydraulics	*Emergency Evacuation*

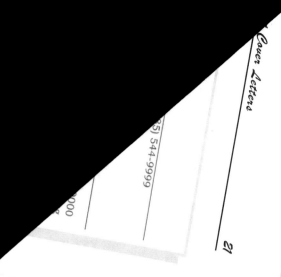

ı fine resume stock (always use the
ɛ) or transmitted electronically, the
ı a lasting impression on the reader,
ɪ you, the job candidate.

nts Its Own Challenges

ınces in which job seekers may find
n challenges when it comes to writing
ɔmmon challenges, we've given you a
ɪt direction. You'll find much more
ıd others in the 100-plus sample cover

If your chaᴜᴇ.ɴ⸣   ɪique and you need even more information
to guide you in preparing a stɪoᴜᴇ⸣ me and compelling cover letter, we suggest
you consult the following resources, all of which were authored or co-authored
by Wendy Enelow:

> *No-Nonsense Guide to Resume Writing* (Career Press)
> *Expert Resumes for Career Changers* (JIST Publishing)
> *Expert Resumes for People Returning To Work* (JIST Publishing)
> *Expert Resumes for Military-to-Civilian Transitions* (JIST Publishing)
> *Best Resumes and Letters for Ex-Offenders* (Impact Publications)
> *College Grad Resumes to Land $75,000+ Jobs* (Impact Publications)

(You can find all of these books and more at *www.wendyenelow.com*.)

Career Change

In any career-change scenario, you should be looking forward, not back.
Your resume should focus on your future career objective and how the skills
you've acquired thus far have prepared you for such an opportunity. Likewise,
your cover letters should be written to match your qualifications with your
current goals, featuring your transferable skills and highlighting keywords that
relate to the new career field you wish to pursue.

A common career change is transition from the military to the civilian
workforce. The most important thing in this situation is to think in civilian terms
and characterize your skills and achievements using language a civilian can
understand. "Experience making critical decisions under highly stressful
conditions, providing leadership to 30 subordinates in the field, and exercising
independent judgment without direct day-to-day supervision" accurately describes
what an infantry officer does in combat. But these same skills are applicable to a
variety of supervisory roles in civilian life.

We suspect that most Military Occupational Specialties (MOSs) are somewhat easier than an infantry officer's to translate into terms a civilian will find meaningful. Procurement, logistics, fleet maintenance, and facilities management are all important military functions, and each of them parallels similar job opportunities in the civilian world.

If your goal is to move from not-for-profit into for-profit, private industry, or vice versa, remember that fund-raising is sales and sales is fund-raising. Each requires the same core skill sets (for example, building relationships, presenting, negotiating, and closing). Likewise, a budget is a budget, regardless of the funding source, and serving a constituency is really just another name for customer service. Simply recognize who your audience is and write your letter using the language and keywords that the reader will understand to be relevant to his or her particular hiring needs.

Similarly, if you plan to transition into (or out of) a teaching career, recognize the transferable skills you offer. For example, teaching and corporate training have strong similarities (whichever direction you're moving), and life experiences can offer some interesting insights that can be brought into the classroom. Once again, consider keywords that relate to your new objective and tailor your cover letters so that they resonate with potential new employers and entice them to act (offering you an interview).

New Graduate

A new graduate can be a traditional student who progressed directly from high school to college and is now ready for the "real world." A new graduate can also be someone who just completed a degree while holding down a full-time job, and who has significant work experience to go along with a freshly minted diploma. Each scenario has its own special considerations.

If you're a recent graduate with no significant professional experience, make the most out of any internship, co-op, or summer job experiences you've had. Highlight on-campus activities that demonstrate your leadership skills (for example, student government, club officer, or intramural sports). And be sure to feature your technology skills, as they are relevant to almost any career track in today's e-based business world and economy.

If you're an "adult learner," who worked for several years and then returned to school, emphasize that you offer the best of both worlds—your recent education that's up-to-date and leading-edge, combined with your experience and maturity. You have current knowledge and the wisdom to make the most of it. This places you in an extremely favorable position in the market.

Return-to-Work

For those of you returning to work after an extended absence, don't worry about addressing employment gaps in your cover letter. Hopefully, your resume is structured in a way that either camouflages the gaps or effectively deals with them. Once you get to the interview, there will be ample opportunity to explain your circumstances and the reasons for any gaps. However, there are individuals who have been out of the workforce for years and this section is written specifically for them.

If you've been on the "mommy (or daddy) track," but are now ready to return to the workforce, it may be effective to feature volunteer activities you've participated in that demonstrate your leadership, organizational, and interpersonal skills. Highlight things such as serving on the advisory board for a charity or preschool, as an officer of the PTA, or as a scout leader. Some creative candidates even use their expertise in managing a household budget as evidence of strong financial management and organizational skills. Also, don't be afraid to draw on professional skills developed before you left the traditional workforce, even if they seem dated.

If you're returning to work after an extended illness, or coping with a physical disability, focus on what you *can* do and don't dwell on things you can't do. In most cases, you'll have some legal protection against discrimination due to your disability and many employers are enthusiastic about employing a motivated worker who genuinely appreciates the opportunity to work.

Ex-offenders perhaps face the toughest challenge when making the transition out of prison and into the workforce. Our best advice is that you should *not* disclose the fact that you were incarcerated on your resume or in your cover letter. You may choose to highlight work experience or training completed "inside the fence," but do so in a manner that does not immediately communicate that you were in prison. Rather, save that discussion for an in-person interview where you can own up to this "life-altering experience" and talk about what you've learned and how you've grown from it. As mentioned earlier in this chapter, consult *Best Resumes and Letters for Ex-Offenders* (Impact Publications) for more advice if you're in this situation.

Relocation

Relocation could mean that you're planning a move to pursue new career options or simply moving to a *better* area for personal reasons. It could also mean that you are the "trailing spouse." Your significant other has landed an opportunity just too good to pass up, and you are the one who needs to find a new job in a new city.

The key in these situations is to convey to the prospective employer that you are committed to the new location, either due to family ties, your love of the area, or recognition of the career potential offered in the new locale. It's helpful if you have an established address in the new location, even if you have to use a friend's while you're transitioning. That way, it looks to employers like you're already there, which they will view as a positive.

Laid Off/Fired From Last Job

In this day and age, layoffs, unfortunately, have become common enough that there's little stigma remaining to being laid off, so don't be self-conscious about it. It's happened to hundreds of thousands of people, so you're certainly not alone! On the other hand, a termination is always a delicate situation to handle. For either scenario, the best approach is to accentuate the positive and de-emphasize the negative. Your cover letters should focus on your skills and achievements, and possibly your longevity with the company. In the case of a termination, it's best to save the discussion of how and why you left your last job for the interview rather than in your resume or cover letter.

Coaching you on how to best deal with these issues in an interview is beyond the scope of this book. If you do find yourself in this situation, here are some wonderful resources that we strongly recommend:

> *Nail the Job Interview* (Impact Publications)
>
> *The $100,000 Job Interview* (Impact Publications)
>
> *How To Choose the Right Person for the Right Job Every Time* (McGraw-Hill)
>
> *Knock 'Em Dead* (Adams Media)

(You can find all of these books and more at *www.wendyenelow.com*. For a copy of *Knock 'Em Dead*, visit *www.amazon.com* or your local bookstore.)

Perceived Job-Hopper

As recently as 10 years ago, if you spent less than three to five years in one job, you were considered a "job-hopper." By today's standards, five years with one company qualifies as long-term employment! Consequently, what can be characterized as job-hopping has shifted over the years, and many professionals now work in occupations and industries where moving from one company to another is the norm.

That said, if you perceive that you may be viewed as a job-hopper by prospective employers, you may want to consider a functional format for your resume that emphasizes your diverse experience and flexibility. Showing that you can adapt easily to new work environments can be seen as a positive by dynamic organizations undergoing significant changes. You may be able to cast yourself as a "change agent," or at the very least as someone who embraces change. Then, be sure that your cover letters reflect the same messages as your resume and embrace the same concepts such as adaptability to change.

Summary

Now that we've explored the six essential truths about cover letters, we'll move on to vital information about cover letter design and format (Chapter 2), cover letter writing (Chapter 3), and the electronic transmission of cover letters (Chapter 4). Following that, Chapters 5–16 offer more than 100 cover letter samples that you can use to create your own winning letters that open doors, generate interviews, and land great new opportunities.

Chapter 2

▶ Simple Truths About
Cover Letter Formatting and Design

When developing your cover letters, there are two important considerations you'll always want to keep in mind: format and design. As with your resume, these elements are essential in preparing your presentation to prospective employers. If you've chosen a unique design for your resume that gives you a distinctive presentation, you'll want your cover letters to be consistent with that design choice so that you present a complete and professional package.

To begin designing your cover letters, ask yourself these questions:

1. Which cover letter format is most appropriate for me to use? Bullet format? Paragraph format?

2. Does the design of my cover letter match my resume? Does the typestyle coordinate with my resume? Does the visual appearance of my letter complement my resume?

As you review the cover letter samples in this book, you'll see dramatic differences in presentation, from conservative to avant garde. A banker or financial analyst would probably design a cover letter on the conservative end of the spectrum, while a media sales representative or graphic artist might want to project a more distinctive visual image. As you read this and later chapters, you should develop a sense of where on that continuum—from conservative to very unique—it's best for your cover letter and resume package to be positioned. This will depend not only on your specific profession (for example, finance, sales, graphic arts, engineering, logistics, or production), but also the specific industry that you are targeting (for example, aerospace, telecommunications, film/television, publishing, or education).

The 4 Simple Truths About Cover Letter Formatting and Design

When you're deciding what design and format to use for your cover letters, you'll want to consider these four essential truths. They are critical to competitively positioning yourself within the job search market by creating letters that are distinctive and memorable.

Truth #1: Effective cover letters contain 10 key components.

Truth #2: Simple designs work best.

Truth #3: Bullet-format letters highlight your skills and achievements.

Truth #4: Paragraph-format letters tell your career stories.

Now, we'll explore each of these truths in much greater detail so you'll understand how to integrate these concepts when designing and formatting your cover letters.

Truth #1: Effective Cover Letters Contain 10 Key Components

As we mentioned in Chapter 1, there are 10 key components that should be part of every effective cover letter, regardless of the particular format and design choices you make. These key elements include:

1. Contact information: The whole point of sending out your cover letters and resumes is to convince prospective employers to contact you for interviews. That being the case, you want to make it as easy as possible for them to reach you. It is essential to include your name, address, phone number, and (personal) e-mail address at the top of each of your cover letters (as well as on your resume).

In the "typewriter era," your address at the top of the page was neat and clean, but generally rather bland in appearance. Today, with all the advantages of modern word-processing software, you can now design a unique and attractive "letterhead" for yourself. A very effective approach is to copy and paste the contact information from your resume onto a blank page and save that document as a "letterhead" that you can reuse each time you need to create a new cover letter. Here are a few examples:

Creating your own letterhead using the heading from your resume:

Example #1:

GARY LUCIANO

716 Wood Lane ~ Rochester, New York 14699

(585) 723-0000   luciano@email.com

Example #2:

MICHELLE S. BATES
24 Bramblebury Lane
Rochester, New York 14699
(585) 544-3333

Example #3:

RYAN R. MITCHELSON   ryanrmitchelson@aol.com

2140 Endicott Drive • Rochester, New York 14699   585-461-8308

2. Date: Your cover letters should include the date the letter is to be mailed, and the preferred format is as follows: December 10, 2006. The date appears just below *your* contact information and above the inside address (which indicates the *recipient* of the letter). Depending on the overall format of your letter (see Truth #2—Simple Designs Work Best later in this chapter), the date can be either flush with the left margin if you're using a block format cover letter (see Karl George sample cover letter on page 34) or indented 4 inches from the left margin if you're using an indented paragraph format cover letter (see Thomas Vincent sample letter on page 35).

3. Inside address: Most frequently, the inside address will include the complete name, title, and business address of the individual to whom you are addressing the letter. This is the most common format and the recommended format when you have all of that information. See example #4:

Example #4: Standard format with complete address:

Mr. Claude Nettles
General Sales Manager
Industrial Supply Associates, LLC
1234 Business Park Road
Roanoke, VA 22334

Dear Mr. Nettles:

In today's job market, however, you will often find yourself frequently responding to an e-mail address or fax number, without knowing the complete address. Examples #5 and #6 show best how to handle such situations.

Example #5: When you only know the e-mail address:

Ms. Rose Gardner
Executive Search Consultant

rgardner@executivesearch.com

Dear Ms. Gardner:

Example #6: When you only know the fax number:

Mr. Randy Gardner
Hiring Director

Fax: (703) 555-9299

4. Reference line: If you decide to include a line that references the position or job posting number for which you are applying, place it between the inside address and the salutation.

5. Salutation: The salutation is the line that says, "Dear Mr. Jones:" You can use "Dear Hiring Authority:" or "Dear Sir/Madam:" if you don't have a contact name. Note that it's accepted practice to refer to all women as "Ms.," unless someone specifically refers to herself as "Mrs."

Following is an integrated presentation showing the inside address, reference line, and salutation as they would appear together.

Example #7: Inside address and salutation with reference line included:

Mr. Sam Sizer, CEO
Amalgamated Industries, Inc.
22 Chester Boulevard, Suite 1202
Rye, NY 15983

Re: Executive Assistant (Posting #06-123EA)

Dear Mr. Sizer:

6. Opening paragraph: Generally, your introductory paragraph will be short (one or two sentences) and will communicate why you're writing to that individual (for example, in response to an advertisement or job posting, to express your interest in employment opportunities with that company, or to follow up on a referral). As you'll read in Chapter 3, there are a variety of strategies and tactics you can adapt for writing your own opening paragraph that will help to distinguish you from the crowd of other candidates.

7. Content/main body of the letter: The main body of your letters is where you'll include the real substance—highlights of your skills, qualifications, employment experiences, achievements, projects, and more that are most relevant to a particular position or company. This is the section that you will use to *sell* yourself and capture an interview. Much of Chapter 3 focuses on the strategies and wording that you can use to create powerful letters that encourage readers to review your resume and extend the opportunity for an interview.

8. Closing paragraph/call to action: The closing paragraph of your letter should explicitly ask for an interview or state your plan for following up whenever possible. Examples of both are shown in Chapter 3. However, there will be instances (for example, blind post office box) in which you will be unable to follow up. In those situations, all you can do is wait to hear back from the company or recruiter.

9. Closing/signature: Immediately following your closing paragraph is the complimentary closing, usually "Sincerely," "Respectfully," or something similarly appropriate. Then add three to four line spaces for your signature, and type your name.

Example #8 shows a closing paragraph and complimentary closing.

Example #8: Closing Paragraph, with complimentary closing and signature:

I am convinced that I can make a significant contribution to your accounting team and would appreciate the opportunity to discuss how my capabilities can serve your needs. Please contact me via phone or e-mail to establish a mutually convenient time for an initial conversation.

Sincerely,

Martin K. Morrison
(your hand-written signature)

Martin K. Morrison

10. Enclosures: Including the word "enclosure" at the end of your letter (two spaces below your typed name) is optional. Whether you mention it or not, you'll be enclosing (or attaching) a copy of your resume, and that's understood. However, you'll find that most people do include the word "enclosure" at the very end of a letter. Here are two examples:

Example #9: Simple reference to an enclosure:

Enclosure

Example #10: Detailed listing of enclosures:

Enclosures: Leadership Profile
Reference List
Job Application

An important note about enclosures: Do not include anything that was not requested. Your resume and cover letter are an introduction to who you are and the value you bring to an organization. Keep it simple and don't overwhelm someone with lots of paperwork they did not request. Trust us when we tell you that this will *not* work to your advantage!

Now that we've detailed each of the key elements that are essential to the design and format of effective cover letters, it's important to see a visual representation. Refer to the next page for a sample cover letter for Dennis Gregory

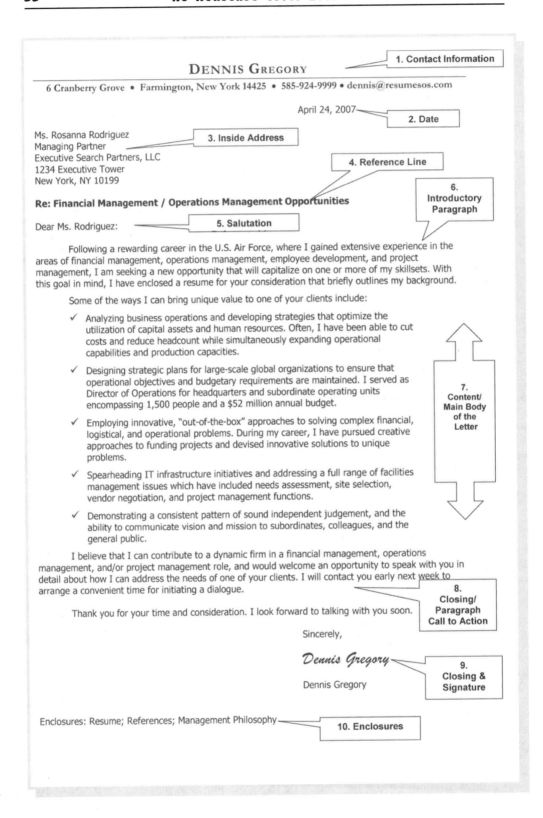

DENNIS GREGORY

1. Contact Information

6 Cranberry Grove • Farmington, New York 14425 • 585-924-9999 • dennis@resumesos.com

April 24, 2007

2. Date

Ms. Rosanna Rodriguez
Managing Partner
Executive Search Partners, LLC
1234 Executive Tower
New York, NY 10199

3. Inside Address

4. Reference Line

6. Introductory Paragraph

Re: Financial Management / Operations Management Opportunities

Dear Ms. Rodriguez:

5. Salutation

Following a rewarding career in the U.S. Air Force, where I gained extensive experience in the areas of financial management, operations management, employee development, and project management, I am seeking a new opportunity that will capitalize on one or more of my skillsets. With this goal in mind, I have enclosed a resume for your consideration that briefly outlines my background.

Some of the ways I can bring unique value to one of your clients include:

✓ Analyzing business operations and developing strategies that optimize the utilization of capital assets and human resources. Often, I have been able to cut costs and reduce headcount while simultaneously expanding operational capabilities and production capacities.

✓ Designing strategic plans for large-scale global organizations to ensure that operational objectives and budgetary requirements are maintained. I served as Director of Operations for headquarters and subordinate operating units encompassing 1,500 people and a $52 million annual budget.

✓ Employing innovative, "out-of-the-box" approaches to solving complex financial, logistical, and operational problems. During my career, I have pursued creative approaches to funding projects and devised innovative solutions to unique problems.

✓ Spearheading IT infrastructure initiatives and addressing a full range of facilities management issues which have included needs assessment, site selection, vendor negotiation, and project management functions.

✓ Demonstrating a consistent pattern of sound independent judgement, and the ability to communicate vision and mission to subordinates, colleagues, and the general public.

7. Content/ Main Body of the Letter

I believe that I can contribute to a dynamic firm in a financial management, operations management, and/or project management role, and would welcome an opportunity to speak with you in detail about how I can address the needs of one of your clients. I will contact you early next week to arrange a convenient time for initiating a dialogue.

8. Closing/ Paragraph Call to Action

Thank you for your time and consideration. I look forward to talking with you soon.

Sincerely,

Dennis Gregory

9. Closing & Signature

Dennis Gregory

Enclosures: Resume; References; Management Philosophy

10. Enclosures

that you first saw in Chapter 1. We've repeated this example to illustrate the specific placement of each of these essential elements in a professionally designed and formatted cover letter. Use this template as the foundation to create your own distinctive cover letters.

Truth #2: Simple Designs Work Best

As already mentioned, the purpose of the cover letter and resume package is to get you noticed by an employer and called for an interview. That's it and nothing more. Resumes and letters do *not* get jobs; only people do! To be sure that you get interviews, you'll want to keep your cover letters inviting, readable, and not overly designed. Remember, you're not creating a brochure or advertisement; you're writing a business letter. Keep it professional!

Font Selection

The first consideration is to select a font (or typestyle) that complements your resume and is easy to read. Most likely, this means using the same font you used for the body of your resume. Commonly used fonts include Tahoma, Verdana, Arial, Bookman Old Style, or Times New Roman. All of these styles are included in the most recent versions of Microsoft Office or have equivalents in other word-processing applications. As such, you can be relatively certain that when you e-mail your resume and cover letter, the integrity of the font will be retained and your e-mail won't come through as garbage.

To be sure that your cover letter is easy to read, we recommend that you use a type size of 10–12 points. Why the range in size? Well, different fonts are larger than others. For example, 10-point Bookman Old Style is easy to read; 10-point Garamond is a little tougher. Conversely, 12-point Bookman is a bit too large and too elementary in appearance, while 12-point Times New Roman is quite readable. You may want to experiment with different fonts and sizes to see which you like best, which looks most professional, and which accommodates the text of your cover letter the best. To help you decide which font is right for you, refer to the Font Comparison Chart on page 49 at the end of this chapter.

Format Selection

The other important consideration to keeping the design of your cover letters simple is whether to use a block format or an indented-paragraph format. Each is completely acceptable; your choice really depends on your personal preferences.

Every element of the block-style letter is flush with the left margin, including the date, signature lines, and opening lines of each new paragraph. In contrast, the indented-paragraph style will have the date and signature lines indented 4 inches from the left margin, with the opening line of each paragraph indented a quarter-inch or half-inch, depending on your preference.

On the following two pages are sample cover letters that illustrate a block-format cover letter and an indented-paragraph cover letter. See which style you like best and which one best complements your resume design and format.

(Block Format Cover Letter)

KARL M. GEORGE

715 Lafayette Boulevard • Rochester, New York 14699 • 585-222-7086 • KMGeorge@resumesos.com

December 19, 2006

Ms. Barbara Barnes
Director of Financial Analysis
Bank of America
1234 Bank Street
Charlotte, North Carolina 29292

Re: Business Analyst Opportunities

Dear Ms. Barnes:

Capitalizing on an MBA in Finance and demonstrated business analysis capabilities, I am seeking a new professional challenge in North Carolina. As a leading firm in the Charlotte market and worldwide, Bank of America is one of the organizations I am seriously interested in joining. Accordingly, I have enclosed my resume that outlines my professional track record.

Some key points that you may find relevant to a position with Bank of America include:

- Demonstrated ability to analyze business processes and identify opportunities for improvement. In various business settings, I have been able to make recommendations for continuous process improvements that have significantly enhanced efficiencies.

- Capacity to develop and utilize reporting and forecasting tools that have provided senior management with strategic information that has enhanced business planning capabilities.

- Experience addressing management and operational issues related to organizational change.

I am confident that my education, experience, and professional enthusiasm would combine to make me an asset to your firm in a Business Analysis / Financial Management role. I would enjoy speaking with you in person to explore the possibilities with Bank of America. I will contact you in a few days to answer any questions and arrange a convenient date and time for us to pursue an initial discussion.

Thank you for your time and consideration. I look forward to speaking with you soon.

Sincerely,

Karl M. George

Enclosure

(Indented Paragraph Format Cover Letter)

THOMAS VINCENT, CPA

616 Penfair Drive • Penfield, New York 14526 • 585-383-8666 • vince@redsuspenders.com

May 6, 2006

Constellation Brands, Inc.
300 Willowbrook Office Park
Fairport, New York 14450

hr@cbrands.com

Dear Hiring Authority:

Your recent postings on Monster.com for a **Tax Compliance Manager** and a **Tax Manager** are both of great interest. Capitalizing on over eight years of tax accounting experience with a leading local CPA firm, I believe my knowledge and expertise are good matches for either of these positions. Therefore, I have attached for your consideration a resume that outlines my qualifications.

Some key points you may find of particular interest include:

- Supervising tax accounting staff, including scheduling and managing projects, reviewing a variety of tax filings, and establishing departmental policy and procedure.

- Ensuring that returns are filed in an accurate and timely manner.

- Advising a broad array of business clients on strategies for minimizing tax liabilities.

- Dealing with tax issues relevant to corporations operating in multiple states.

- Representing clients' interests during IRS audits and tax compliance proceedings.

- Utilizing leading-edge tax software to address client needs.

In addition, I have distinguished myself as someone who has exceptional customer relations skills and the capacity to balance multiple projects during the fast-paced tax season at a busy CPA firm. I would enjoy meeting with you to discuss how I can meet or exceed your needs for either of these positions and encourage you to contact me to arrange an initial interview.

Thank you for your time and consideration. I look forward to speaking with you soon.

Sincerely,

Thomas Vincent, CPA

Enclosure

Truth #3: Bullet-format Letters Highlight Your Skills and Achievements

Bullet-format cover letters have become increasingly popular over the past decade. In essence, the bullet format is one in which a cover letter is composed of an introductory paragraph followed by several "bullet points" that highlight key information the writer (job seeker) wishes to convey to the reader (HR representative, hiring manager, or recruiter). One significant advantage of bullet-format cover letters is that they appear more readable. Employers who are quickly reviewing cover letters and resumes can zero in on the bullet points and get the essence of your message, even if that's all they read during their initial screening.

There are two situations in which bullet-format cover letters are most effective. The first is when you want to briefly highlight a list of achievements or work experiences that relate to the types of positions for which you are applying. The second is when you want to respond point-for-point to the specific qualifications an employer is seeking in a candidate.

The first scenario, listing skills and experiences that you, as a candidate, have to offer, works well for broadcast or networking letters. Broadcast letters (also referred to as cold-call letters) are those that you would send to employers and/or recruiters when you are not applying for a specific opening, but are "broadcasting" your availability and key capabilities by sending essentially the same letter to a mailing list of contacts.

Networking letters are those that you would send to acquaintances (warm networking contacts) or people you'd like to meet (cold networking contacts). The goal is to advise these contacts of your job search and ask for their assistance. Here is a set of sample bullet points as they might appear in either a broadcast or networking letter:

Example #11: Bullet points highlighting skills and experience:

Some of the key talents that I can bring to a position with your firm include:

- Experience administering Defined Benefit and Defined Contribution Pension Plans which include monitoring compliance, tracking terminations and new submissions, and communicating with plan sponsors, participants, and accountants.

- General Accounting experience that includes exposure to Accounts Payable, Accounts Receivable, Payroll, and General Ledger. I have also prepared financial reports and projections, and participated in budget-planning activities.

- Experience coordinating benefits enrollment including processing applications, communicating with employees on key issues, and resolving problems for employees.

The other scenario in which bullet-format letters are most useful is when responding to specific job requirements. Often, a job posting will include its own set of bullet points, outlining the requirements the employer seeks in a candidate. In such cases, it works to your advantage to tailor your cover letter so that it answers each bullet point from the job posting with an example of your skills, experiences, or achievements that demonstrate your capabilities. By following this pattern, you can clearly communicate your value as it specifically relates to the employer.

In the following example, first look at the employer's requirements (essential duties) and then see how bullet points from the corresponding cover letter answer those requirements. (Note that in this example, only the cover letter bullet points should be included in the actual letter; not the "Essential Duties" as outlined by the employer.)

Example #12: Job Posting—Essential Duties:

- Plans the annual budget and controls expenses for the department; enforces cost controls and establishes cost measurements to ensure budget compliance.

- Develops goals and objectives of the department; directs and administers the work performed by the department; and ensures projects are completed on time.

- Hires, supervises, and assigns work to subordinates; mentors employees; and evaluates team members' performance.

- Plans and allocates resources to ensure efficient operation of the organization.

- Establishes long-range goals, objectives, and overall direction for the department; monitors and reviews strategic plans; ensures that long-range objectives are met.

- Provides information on key issues and trends to community groups, organizations, and media on a regular basis.

Corresponding cover letter bullet points:

- ***Budgeting and cost controls.*** *Faced with cuts from primary funding sources, I contained costs by exploring innovative ways of delivering services and developing revenue alternatives.*

- ***Articulating goals and objectives.*** *As Executive Director of the Finger Lakes Collaborative, I established a vision for future development, created a capital improvement plan that was completed two years ahead of schedule, and championed a leading-edge technology plan.*

- *Hiring, supervising, and evaluating employees.* *The selection and retention of key personnel have always been a vital component of my leadership success. I have also endeavored to be a mentor and coach to those under my supervision, helping them achieve their professional potential.*

- *Planning and allocating resources.* *As part of addressing budgeting and funding issues, I have always been mindful of utilizing both physical assets and human resources to most efficiently deliver services.*

- *Communicating policies, standards, and objectives.* *Throughout my career, I have identified both deficiencies and best practices related to service delivery, and developed strategies for improving processes and implementing these improvements.*

- *Providing information on key issues to the community.* *For the past 13 years, my high-profile leadership positions have encompassed a heavy schedule of public speaking as well as one-to-one communication with key stakeholders.*

One other variation on the bullet-format cover letter is the comparison, or "T-chart," letter. This style shows the employer's requirements and the candidate's qualifications side-by-side in a chart. This format is less common than the others already illustrated, but you may want to use it in certain situations in which you want to explicitly demonstrate how your skills match an employer's needs. An example of a "T-chart" appears below:

Example #13: "T-chart" letter with employer's requirements and candidate's skills:

Your Requirements:	*My Relevant Qualifications:*
- Lean Six Sigma Certification	- Green Belt Certified; currently pursuing Black Belt
- Experience with Kaizan Events	- Championed four successful Kaizan events over a three-year period
- Ten years of Manufacturing Experience	- Five years as machine operator, followed by seven years as production supervisor
- Proficient in MS Project	- Advanced training and practical experience with MS Project
- ISO-9000 Experience	- More than 12 years in QS-9000 environment (auto industry equivalent of ISO-9000)

One of the biggest advantages of using bullet-format or T-chart cover letters is their "modularity." In other words, you can easily remove one bullet from an existing letter and "plug in" a new bullet to quickly modify it when responding to a different, but related, position. As you'll learn in Chapter 3, when we discuss *writing* your cover letters, you may want to create several prototype, or general, cover letters that encompass the key points you will communicate to prospective employers. Then, as you respond to specific job postings, you can easily modify these bullet-format prototype letters to be more relevant to particular openings by adding, subtracting, and/or reordering the sequence of your bullets. If you are applying for several opportunities each week, this approach can be very efficient.

The one disadvantage of the bulleted format is that it can significantly reduce the amount of information you can include in a one-page cover letter. Your bullet points must be concise and to-the-point in order to have the desired impact. If your experiences require more of a narrative, storytelling approach, the paragraph format may be your best choice.

Examples of bullet-format, indented cover letters are shown on pages 40, 41, and 42.

Truth #4: Paragraph-Format Letters Tell Your Career Stories

There will be instances when either the requirements of a position or the circumstances of your work history are best presented in a narrative or storytelling approach. Resume-writing professionals and career coaches frequently advise their clients to use the Problem-Action-Result (PAR) or Challenge-Action-Result (CAR) method to develop success stories that can be used in a job interview, incorporated into a resume, or, for our purposes here, included in a cover letter.

In such cases, formatting your cover letter in paragraphs, instead of bullets, affords you the opportunity to sell yourself with examples of your successes. You can include more detail about one or more specific situations that may be of particular interest to the potential employer and, ideally, set the stage for pursuing a dialogue about these successful scenarios during an interview.

In Chapter 3, when we discuss *writing* your cover letters, we will explain further how to develop your CAR stories. Briefly stated, you'll want to identify a *Challenge* that you faced, describe what *Actions* you took to address that challenge, and showcase the *Results* you were able to deliver that resolved the key issues or delivered the most value. To have the most impact, those results should be as quantifiable as possible (for example, percentage of increase in sales, reduction in equipment downtime, or improvement in quality ratings). In other words, you want to include whatever statistics you have available that support your individual success stories.

TIMOTHY L. MICHAELS

22 King Street • Fairport, New York 14450 • 585-555-9898 • timm2@localnet.net

January 25, 2007

Mr. William Dorman
Chief Information Officer
Important Industries, Inc.
1234 Industrial Parkway
Rochester, New York 14699

Dear Mr. Dorman:

Capitalizing on a 12-plus year career with the Yellow Box Company that has encompassed Systems Administration, IT Project Management, and Business Analyses experiences, I am seeking to utilize my broad-based IT knowledge in a challenging position with your firm. In pursuit of that goal, I have enclosed for your review a résumé that outlines my professional background.

Some of the key capabilities that I can bring to a position with your firm include:

- **Supporting precision manufacturing operations, including clean room environments. During the start-up and launch of YBC's thin film manufacturing facility, I was accountable for setting up and maintaining process control, inventory management, and resource planning applications that contributed to the efficient and profitable operation of that plant.**

- **Managing database tools that allow sales and marketing teams to capture customer information, track market trends, and plan sales/marketing strategies. In my current assignment, I maintain applications that are utilized by 100 managers in the field, plus close to 100 marketing and headquarters staff, to manage relationships with a customer base exceeding one million total accounts.**

- **Implementing and maintaining HR applications and e-mail utilities to serve up to 500 end-users. As a Senior Systems Analyst with the team that launched the Office Imaging Group, I had responsibilities in these areas, including controlling user access and establishing accounts.**

- **Serving in Business Analyst roles that have included using then innovative IT solutions to streamline and optimize various materials forecasting functions.**

I believe that the knowledge and expertise developed over the course of my career can be a valuable asset to a smaller firm on the rise. I would enjoy meeting with you to explore how I can best serve your current and future needs, and encourage you to contact me to arrange an initial interview.

Thank you for your time and consideration. I look forward to speaking with you soon.

Sincerely,

Timothy L. Michaels

Enclosure

WALTER E. ELLIS
75 Clover Street
Rochester, New York 14610-4261
585-777-9988 (Home) / 585-888-9988 (Cellular)
walteree@resumesos.com

November 27, 2006

Mr. B. Thomas Golisano
President & CEO
Paychex, Inc.
911 Panorama Trail, South
Rochester, New York 14625

Dear Mr. Golisano:

Capitalizing on a career that encompasses broad-based experience in brand marketing, public relations, and customer relations, I am seeking an opportunity to apply these skills in a marketing communications position that will offer the potential for advancement based on performance. I believe that I possess knowledge and expertise that can be an asset to your firm and have, therefore, enclosed for your review a résumé that outlines my professional background.

Some key points that you may find relevant to a marketing communications role with your organization include the following:

- *Identifying target audiences and developing marketing messages that reach those audiences. In both business-to-business and consumer products settings, I have been successful in researching potential market segments and creating strategies that effectively communicate product features and promote brand awareness.*

- *Implementing innovative, technology-based approaches to marketing, including championing e-commerce initiatives that both augment product sales and afford opportunities to gather information about customers.*

- *Spearheading public relations efforts that coordinate with marketing strategies and advance overall business goals. These have included placement of features in both electronic and print media, participation in high-profile public events, and implementation of "strategic philanthropy" initiatives.*

- *Directing an array of brand management activities, which have encompassed graphic design, copy writing, and production of collaterals, point-of-sales materials, and product packaging.*

I am confident that my experience, education, and enthusiasm will allow me to make a meaningful contribution to your ongoing business success. I would enjoy meeting with you to discuss in detail how my capabilities can best serve your marketing communications needs. Please contact me to arrange a mutually convenient date and time when we might initiate a dialogue.

Thank you for your time and consideration. I look forward to speaking with you soon.

Sincerely,

Walter E. Ellis

Enclosure

CONRAD JAMES

122 Pine Bluff Circle • Manlius, New York 13105 • 315-271-7551 • conniej@yahoo.com

October 26, 2006

Ms. Sally Close
Vice President for Sales & Marketing
Sunshine Industries, Inc.
1234 Seminole Boulevard
Orlando, Florida 33333

Dear Ms. Close:

Capitalizing on close to six years of experience in sales and management roles with customer-oriented organizations, I am seeking an opportunity in a corporate setting where my capabilities can further your business objectives, while offering career development opportunities. With this goal in mind, I have enclosed for your consideration a résumé outlining my experience.

Some key points you may find relevant to a sales, marketing, and/or management trainee role with your firm include:

- *Selling capital equipment to business and government accounts, including developing long-term, consultative relationships with customers.*

- *Supporting sales operations by developing specifications, responding to competitive bid requests, and managing a variety of vendor relations functions.*

- *Managing capital projects, including $500K and $750K renovations of restaurant facilities, as well as the assembly/fabrication of custom equipment for municipal highway departments.*

- *Providing leadership to groups of up to 24 customer service employees in retail and hospitality business environments, including recruiting and training team members.*

I am convinced that my skills can contribute to your ongoing business success, and that my professional development can significantly benefit from joining a leading organization such as yours. I would enjoy speaking with you in person about potential opportunities and ways that I can address your needs. I will be visiting Orlando the week of May 21st and would be pleased to meet with you during that time. Please contact me to arrange an initial interview.

Thank you for your time and consideration. I look forward to talking with you soon.

Sincerely,

Conrad James

Enclosure

Paragraph-format cover letters are also effective when you want to *tell the story* of your career path. Maybe you were promoted quickly or had a great mentor who helped you advance your career. Perhaps you've worked or traveled internationally, giving you experiences that uniquely enrich your capabilities for a particular job. The paragraph format gives you the opportunity to tell such stories in a compelling way, which a bullet-format letter just doesn't allow. Here's an example of the middle paragraphs from such a letter:

Example #14: Unique and compelling story of a candidate's career track:

> Even though my father owned the company, he was determined that I learn the business from the ground up. After college, he arranged for me to have six-month internships with four different companies that were either suppliers or customers. These experiences, in each case on the shop floor, broadened my understanding of the products and processes involved in our industry. Because my coworkers assumed I was just another employee, they treated me as "one of the gang," and I greatly enhanced my ability to relate to and build rapport with diverse groups of people at all levels.
>
> When I returned to Acme Products, first in a production planning role and later as an Account Manager, I was able to apply the knowledge and expertise gained during my internships in ways that enhanced customer satisfaction and improved both productivity and product quality.
>
> Now that Acme has been profitably sold to Consolidated Industries, I feel that my unique professional development program has prepared me to assist your firm in meeting the needs of your customer base, which substantially overlaps that of Acme.

One other advantage of paragraph-format cover letters is that you can usually fit more information on the page, but that's a double-edged sword, because your letter can be perceived as dense if you include too much copy. However, by writing compelling success stories (such as the one above) and making judicious use of white space and type effects (**bold** and *italics*), you can make this cover letter format work to your advantage.

On the following pages are two sample paragraph-format cover letters. The first is prepared in block style (flush-left format); the second uses indented paragraphs. Either format is acceptable.

Then, on page 46, you'll find a chart that compares bullet-format and paragraph-format cover letters. This chart gives you a quick reference guide to the characteristics of each style of letter, summarizing when it's best to use each and providing tips on mistakes to avoid.

MORTON D. JOSEPH
18714 Eagle View Terrace
Victor, New York 14564
(585) 924-9999
MJoseph@ResumeSOS.com

November 29, 2006

Mr. Burton Nance
Tarheel Tours
P.O. Box 999
Raleigh, NC 28699

Dear Mr. Nance:

Following up on our conversation of last week, I am enclosing a current resume as an expression of my interest in professional opportunities with your firm. I offer strong customer service and management experience, and believe that my leadership skills and management expertise could be valuable to your organization in an Operations Manager / Customer Service Manager role.

As you know, I am currently Director of Operations for Upstate Tours, with total accountability for the scheduling and movement of 60 drivers. In recent weeks, I have successfully dealt with a range of customer satisfaction issues through careful attention to customers' wants and needs, combined with collaboration with other carriers. Over the past 60 days, I have saved the company over $200,000 in revenues by avoiding potential trip cancellations.

Earlier, as a Department Head at the Syracuse *Herald-Journal*, I supervised call center and customer service employees, with accountability for serving the needs of 237,000 customers on a daily basis. By implementing new call center technology and promoting employee development initiatives, I was able to achieve a 36% improvement in our Customer Satisfaction Index, which translated into a 15% increase in subscriber retention over a two-year period.

I am confident that I can make a substantial contribution to your continuing success, and I would welcome further discussion of how my capabilities can serve your needs. Please contact me to arrange a convenient date and time to talk.

Thank you for your time and consideration. I look forward to speaking with you soon.

Sincerely,

Morton D. Joseph

Enclosure

NEIL SHANNON
1571 Creek Road
Walworth, New York 14566
(585) 715-8682
Shannon13@ResumeSOS.com

September 30, 2006

Ms. Ebelise M. Torres
Assistant Superintendent for Personnel
North Irondequoit Central School District
1234 School Road
Rochester, NY 14699

Dear Ms. Torres:

As an aspiring teacher anticipating completion of a certification program in **Elementary Education (N-6)** at SUNY Brockport in December 2006, I am seeking an opportunity to join your teaching staff on either a full-time interim or permanent basis beginning in **January 2007**. Accordingly, I have enclosed for your consideration a resume that outlines my qualifications.

Over the past two school years, I have substituted extensively with a number of local districts, including Batavia City, Newark, Wayne Central, and Red Jacket. I have been exposed to all grade levels and subject areas for Grades K-5, as well as teaching Art, Music, and Physical Education.

During an eight-week assignment at Thomas Edison Elementary School in the Wayne Central School District, I taught in a 12:1:1 self-contained Special Education classroom. With the assistance of the assigned para-professional, I developed and implemented teaching strategies appropriate to the needs and abilities of the 12 students for which we were responsible.

For 10 years prior to my decision to pursue a teaching career, I worked for a firm that distributed books and periodicals throughout western New York and Pennsylvania. An integral part of this job was maintaining knowledge of the works offered by various publishing houses. This, combined with my B.A. in English, helped to hone my own interest in reading, which allows me to bring an enthusiasm for literacy into the classroom.

I am confident that my background and education provide me with the necessary tools to have a significant positive impact on the educational lives of your students. I would enjoy meeting with you in person to discuss how I can best serve your teaching needs and will phone next week to schedule an interview.

Thank you for your time and interest. I look forward to speaking with you soon.

Sincerely,

Neil Shannon

Enclosure

Comparison of Bullet- and Paragraph-Style Cover Letters

	Bulleted Letters	Paragraph Letters
Audience	➤ Recruiters ➤ HR representatives ➤ "Cold" networking contacts	➤ Hiring managers ➤ Recruiters ➤ "Warm" networking contacts
Situation	➤ Listing qualifications ➤ Responding to specific requirements in job posting ➤ Providing quick overview of capabilities ➤ Highlighting special projects and achievements	➤ Relating problem-solving skills ➤ Describing achievements or successes ➤ Demonstrating ability to address similar challenges in new job setting ➤ Summarizing your "career story"
Characteristics	➤ Direct and to-the-point ➤ Easy to read	➤ Tells a story (challenge/action/result)
Format/Effects	➤ Use **bold** or *italics* to make bullets stand out ➤ Keep letter on one page	➤ Use text effects sparingly ➤ Maintain proper amount of white space ➤ Keep letter on one page
Things to Avoid	➤ Too many bullets ➤ Not enough white space ➤ Lengthy bullets	➤ Text too dense ➤ Not enough white space ➤ Too much detail

10 Critical Mistakes to Avoid

1. **Choosing the wrong format.** As discussed earlier in this chapter, bullet-format letters and paragraph-format letters each have their appropriate uses. Choosing the wrong format for a particular situation can harm your chances with a prospective employer. This relates back to advice from Chapter 1 about knowing your target audience and crafting a document with *format* and *content* that will appeal to that specific audience.

2. **Dense copy; overly long letter.** If you have too many words crammed on a page, your letter becomes less readable and may be passed over by an employer. As with resumes, make strategic use of white space to keep your cover letter visually appealing. Likewise, limiting the letter to one page increases the chances that an employer will take the time to read it. Except for special situations, strive to keep your cover letters to a single page.

3. **A too-tiny font.** Resist the temptation to reduce the type size just to fit more on the page. Stick with 10-point or larger and, if necessary, edit the content of the letter to keep it to one page. It's much more important to maintain the readability of your letters and give the reader an attractive presentation than to strive to squeeze in that extra sentence or two. Refer to the chart on page 49 for a comparison of some of the common fonts and how they look in various sizes.

4. **Overuse of bold,** *italics,* **and** underlining. These design elements can effectively enhance your cover letters, but overuse of them can be a distraction. As you review the many sample cover letters in later chapters of this book, take note of how **bold,** *italics,* and underlining are used to improve readability and visual impact without detracting from the letter.

5. **An untidy letter.** Dog-eared pages, wrinkled pages, or coffee stains all detract from your presentation and are completely unacceptable.

6. **A poorly reproduced letter.** If at all possible, use a laser printer to print all of your job search documents. It may well be worth visiting your local library or copy center, where they should be able to provide you with laser prints for a modest fee. If, for the sake of expediency, you decide to print your letters on an inkjet printer, set the printer at its highest-quality setting and make sure the ink is thoroughly dry before handling your letter.

7. **Inappropriate paper.** Just as exotic, hard-to-read fonts can negatively affect your presentation, so can the use of paper that has a bold color or background that makes it hard to read. If your documents are faxed at some point, either by you or the employer, a color or patterned background can detract from the quality of the transmission. As with your resume, your cover letters should be

printed on quality, watermarked paper. A variety of moderately priced, attractive choices are available at office supply stores or copy centers. The paper your cover letters are printed on should match your resume; the best color choices are white, natural white (cream), ivory, or light gray.

8. **Handwritten changes.** Handwritten changes on your job search documents are not acceptable! Presumably, you've spent a great deal of time writing and formatting a top-notch resume, plus additional time composing a cover letter targeting your ideal job. Doesn't it make sense to take the extra few minutes to make the necessary changes on the computer and print out a clean copy of your letter? Again, if computer access is an issue, many public libraries offer free access to anyone with a library card (they may charge for printing documents for you), and copy centers generally allow access to computers for a nominal fee.

9. **Odd-sized paper.** Although many job seekers may perceive this as a competitive advantage, believe us when we tell you that is not the case. If you're looking for a position in the United States, be sure to print your cover letters and resumes on paper that is 8.5 × 11 inches. Perhaps if you're an artist or designer, you might come up with some-thing unique, but that's a rare exception to the rule. Some executives use an "executive" or "monarch" size paper which is slightly smaller (7.5 × 10.5 inches), but, again, this is an exception.

    If you're applying for jobs internationally, there is a different standard sheet size, known as "A4" (8.27 × 11.69 inches in the U.S. system of measurement), which is used in Europe, Australia, and various parts of Asia. However, if a company is accepting applications from U.S. residents, it's likely that they will accept our standard letter-size sheet.

10. **Typographical errors.** Typographical, grammatical, and word usage mistakes are totally unacceptable. After spending considerable time preparing your job search documents, it would be a shame to make a poor impression on an employer by allowing such errors to slip through. Of course, you should run "spell-check" as a preliminary step, but don't count on it to catch every mistake. The classic example is the misuse of the words, "to," "two," and "too." Each is a properly spelled English word, but each has a different meaning and usage. Your computer's spell-check cannot reliably detect if you're using the correct one in the right context. The solution is to proofread, proofread, and then proofread again. Reread the documents yourself; set them aside and come back to reread them again; then, have a trusted friend (with a strong command of written English) read them; read them aloud to yourself. You only have one opportunity to make that first impression, and you should do everything you can to make it a strong and positive one.

Comparison of Common Cover Letter Typestyles and Sizes

Size	Roman	Bold	*Italic*
10 pt.	Arial Bookman Old Style Garamond Tahoma Times New Roman Verdana	**Arial** **Bookman Old Style** **Garamond** **Tahoma** **Times New Roman** **Verdana**	*Arial* *Bookman Old Style* *Garamond* *Tahoma* *Times New Roman* *Verdana*
10.5 pt.	Arial Bookman Old Style Garamond Tahoma Times New Roman Verdana	**Arial** **Bookman Old Style** **Garamond** **Tahoma** **Times New Roman** **Verdana**	*Arial* *Bookman Old Style* *Garamond* *Tahoma* *Times New Roman* *Verdana*
11 pt.	Arial Bookman Old Style Garamond Tahoma Times New Roman Verdana	**Arial** **Bookman Old Style** **Garamond** **Tahoma** **Times New Roman** **Verdana**	*Arial* *Bookman Old Style* *Garamond* *Tahoma* *Times New Roman* *Verdana*
11.5 pt.	Arial Bookman Old Style Garamond Tahoma Times New Roman Verdana	**Arial** **Bookman Old Style** **Garamond** **Tahoma** **Times New Roman** **Verdana**	*Arial* *Bookman Old Style* *Garamond* *Tahoma* *Times New Roman* *Verdana*
12 pt.	Arial Bookman Old Style Garamond Tahoma Times New Roman Verdana	**Arial** **Bookman Old Style** **Garamond** **Tahoma** **Times New Roman** **Verdana**	*Arial* *Bookman Old Style* *Garamond* *Tahoma* *Times New Roman* *Verdana*

Chapter 3

▸ # Simple Truths About
Writing Your Cover Letters

Each of the chapters in this book is critically important to writing powerful and effective cover letters that get you and your resume noticed, set you apart from the crowd, and entice a prospective employer to offer you an interview. However, this chapter is perhaps the most important, demonstrating step-by-step how to write each section of your cover letter. You'll also want to refer to Appendix A, where you'll find a cover letter worksheet that you can use as a foundation to collect all the information you will need to write each of your letters. If you need more forms than we've provided, feel free to make copies so that you have ample materials to see you through the writing process.

Before we begin to explore each of these sections, it's important to review the key concepts—the simple truths—from each of the two preceding chapters. In Chapter 1, you were introduced to the six simple truths about cover letter writing:

Truth #1: Effective cover letters contain 10 key components.

Truth #2: Cover letter writing is sales.

Truth #3: Cover letter writing is all about strategy.

Truth #4: Targeted letters work best.

Truth #5: The cover letter must match the resume.

Truth #6: Each circumstance presents its own challenges.

If you can't remember the specifics of each of these truths, take a few minutes to review Chapter 1 again, as these concepts are essential to understand and apply when you begin to actually write your letters.

Then, in Chapter 2, you were introduced to the four simple truths about cover letter design and formatting:

Truth #1: Effective cover letters contain 10 key components.

Truth #2: Simple designs work best.

Truth #3: Bullet-format letters highlight your skills and achievements.

Truth #4: Paragraph-format letters tell your career stories.

Again, if you can't remember the specifics of each of these truths, take a few minutes to reread Chapter 2, as these concepts are also essential to understand and apply when you begin to write your letters.

Now that you have a clear grasp of strategic and design considerations for your cover letters, it's time to move on to the critical elements of the actual writing process. Similar to when you wrote your resume (if you followed the step-by-step process outlined in our companion book, *No-Nonsense Resumes*), writing your cover letters requires a unique blend of art and science, allowing you to use a *creative* approach to present *factual* information about yourself and your career. A cover letter is no longer simply a transmittal letter that accompanies your resume. Rather, today's cover letter is a sales document that should be written to promote the very best you have to offer to a company. Bottom line: That's the only goal of your cover letter—to grab a hiring manager's or recruiter's attention (along with your resume) and help you get job interviews.

In this chapter, we're going to introduce you to the strategies and techniques that we, as professional resume writers, use to write powerful cover letters with a simplified and streamlined process. If you follow these instructions, you too will be able to craft cover letters that portray your very *best* you!

The 5 Simple Truths About Cover Letter Writing

Just as many other business-related activities, cover letter writing is a process. In many ways, it's much akin to writing a technical report in that the final document (1) has a very specific purpose, (2) must clearly and concisely convey a particular message, and (3) must appropriately communicate that message to its target audience.

With that in mind, it's easy to understand that writing cover letters and other job search communications is *not* at all like creative writing (for example, novels, short stories, and poems), for which you stare at a blank piece of paper waiting for inspiration. Rather, cover letter writing is closer to following an outline or connecting the dots. With our help, you'll be able to connect *your* dots and write cover letters using a very methodical and logical process.

We'll begin with the five simple truths for writing winning cover letters:

Truth #1: Four key components are essential for success.

Truth #2: It's all about positioning.

Truth #3: There are five basic types of cover letters.

Truth #4: You don't have to write in order.

Truth #5: The language should be different than in your resume.

The remainder of this chapter will explore these simple truths in much greater detail, and provide you with essential how-to information for writing cover letters that are intelligent, distinct, and filled with information that will encourage a recruiter to invite you for an interview. Remember, cover letters do not get jobs; their only "job" is to help get *you* an interview!

Truth #1: 4 Key Components Are Essential for Success

As presented in Chapter 1 and Chapter 2, there are 10 key components of every effective cover letter:

1. Contact information
2. Date
3. Inside address
4. Reference line
5. Salutation
6. Opening paragraph
7. Content—main body
8. Closing paragraph/call to action
9. Complimentary closing/signature
10. Enclosures

However, of these 10, there are four—contact information, opening paragraph, content, and closing paragraph—that stand out as most important. That's what we will focus on in this section.

Contact Information

The very first thing that you're going to include on your cover letter is your contact information—name, mailing address, phone number(s), and e-mail address. Here are three standard formats that you can select from:

Format #1: Standard

JOSHUA L. FARMER
22 Glen Cove
Ames, IA 39872
Home (308) 555-2937 / Cell (308) 555-0972 / jfarm@msn.com

Format #2: Modified

MARIA FERNANDEZ

987 Derby Run Road
Finksburg, MD 20972

(301) 555-9038
fernanm@aol.com

Format #3: College Student (similar format—with two addresses—could be used for relocation or "trailing spouse")

SALLY R. SIMMONS

SallyS85@hood.edu

Permanent Address:
665 Williamson Road
Dover, DE 19903
Cell (302) 555-2983

Current Address:
Grayson Hall, Rm. 422
Hood College
Frostburg, MD 22925

Although including your contact information should be a snap, sometimes there are unusual circumstances or special considerations. Pay close attention to these recommendations:

1. If you have a gender-neutral name, consider using one of the following formats so that someone knows how to address you:

   Mr. Lynn F. Gundersen

   Ms. Tracey S. Simpson

2. If you have a first name that's difficult to pronounce, or go by a *call name* other than your first name, consider using one of the following formats so that someone knows how to address you:

   Ranguswamy "Roger" Abdellah

   Melissa C. "Chris" Miller

   HR people and hiring managers are human, and this approach helps put them at ease in contacting and communicating with you, and gives them one less reason to screen you out.

3. If you don't yet have a personal e-mail address, get one! Today's job search market has gone electronic and many prospective employers will want to communicate with you via e-mail. However, it is inappropriate to use your current work e-mail to conduct your job search. Rather, get a free e-mail account with Yahoo!, Hotmail, Gmail, or any one of a number of other providers that will allow you to access

your e-mail account from any computer with an Internet connection. When setting up your account, be sure to use a professional-sounding screen name (for example, AJSmith13@hotmail.com) and *not* something cute or unprofessional (for example, HoneyBear@yahoo.com).

4. Be very careful if you decide to include your work phone number on your resume, and only do so if you have a direct number. Even in that situation, it's preferable to have people contact you on your private cell phone or at your home number. You're not at your current job to spend your days conducting your job search!

   While we're on the topic, make certain that your outgoing voice mail message, whether on your cell phone or home answering machine, sounds professional (for example, "You have reached 555-1234. I'm unable to take your call right now, so please leave a message at the tone," is *much* more acceptable than, "Hey, dude! You know the drill—if you're a telemarketer, drop dead"). One person's humor is another person's poor taste.

5. If you have an online version of your resume (see Chapter 4 in *No-Nonsense Resumes* for more information on creating e-based resumes), be sure to include the Website address (URL) in the contact information section of your letter so people can go online to read more about you and your career.

Opening Paragraph

The opening paragraph of your cover letter serves as an introduction that is designed to communicate the following:

1. Why you're writing the letter, which is generally either in response to an advertisement or because you're interested in employment opportunities with a specific company.

2. Your particular area of expertise, your profession, or your industry of choice.

3. A brief summary of the value you bring to that organization.

To best demonstrate how to write a strong introduction for your cover letters, carefully review the following examples:

Example #1: Opening paragraph when responding to an advertisement:

Enclosed is my resume in response to your advertisement for a Public Relations Professional. In reviewing your specific qualifications for the position, I discovered that I have precisely the experience that you are seeking in a candidate. As such, several of my most notable projects are highlighted below.

Example #2: Opening paragraph when writing directly to a company to express your interest in employment opportunities:

When I joined PRM in 2004, the company was fraught with organizational challenges and issues. Today, our organization is strong, our cash flow is positive, our member retention is outstanding, and we are technologically on the "cutting edge." Now, I'm looking to make the same contributions to another company and would be delighted to interview for an executive assignment with CCM Associates.

Example #3: Opening paragraph when writing to a recruiter:

Currently, I serve as Director of Production Operations for a large chemical manufacturing facility in Houston, but am ready to make a career change. As such, I am contacting you about potential opportunities with any of your clients that will capitalize on my strong qualifications, and have enclosed my resume for your review.

Content/Main Body of the Letter

The content of your cover letter—the text between the opening paragraph and the closing paragraph—is the most vital component of the letter. It is this section that allows you to briefly, yet comprehensively, communicate the skills, experiences, and achievements of your career that are most relevant to the particular position for which you are applying or the specific company you are contacting. We often refer to this section as the *meat* of the cover letter.

There are hundreds of examples we could provide that demonstrate how to formulate the content section of your cover letters. However, the best resource you have is right in your hands—all the letters we've included in Chapters 5–16. Be sure to review all those appropriate to your career field to get ideas on how best to write the content of your letters.

Basically, there are three different formats that you can use to present this section of your letter—the bullet format, the paragraph format, and the combination format—and each has its own purpose. If your goal is to communicate specific information about your skills, achievements, projects, and experiences, then a bullet-format cover letter will generally work best, because it allows you to include specific information in a brief and easy-to-read style.

Example #4: Bullet format

With a total of 17 years of experience in construction and facilities management, I bring to Engelhard excellent skills in:

* All major construction trades including HVAC, electrical, roofing, framing, concrete forming and finishing, carpentry, ceramic tile, and painting.
* Evaluating project costs and developing accurate project budgets.
* Selecting, negotiating contracts with, and managing project subcontractors.
* Managing projects to comply with state and local building codes and regulations.

On the other end of the continuum is the paragraph format, which is best used when you want to communicate a *story* about your career that might focus on rapid promotion, unique opportunities, and the overall strength of your experience. Note that you should keep your cover letters to only two or three short paragraphs.

Example #5: Paragraph format

Throughout the past 12 years, I have built and profitably managed high-volume, multi-site retail operations. My strength lies in my ability to integrate all the finite elements of retailing—most critically, sales—with marketing, advertising, merchandising, inventory, personnel, customer service, finance, facilities, and other supporting business infrastructures. What makes my qualifications so unique is the fact that I have worked in a number of different retail situations—new ventures, acquisitions, turnarounds, and growth operations.

During my tenure with ABC Stores, I have repeatedly demonstrated my success by providing strong financial results. In one situation, sales grew to over $40 million; in another, revenues increased at a rate of better than 35% annually. This has been achieved largely as a result of my efforts in providing a strong strategic vision and a business structure to support success.

Between the two extremes of the bullet format and the paragraph format lies the combination format, which integrates both bullets and paragraphs to tell a story *and* highlight the resulting achievements. The following sample is a perfect example of how to best create this type of letter.

Example #6: Combination format

Currently, as the Group Account Manager for Excel Communications and its primary business units (including emerging online and multimedia technologies), I spearhead a dynamic media marketing organization. My challenge has been to expand and strengthen market presence through the introduction of a diversified portfolio of advertising, business development, promotional, and strategic alliance initiatives. Results have been significant and include:
- Capture of an 11% gain in overall primetime cable share.
- Creation of "standardized" programming and scheduling to attract and retain a loyal audience.
- Development of innovative multimedia advertising and promotional strategies.
- Expansion into new media applications.

Closing Paragraph(s)/Call to Action

The closing paragraph, as the name implies, is the section that you use to close, or end, your cover letter. Specifically, it should incorporate a "call to action," and should state either how you plan to follow up (the proactive approach) a request for an interview (the more passive approach). We strongly recommend that you take the proactive approach and follow up whenever possible. Unfortunately, it's not always possible if you're responding to a blind ad or post office box with no company or contact information.

You can also use the closing paragraph to include any additional information that may have been requested in an advertisement (for example, salary history, salary requirements, or geographic requirements). And finally, be sure to express your appreciation to that individual for taking the time to review your resume and consider your qualifications.

Here are several different examples you can use as the foundation from which to write your own closing paragraphs:

Example #7: Closing paragraph when responding to an advertisement:

I would welcome the chance to interview for the Sales Associate position with your firm and can guarantee that the strength of my financial and operating experience will add measurable value to MTB Unlimited. I'll follow up next Thursday to schedule an interview. Thank you for your time and consideration.

Example #8: Closing paragraph when writing directly to a company to express your interest in employment opportunities:

My goal is a senior-level management position where I can direct sales, marketing, and customer service for an organization in Europe—quite similar to the responsibilities I manage today. However, my goal is to affiliate with an organization offering stronger opportunities for professional growth, management, and leadership. Please note that I am conversational in five different languages and have a wealth of cross-cultural business experience. I appreciate your time in reviewing my qualifications and look forward to speaking with you to pursue opportunities with Merrill Lynch.

Example #9: Closing paragraph when writing to a recruiter:

At this point in my career, I am confidentially exploring new professional challenges and opportunities, and would welcome the chance to discuss any specific search assignments that are appropriate for an individual with such an extensive background in the building trades industry. Be advised that I am open to relocation and that my salary requirements are $60,000+. Thank you.

As you review all of the sample cover letters in this book, you'll find scores of examples that you can adapt to create the exact wording of your opening paragraph, main body, and closing paragraph of your cover letters—language that will generate interest and enthusiasm on the part of your new employer.

Truth #2: It's All About Positioning

In Chapter 1, we discussed the concept of positioning—of *painting a picture* of yourself that you want a hiring manager or recruiter to see. Your goal is to position yourself in the cover letter as an individual who is well-qualified for the opportunity you are pursuing.

Consider the following: Suppose that your entire career has been in accounting (with lots of training and supervisory responsibilities), and you now want to pursue a career in human resources. If that's the case, you want your letter to position you as an HR professional and *not* as an accountant. As such, you'll want to highlight your experience in employee training, development, supervision, and performance evaluation more prominently than your experience in day-to-day accounting operations.

Or perhaps you've been a nurse for 10 years and now want to transition into pharmaceutical sales. Be sure that your letter positions you as an individual qualified for a sales position by emphasizing your communication skills, ability to manage relationships with physicians, and your background in working with pharmaceutical reps to place orders and evaluate new products.

There are thousands of examples similar to these that we could use to demonstrate the concept of *positioning*. Perhaps the most important concept is that of *reweighting,* or shifting the emphasis away from your *current* core responsibilities and focusing on ancillary responsibilities that are more supportive of your current job objectives.

One word of caution: When you are reweighting your skills and experience, you must *remain in the realm of reality.* Don't overstate or oversell your qualifications if you cannot live up to what you wrote in your cover letter when you get to the interview. If you have to defend something that you wrote, you will most likely have lost that opportunity. Trying to back-pedal generally does not work to your advantage. Honesty and accuracy are essential!

On the opposite side of this discussion are candidates who are seeking a position within their current occupation or profession (for example, a production supervisor seeking a new, higher-level position as a production manager). In this situation, the issue is not *reweighting,* but rather *heavily weighting* the skills and experiences that you already have so that you're positioning yourself as an extremely well-qualified production manager in your cover letter. In this example, the candidate wants to place an equal emphasis on both his or her production talents and supervisory/management experience so that he or she paints just the *right* picture.

As you can see, the concept of positioning is critical to all job seekers, whether they're pursuing a similar career path or changing careers for new opportunities. Think carefully about how you want to position yourself in your cover letters based on the specific opportunities you are pursuing. Once you know your position, writing cover letters will be easier and more efficient, and the result will be cover letters that proudly portray your relevant qualifications.

Truth #3: There Are 5 Basic Types of Cover Letters

As you review the sample cover letters in this book, it may appear that there are countless different "varieties" of cover letters. They do seem to come in all shapes and sizes. However, if you look closely, you'll see that there are really only five distinct types or categories of letters:

▶ **Company Ad-Response Letters**

▶ **Recruiter Ad-Response Letters**

▶ **Company Cold-Call Letters**

▶ **Recruiter Cold-Call Letters**

▶ **Referral Letters**

You'll find that there are strikingly similar characteristics among these categories of letters, as well as strikingly different characteristics that clearly distinguish one from the other. It is imperative that you understand how best to write each type of letter so that you're well equipped for each situation that may arise during your job search. In fact, it is quite likely that you and most other job seekers will use all five of these letters repeatedly throughout your search.

Remember, regardless of the specific category of letter you're writing, you will always want to heed the information presented in Truth #1 earlier in this chapter, where we outlined the four key components of every effective cover letter—contact information, introduction, content, and closing. Now, let's explore what makes each of the five categories of letters unique.

Company Ad-Response Letters

Company ad-response letters are just what you would imagine; letters written in response to specific advertisements you might see in a newspaper, journal, or other print publication, as well as letters that you'll send in response to online job postings.

Unique Characteristics:

▶ These letters specifically refer to each job title or job announcement, either in a subject line at the beginning of the letter or in the first paragraph of the letter. You want to immediately *connect* yourself to the position so that it is clear what opportunity you are pursuing.

> These letters often include an introductory paragraph that immediately communicates your value, skills, and qualifications for that particular position. For example, if you're applying for a position as a sales representative, you might consider an opening paragraph such as:

> > *Building market value is my expertise. Whether establishing a new market or accelerating sales within an existing market, I have consistently increased sales revenues and expanded the size of the customer base. This is the value I bring to the Sales Manager position at Sims, Incorporated.*

> Note that this introductory paragraph effectively accomplishes two things: (1) immediately communicates the value of the candidate (in building revenues and capturing customers) and (2) identifies the position for which this candidate is applying.

> Even if an advertisement requests that you provide salary information, it is not necessary to do so. In survey after survey, it has been proven that a company will contact you if they're interested, regardless of whether or not you responded to their request to provide salary information. If you're comfortable including the information, then do it. If you're not, then it's fine to omit it.

> *One important recommendation:* Rather than tie yourself to a specific salary number, if you're asked to provide salary requirements, you might considering providing a range (for example, "My salary requirements are $60,000 to $70,000 a year"). This gives both you and your interviewer some flexibility when negotiating your best salary.

> *One important insight:* Surveys have also indicated that most interviewers have the authority to negotiate a salary up to 10 percent higher than what they may have originally told you. Knowing that, you *always* want to negotiate. In fact, hiring managers have told us that they *expect* candidates to negotiate and are often surprised when they don't. Take advantage of the opportunity and negotiate for your very *best* salary.

Refer to the Abelson company letter on page 67 for an example of a company ad-response letter.

Recruiter Ad-Response Letters

Just as with company ad-response letters, these letters written to recruiters are just what you would imagine: letters written in response to specific print and online advertisements.

Unique Characteristics:

> These letters specifically refer to each job title or job announcement, either in a subject line at the beginning of the letter or in the first paragraph of the letter.

▶ As with letters directed to companies, these letters frequently include an introductory paragraph that succinctly communicates your value, skills, and qualifications for the advertised position. For example, looking again at our hypothetical sales representative position, you might consider this opening paragraph:

> *Building market value is my expertise. Developing new markets and increasing penetration in existing markets are capabilities that I can bring to a Sales Manager role with your client, Sims, Inc. My track record of consistently increasing revenues and expanding account bases demonstrates my capacity to address Sims' immediate challenges and contribute to its future growth.*

Again, as with the company-directed letter, this introductory paragraph immediately communicates the value of the candidate and identifies the position for which this candidate is applying.

▶ These letters *do* include salary history and/or salary requirements as requested in the advertisement. It is important to fully disclose your salary expectations to recruiters so that you're not wasting their time or yours. If you're looking for an annual salary of $75,000, you certainly don't want to spend an afternoon interviewing for a $45,000/year position! When you share your salary expectations, you'll be helping a recruiter find just the *right* opportunity for you.

▶ These letters also include, in the closing paragraph, other *personal* information that is important to your search. This may include your geographic preferences, your need to be in an area with special medical and/or educational facilities, and other information that may be pertinent to the opportunities that interest you. Again, don't waste your time or a recruiter's time. Here are two examples:

> *At this point in my career, it is important that I remain in the Northeastern U.S. as I have a special-needs child enrolled in a private residential school in Boston. Obviously, my family and I want to remain within a few hours driving distance so that we can continue to visit him on a regular basis.*

> *Currently I serve in a volunteer capacity as the Director of the Shore Lakes United Way Campaign, a position I've held for the past three years and one that I find tremendously rewarding. As such, I am only available for opportunities in the Southern California area.*

Refer to the Abelson recruiter letter on page 68 for an example of a recruiter ad-response letter. Note the differences between the Abelson company letter on page 67 and the Abelson recruiter letter on page 68 (differences are highlighted in bold print).

Company Cold-Call Letters

Company cold-call letters are written to express your interest in employment opportunities with a particular organization—not in response to any particular position announcement. They're known as "cold" letters that you're using to introduce and market yourself to the company in anticipation that they may have an unadvertised opportunity for which you would be an ideal candidate.

Unique Characteristics:

▶ These letters specifically refer to the type of position you are pursing, generally in the first paragraph of the letter. You want to immediately *connect* yourself to a particular career path so that it is clear to the reader what type of position you are pursuing.

▶ These letters generally begin with an introductory paragraph that immediately communicates your value, skills, and qualifications as they relate to a particular company. For example, if you're interested in an opportunity in manufacturing operations, you might start your letter with an opening paragraph such as:

> *Improving manufacturing output and product quality are what I do best. Throughout my 12-year career in manufacturing operations, I have been successful in increasing throughput by as much as 35% and reducing product rejects by an unprecedented 72%. This is the value I bring to AMN and am hoping you are in the market for a candidate with precisely my qualifications.*

Note that this introductory paragraph effectively accomplishes two things: It (1) immediately communicates the value of the candidate (in building revenues and capturing customers) and (2) identifies the type of career opportunity the candidate is pursuing.

▶ These letters *never* mention salary history or salary requirements. That discussion is better left for a second, third, or fourth interview, and is never appropriate to include in a cold-call letter.

▶ Your only objective in writing this type of letter is to generate interest on behalf of the employer and get a phone call or e-mail message offering you the opportunity for an interview.

Refer to the Madras company letter on page 69 for an example of a company cold-call letter.

Recruiter Cold-Call Letters

Recruiter cold-call letters are written to express your interest in employment opportunities within a particular profession or industry—not in response to any particular position announcement. They're known as "cold" letters that you're using to introduce and market yourself to a recruiter in anticipation that he or she may have a current search assignment for which you would be an ideal candidate.

Unique Characteristics:

▶ These letters specifically refer to the type of position or industry you are pursing, generally in the first paragraph of the letter. You want to immediately *connect* yourself to a particular career path so that it is clear to the recruiter what type of position you are pursuing.

▶ These letters generally begin with an introductory paragraph that is short and to the point. For example, if you're interested in an opportunity in accounting management, you might start your letter with an opening paragraph such as:

> *As a corporate accountant with eight years of increasingly responsible experience, I am currently exploring new mid-level accounting management opportunities. Enclosed for your review is my resume in anticipation that you may have a current search assignment for a candidate with my qualifications.*

Recruiters often receive hundreds of unsolicited resumes each week. If you can make their job easier by identifying your particular area of interest, without requiring them to read all of your material, you'll be much more likely to capture their interest and, perhaps, get an interview with either the recruiter or one of his or her client companies.

▶ These letters *always* mention salary history or salary requirements. Just as with ad-response letters that you write to recruiters, you want to be sure to include your salary requirements and any relevant personal information (for example, geographic preferences and educational requirements) when writing to recruiters. Remember, you don't want to waste anyone's time!

▶ Your only objective in writing this type of letter is to generate interest on behalf of the recruiter and get a phone call or e-mail offering you the opportunity to interview for a search assignment that the recruiter may currently have or anticipates in the near future.

Refer to the Madras recruiter letter on page 70 for an example of a recruiter cold-call letter. Note the differences between the Madras *company* letter and this Madras *recruiter* letter (differences are highlighted in bold print).

Referral Letters

Referral letters are letters that you will write when a specific person refers you to another person or a company. These letters can be extremely powerful in opening doors and generating interviews because a third-party referral is a great testimonial to your qualifications. This, in and of itself, speaks highly of your skills and performance.

Unique Characteristics:

▶ These letters begin with an immediate mention of the individual who referred you, in order to leverage that relationship. In fact, that is principally what distinguishes referral letters from both company ad-response and company cold-call letters.

▶ Just as with cold-call letters to companies, these letters specifically refer to the type of position you are pursing, generally in the first paragraph of the letter. You want to immediately *connect* yourself to a particular career path so that it is clear to the reader what type of position you are pursuing.

▶ Following the mention of your mutual friend/colleague, these letters generally begin with an introductory paragraph that immediately communicates your value, skills, and qualifications as they are appropriate to that company. Here's an example demonstrating how best to write an opening paragraph that incorporates all three of these essential elements:

> *John Bower, a close colleague of mine, suggested I contact you immediately to let you know of my interest in a position as a Logistics Manager with RDL. John speaks so highly of you and the organization, and felt that my skills would be a perfect match for your firm. My resume, highlighting my extensive experience and successes in logistics management, is enclosed for your review. Most notable has been my success in increasing the volume of material that we're currently moving at Atlas Equipment by 24% and reducing our annual vendor expenses by an average of 18%.*

Note that this introductory paragraph effectively accomplishes three things: It (1) states the name of the individual referring the candidate at the very beginning of the letter; (2) identifies the type of career opportunity the candidate is pursuing; and (3) highlights the value of the candidate (in increasing product movement and reducing vendor costs).

▶ These letters *never* mention salary history or salary requirements. That discussion is better left for a second, third, or fourth interview and is never appropriate to include in a referral letter.

▶ Your only objective in writing this type of letter is to generate interest on behalf of the employer and get a phone call or e-mail offering you the opportunity for an interview.

▶ Keep in mind that the person to whom the letter is addressed may *not* be involved in the ultimate hiring decision. This is fine, because, hopefully, he or she can introduce you to the right person, or at least direct your resume to the right person. This is important to remember, because it may impact the tone of your letter and what you are specifically asking the reader to do for you.

See the Williams letter on page 71 for an example of a referral letter.

Truth #4: You Don't Have to Write in Order

Give yourself a break! If you're struggling to write a cover letter, consider writing the letter "out of order." This is one of the most valuable insider tips that we can pass along, a strategy that many professional resume writers use over and over when they hit a stumbling block.

Often, the closing paragraph is the easiest to write, so start with that. Take a look back at the sample closing paragraphs earlier in this chapter and you'll see that they generally comprise three key components: (1) a thank-you to the recipient for taking the time to review your materials; (2) information on how to best contact you; and (3) information about how you will follow up, or that you'll wait for the recipient to contact you. As stated previously, we strongly recommend that you, the job seeker, follow up when possible.

Because the closing paragraph is strong and generally "factual" information, it should be quick and easy to write. *Estimated time for completion: 5 minutes.*

Once you've written the closing paragraph, you may find it easier to write the "meat" of the letter next. This will be the information that you'll include either in your paragraphs or bullets—the information about you and your career that is most relevant to the position or company to which you are applying. Again, refer to the samples earlier in this chapter to determine how you can best present your qualifications in a short and hard-hitting cover letter. Have the position description, job posting, and any other research materials handy as you write to help expedite the process. *Estimated time for completion: 30 minutes.*

Now, it's time to write the introductory paragraph, which can be the most difficult. As we discussed earlier in this chapter, it's always best to start your letters with information that will grab a reader's attention, rather than the more traditional, *I am writing in response to your advertisement for an Accounting Clerk as posted on Monster.com.* You want your letters to instantly spark the reader's interest and communicate the value you bring to a position or company within the first few words of your cover letters whenever possible.

Take some time to think about what is most important to communicate to each specific employer and then use that information as the foundation for your introductory sentence and paragraph. *Estimated time for completion: 20 minutes.*

When you write your cover letters from the "bottom to the top," you may find that the writing process is much easier and faster. Next time you're struggling with a letter, try this strategy and see if it works for you. Once you've written a few cover letters, the process will get easier (and faster). Plus, as you'll see when you read the next section, your existing letters can serve as a "template" or starting point for other letters, saving you significant time and energy.

(Company Ad-Response Letter)

MARCIA ABELSON

2209 Speedway Drive
Toledo, OH 40928

(909) 555-7352
abelsonm@msn.com

July 21, 2006

Elisabeth Suter
President & CEO
Kramer Technologies, Inc.
1000 Kramer Boulevard
Boston, MA 02983

RE: Executive Vice President – Product Development & Marketing

Dear Ms. Suter:

To gain a competitive lead in today's technology-driven marketplace requires an executive with a record of innovation and performance success across the full array of core business functions – from organizational design and leadership to product development and market positioning to global sales leadership to bottom-line financial results.

With more than 16 years of senior management experience in start-up, turnaround, high growth and Fortune 500 technology companies, I have created the vision, developed the strategies and executed the tactical actions to increase revenues and customer loyalty, reduce operating costs, expand market penetration, strengthen organizational performance and improve bottom-line profits. This is the value I bring to Kramer Technologies.

My success is a direct result of my ability to leverage the strengths of each organization's personnel, technology and capital resources. Under my leadership, I have been instrumental in:

- Restructuring and revitalizing non-performing organizations to achieve record financial results.
- Establishing best-in-class operations that have been the benchmark for numerous ventures.
- Recruiting and leading top-performing field and corporate teams to unprecedented performance.
- Structuring joint partnerships and strategic alliances to leverage opportunities worldwide.
- Identifying and negotiating corporate and technology acquisitions to strengthen strategic position.

My approach is hands-on, with a true commitment to the success of my team, my organization and the corporation at large. Never daunted by challenge, I view each obstacle as an opportunity to build, lead and deliver. What's more, I have consistently demonstrated my ability to outperform the competition, dominate the marketplace and accelerate revenue growth beyond corporate, investor and shareholder expectations.

I would welcome the opportunity to interview for the above-referenced position and can guarantee that the strength of my experience and knowledge of our industry and its major players will add measurable value to Kramer Technologies. I'll follow up next week to schedule an interview and thank you for your consideration.

Regards,

Marcia Abelson

Enclosure

(Recruiter Ad-Response Letter)

MARCIA ABELSON

2209 Speedway Drive
Toledo, OH 40928

(909) 555-7352
abelsonm@msn.com

July 29, 2006

Drew Montgomery
Technology Recruiter
Lewis & Morton Recruiting
900 Main Street
Boston, MA 02965

RE: Executive Vice President – Product Development & Marketing – Fortune 500 Technology Company

Dear Mr. Montgomery:

Please accept this letter and resume in consideration for the above-referenced position. I bring a unique blend of IT leadership talent to the position with my most notable achievements in organizational design and leadership, product development, market positioning, global sales leadership and bottom-line financial management.

With more than 16 years of senior management experience in start-up, turnaround, high growth and Fortune 500 technology companies, I have created the vision, developed the strategies and executed the tactical actions to increase revenues and customer loyalty, reduce operating costs, expand market penetration, strengthen organizational performance and improve bottom-line profits. This is the value I bring to Kramer Technologies.

My success is a direct result of my ability to leverage the strengths of each organization's personnel, technology and capital resources. Under my leadership, I have been instrumental in:

- Restructuring and revitalizing non-performing organizations to achieve record financial results.
- Establishing best-in-class operations that have been the benchmark for numerous ventures.
- Recruiting and leading top-performing field and corporate teams to unprecedented performance.
- Structuring joint partnerships and strategic alliances to leverage opportunities worldwide.
- Identifying and negotiating corporate and technology acquisitions to strengthen strategic position.

My approach is hands-on, with a true commitment to the success of my team, my organization and the corporation at large. Never daunted by challenge, I view each obstacle as an opportunity to build, lead and deliver. What's more, I have consistently demonstrated my ability to outperform the competition, dominate the marketplace and accelerate revenue growth beyond corporate, investor and shareholder expectations.

I would welcome the opportunity to interview for the above-referenced position and am available for relocation. As requested, my recent compensation has averaged $175,000 and I would anticipate a new position would afford me a package well in excess of $200,000. I look forward to hearing from you.

Regards,

Marcia Abelson

Enclosure

(Company Cold-Call Letter)

SAL MADRAS

22 Canal River Street
Menlo Park, CA 90993

salmadras@msn.com
494-555-9827

August 20, 2006

George Glenn
Chief Technology Officer
The XMIZ Corporation
22 Boonsboro Boulevard
San Mateo, CA 98372

Dear Mr. Glenn:

Building high-performance technology organizations is my expertise. Whether challenged to develop a strategic IT plan, spearhead development of new technologies, or enhance the quality and reliability of existing systems, I have consistently surpassed all performance objectives and built IT functions that have supported mission-critical business operations.

My greatest strength lies in the combination of my leadership and technology qualifications. In my current position, I lead a team of 40 IT professionals developing, implementing and supporting a portfolio of advanced technologies for a $200 million business unit. The range of my responsibilities is vast and includes strategic IT planning, staff training and development, project management, budget preparation and justification, and leadership of the entire IT development and support organization. I have included the most prominent projects on my resume – projects that have delivered measurable gains in business productivity, quality and revenue performance as a direct result of IT initiatives that I have spearheaded.

Of particular note, I have been the forerunner within the organization in utilizing offshore personnel in China to supplement U.S.-based operations, a huge endeavor that has been extremely effective for Myerson Technologies. This has allowed me to further demonstrate my strong leadership and motivational abilities while working within a cross-cultural, multi-lingual environment.

Although secure in my current position, I am confidentially exploring new management challenges and opportunities where I can continue to provide strong and decisive technology leadership. As such, I would welcome a personal interview to discuss how my qualifications can strengthen and support your IT organization and help achieve your long-term technology goals. I thank you for your time and will follow up with you next week.

Sincerely,

Sal Madras

Enclosure

(Recruiter Cold-Call Letter)

SAL MADRAS

22 Canal River Street   salmadras@msn.com
Menlo Park, CA 90993   494-555-9827

August 20, 2006

Leslie Greene
The Adams Technology Recruitment Group
909 Blair Smith Road
San Francisco, CA 98263

Dear Mrs. Greene:

Anticipating that one of your clients may be seeking a senior-level IT executive, I have enclosed my resume for your review. The value I can bring to a leading edge IT firm is my success in building high-performance technology teams and organizations. Whether challenged to develop a strategic IT plan, spearhead development of new technologies, or enhance the quality and reliability of existing systems, I have consistently surpassed all performance objectives and built IT functions that have supported mission-critical business operations.

My greatest strength lies in the combination of my leadership and technology qualifications. In my current position, I lead a team of 40 IT professionals developing, implementing and supporting a portfolio of advanced technologies for a $200 million business unit. The range of my responsibilities is vast and includes strategic IT planning, staff training and development, project management, budget preparation and justification, and leadership of the entire IT development and support organization. I have included the most prominent projects on my resume – projects that have delivered measurable gains in business productivity, quality and revenue performance as a direct result of IT initiatives that I have spearheaded.

Of particular note, I have been the forerunner within the organization in utilizing offshore personnel in China to supplement U.S.-based operations, a huge endeavor that has been extremely effective for Myerson Technologies. This has allowed me to further demonstrate my strong leadership and motivational abilities while working within a cross-cultural, multi-lingual environment.

Although secure in my current position, I am confidentially exploring new management challenges and opportunities where I can continue to provide strong and decisive technology leadership. **As such, I would welcome a personal interview to explore any current search assignments that would be appropriate for a candidate with my qualifications. Please note that I am open to relocation and would anticipate a compensation package of $125,000 to $150,000 annually. Thank you for your time and consideration.**

Sincerely,

Sal Madras

Enclosure

(Referral Letter)

MARTIN R. WILLIAMS
williamsmr@comcast.net

29837 Gregson Boulevard
Tucson, Arizona 85026

Home: 612.555.9924
Cell: 612.555.1783

September 19, 2006

Lisa Peterson
Executive Vice President
Cold Stone Creamery
9009 Del Rey Boulevard
Tucson, AZ 85100

Dear Ms. Peterson:

Barry Levitt of RMS Confectioners suggested I contact you. I've known Barry since our days together at RMS and when he heard I was in the market for a new opportunity, he immediately thought of Cold Stone. As such, I've enclosed my resume for your review in anticipation that you may be interested in a management candidate with my qualifications in the industry.

A few brief highlights include:

- Member of the executive management team that grew a small retail venture from 2 stores to 99 locations (California to Maine), 1100 employees and $200+ million in annual revenue.

- Unique blend of leadership, operating management, marketing and organizational development talents.

- Keen eye for sourcing and selecting the "right" retail locations and negotiating favorable lease terms and conditions.

- Substantial experience in corporate finance supporting accelerated growth and expansion (e.g., mergers, acquisitions, venture capital funding).

- Strong background in recruiting, training and leading teams of top-producing professionals nationwide.

- Superb presentation and negotiation skills.

I know from what I have read and learned about Cold Stone, your executive team, business model and operations that it is a company that closely matches my values and my vision for success. Further, it is my expectation that the energy of the people and organization at Cold Stone is remarkable, and I would welcome the opportunity to become a part of it all.

I will call you Tuesday morning to see when we can schedule an interview and do appreciate your time.

Sincerely,

Martin R. Williams

Enclosure

Truth #5: The Language Should Be Different Than in Your Resume

Do not repeat—word for word—information that you've written in your resume in your cover letters. It's very easy to copy and paste from one document to the other, but we strongly recommend that you do *not* do this. Your cover letter should be written to *complement* your resume by providing any one (or a combination) of the following items:

➤ Additional professional information that you did not mention on your resume that is particularly relevant to that specific employer.

   Example: It may be that you did not include certain information on your resume because you did not think it would be important for most of the positions you are pursuing. If and when it does become important to a particular company or opportunity, then your cover letter is the perfect vehicle for sharing that information. Here's a great example:

   One of the most challenging and rewarding projects I ever worked on was the back-end design of a new accounting management and reporting system for Chase Manhattan Bank. This 2-year, $8 million project involved more than 100 team members from IT departments throughout the organization, with my specific role as the lead software engineer.

   Including this type of "additional" information is crucial to positioning yourself as a top candidate.

➤ A "summary" of the overall skills and qualifications you bring as they relate to a particular company or position.

   Example: To be effective, your cover letters must focus on the specific skills, qualifications, and experiences that will be of most interest to a specific company. Most, if not all, of these will likely have been included in your resume. Your challenge, therefore, is to restate that information concisely, without repeating it verbatim. For example,

   Over the past 10 years, I've acquired a wealth of experience throughout the entire supply management chain, with particular emphasis on logistics, distribution, warehousing, vendor management, and long-range quality improvement.

   This type of "summary" sentence allows you to encompass experience from all facets of your career.

➤ A "summary" of your key achievements, projects, and specific contributions that are most relevant to the position you are applying for or the company you are contacting.

   Example: If you're a sales representative and you've included your notable sales achievements for each position in your resume, you don't want to repeat those identical achievements in your cover letters. Rather, "summarize" the information by combining your achievements:

Over the past five years, I increased regional sales by an average of 22% despite intense market competition.

This sentence highlights the candidate's average sales performance while employed with three different companies, totally eliminating the need to repeat the same statistics already presented on the resume.

➤ Personal information that is directly related to a specific company, position, or geographic region that will definitely position you as an even stronger candidate.

Example: If you're relocating back to an area that you're familiar with, be sure to highlight that in your letter. It's always a strong selling point if you're established in a certain region. Here's an example of what you might write:

I was born and raised in Toledo and, as such, have extensive contacts throughout the area who will be valuable in building my network and customer base. My ability to hit the ground running will allow me to immediately become a productive member of your team.

This sentence clearly communicates that this candidate is already a part of the "community."

Streamlining Your Writing Process

Just as with any other activity, cover letter writing gets easier and faster the more often you do it. We recognize it's not something that most job seekers do on a regular basis, so here are a few *tricks of the trade* that should make writing your cover letters easier and faster.

1. **Write when you're fresh.** Professional writers know that they have a certain time each day when they're freshest and do their best work. For one of us, it's first thing in the morning. For the other, it's late at night. Determine when your own *prime time* is and be sure to write your cover letters then.

2. **Write alone.** You'll find that it will be much easier to work on your cover letters if you do it when it's quiet and you have no distractions. Bottom line: You're going to need to think and think hard about what information to include, how to include it, where to include it, and more. The less noise around you, the better. Ignore the phone, ignore your e-mail, and focus 100 percent of your energies on writing.

3. **Be smart and use available resources.** This book contains more than 100 sample cover letters. If you're stumped on how to approach a cover letter, can't find the right words, or are unsure about which

format to use, you're almost always sure to find a letter that you can use as an example to inspire your own creativity. And don't restrict yourself to just this cover letter book. There are other terrific books available that can give you new ideas and strategies to make your letters the very best they can be.

4. **Write from the bottom to the top.** Remember our earlier discussion about Truth #4—You Don't Have to Write in Order? One of the tricks that many professional writers use is to write letters from the bottom to the top, starting with the closing paragraph, then the real content of the letter, and finally the introductory paragraph. Try it and you'll see that letter writing can be much easier and faster.

5. **Write one great cover letter and then use it over and over again.** If you take the time to write one great cover letter, you can often customize that letter to use when applying to a variety of positions. With just a few minor edits (for example, adding another achievement, including a new project, or mentioning a particular skill you have that is most relevant to a particular company's hiring requirements), you can often adapt the letter so that it's perfect for another opportunity. What's more, it should only take you a few minutes!

Chapter 4

▶ Simple Truths About
Electronic Cover Letters

By now, you've probably spent a great deal of time writing and designing at least one cover letter, if not more, to accompany your resume. After having read the first three chapters of this book, you now know the most critical considerations for a powerful and effective cover letter:

▶ Identifying your target audience.

▶ Advantages and disadvantages of bullet-format letters.

▶ Advantages and disadvantages of paragraph-format letters.

▶ Strategies for communicating your unique value.

▶ Differences between letters written to employers and letters written to recruiters.

▶ Importance of matching your cover letter to the format and design of your resume to create an integrated and compelling package.

▶ Using the right language and tone to write cover letters that effectively *sell* you and your unique skills.

What you have created through this process is a "conventional" printed cover letter, which is what you most likely imagine when you think about letters. Even though it probably exists as an electronic, word-processed document, this is the version you will mail or fax to prospective employers and recruiters and use as an introductory and networking tool. In fact, we prefer to call it the *human-eye* version because the style, overall format, presentation, and paper choice are all designed to appeal to readers as they hold the document in their hands, making that all-important, attention-grabbing first impression.

Now that you've created one or more powerful cover letters that can be mailed or faxed to prospective employers and recruiters (along with your resume, of course), you'll also want to think about other versions of your cover letters that you'll most likely need during the course of your job search. This is where technology enters the picture.

In today's job market, employers and recruiters are relying more and more on e-mail and other online methods of transmitting and tracking information about you, the job candidate. It's vital for the soon-to-be successful job seeker (*you*) to have the proper electronic versions of your cover letters to complement your attention-grabbing electronic resume. If you haven't had the opportunity to read our companion book, *No-Nonsense Resumes* (Career Press, 2006), we recommend closely reviewing Chapter 4 in that book for detailed information on preparing resumes for electronic distribution. That advice works hand-in-hand with the recommendations in the rest of this chapter about the design and production of electronic cover letters.

E-letters Work in Today's E-search Environment

Electronic job search documents (resumes and cover letters) offer two distinct advantages over the more traditional, printed cover letter. First, using the latest technology allows you to get your materials into the hands of the appropriate hiring authority quickly and efficiently. No need to wait for "snail mail," when you can immediately transmit your information via e-mail and have it in the hiring authority's hands within minutes. What's more, that individual can then conveniently share your cover letter and resume with others throughout the organization. For example, a human resources manager can quickly and effortlessly forward your "package" to the manager who will ultimately be making the hiring decision. Use of this electronic approach has streamlined the job search process and provided all of us with the ability to submit documents to a prospective employer in *real time*.

Second, and just as important, e-letters afford you the capability to circumvent "gate keepers" and communicate directly with decision makers. When you are engaged in a job search, we strongly recommend making direct contact with the hiring manager (the person who makes the ultimate decision, and probably your boss if you get the job) whenever possible. In today's business world, snail mail and phone calls are still often screened by support personnel. As such, your mailed cover letter and resume package may get redirected to human resources, or your repeated phone calls to "Mr. Big" or "Ms. Important" may result in being told he or she is *always* in a meeting.

In contrast, most business people, even at the highest levels, read their own e-mails. This means there's a good chance that if you e-mail your cover letter and resume to a key person, they just might see it and read it, subject line grabs his or her attention and the opening lines o are compelling.

Before we proceed with our discussion of the actual cc and transmission of electronic cover letters, it is important to note that are four basic types of e-letters.

1. E-mail letters

2. ASCII text letters

3. Word-processed letters

4. Scannable letters

The remainder of this chapter will discuss these four types of letters in detail—what they are, how to produce them, and how they are transmitted. First, however, we'll discuss the importance of the subject line, which is relevant to whatever type of cover letter you're writing and sending.

Capture Your Reader With the Subject Line

The first step in developing a powerful and compelling electronic letter is to write a subject line that piques the reader's interest, without being so sensational that it causes the reader to assume it's spam. It should be professional and to the point.

Specifically, the subject line in a job search e-mail should include the title of the position for which you are applying (and the job/vacancy announcement number, if applicable). In addition, we recommend that you include the words "Resume of" followed by your name. This format immediately alerts the recipient that you're responding to a specific job announcement and have forwarded your resume. Here's an example:

VP of Manufacturing (#45893) – Resume of Jonathan Johnson

If you're not responding to a specific job announcement and are simply e-mailing your resume to a prospective employer or recruiter in anticipation that they may have an opening for a candidate with your qualifications, use a *headline* similar to what you may have used in the summary section of your resume. This clearly identifies *who* you are and the type of position you are seeking. For example:

Vice President of Sales / Director of Business Development

E-mail Letters Are Different Than Traditional Cover Letters

When preparing cover letters to be included in the body of an e-mail message, the first thing you want to do is consider the medium. Just as spoken language is quite different from the written word, e-mail messages (and letters) have evolved into a form that is much more succinct and direct than formal correspondence, such as cover letters. We're not recommending that you resort to using slang abbreviations, symbols, or other electronic "shortcuts" that have become popular in today's online communities, but we do suggest that you keep in mind that most people reading e-mail are in a hurry and read quickly.

As such, e-mailed cover letters must be straightforward, to the point, and instantly communicate your value to that prospective employer. Your goal with an e-mail letter is to hook the reader and grab his or her attention.

If you choose to use this type of e-letter, you will want to open with a formal salutation (for example, Dear Mr. Smith:, Dear Ms. Jones:, Dear Hiring Authority:). Follow that with a brief opening paragraph (briefer than what you might use in a conventional letter), and then several bullet points outlining how you match the requirements of the opening (or your targeted position).

Your closing paragraph should reference your attached resume as a Microsoft Word document. Or if you're particularly tech-savvy, you can include a hyperlink to an online version of your resume or Web portfolio.

You can compose your e-letter directly in your e-mail window, if you choose, but we believe that writing the letter first as a Microsoft Word (or other word-processing) document gives you the chance to more carefully edit the letter and ensure there are no mistakes before clicking that irrevocable "Send Now" button.

Following are two examples of cover letters included within the body of an e-mail message. Use these as samples when you produce your own e-mail cover letters.

Example #1: E-mail cover letter included in the body of the e-mail message (applying for a specific opening):

SUBJECT LINE: **DRIVER (JOB # A06077) / RESUME OF MIKE KOHL**

Dear Mr. Brennan:

Your ad for a Driver at Plum Hollow Independent Living Center is a superb match for my professional experience and capabilities:

• An excellent driving/safety record, a Class B CDL, and training as a school bus driver.

- Strong knowledge of Niagara Falls / Buffalo and
  Niagara / Erie County streets, including the most
  efficient routes between key destinations.

- Experience dealing with residents and employees
  of a leading long-term care facility as a 20-year
  employee of St. Matthew's Senior Care Community.

Attached for your consideration is my resume (Microsoft
Word document) that outlines my qualifications in further
detail. This document can also be viewed or downloaded at
www.resume.com/mkohl.

I will follow up with you next week to establish a mutually
convenient time for an initial interview. In the meantime,
please feel free to call me at (716) 454-9876. I look
forward to speaking with you soon.

Sincerely,

Mike Kohl

Attachment

Example #2: E-mail cover letter included in the body of the e-mail message (broadcast/networking letter):

SUBJECT LINE:

**REFERRED BY FLORENCE KAY - ACCOUNTING / PENSION
ADMINISTRATION**

Dear Mr. O'Shaunessy:

Florence Kay suggested I contact you regarding potential
Accounting and Pension Administration opportunities with
your firm. Some of the key talents I offer include:

- Experience administering Defined Benefit and
  Defined Contribution Pension Plans including
  monitoring for compliance, tracking terminations
  and new submissions, and communicating with
  sponsors, participants, attorneys, and
  accountants.

- General Accounting experience that includes
  Payables, Receivables, Payroll, and General
  Ledger. I have also prepared financial reports,
  forecasts, and budget projections.

- Experience coordinating benefits enrollment including processing applications, communicating with employees, and resolving problems.

- Strong computer literacy and excellent customer relations / interpersonal skills.

I believe that I can be a valuable asset to your firm and would enjoy speaking with you further to discuss the possibilities. My professional portfolio, including a downloadable resume, may be viewed at www.jannelcopeland.com. I have also attached a Microsoft Word version of my resume. Should mutual interest exist, please call me at 315-585-3233 to arrange a meeting. Thank you.

Sincerely,

Jannel Copeland
www.jannelcopeland.com

Regardless of the *general* advice we have just given you, always follow the specific instructions the employer provided in the job posting. Some employers *require* you to attach your resume as a Microsoft Word document; others may *require* that the resume be submitted as ASCII text pasted into the body of the e-mail. (You'll read more about ASCII text files in the next section of this chapter.) There are various technical reasons why an employer (or recruiter) may insist on a certain format. Suffice it to say that if they spell out in the posting which method they prefer, it's important for you to comply with their request, whether or not it's consistent with our specific recommendations and preferences.

Creating and Using ASCII Text Files

As e-mail technology has evolved over the past few years, you may be able to simply copy and paste your letter directly into the e-mail window without losing the format or typestyle. However, you cannot assume this will always work, so we recommend that you send a few test e-mails to friends to see what happens. The more foolproof approach is to convert your cover letter into an ASCII text file before copying and pasting it into your e-mail message. This will ensure that the integrity of your letter is maintained (for example, characters, spacing, and basic format).

In addition, some recruiters and employers may insist on receiving an ASCII text version of your documents (cover letter and resume). If this is the case, pasting the ASCII text version of your documents into an e-mail message is the only way to send it electronically to those organizations.

What's more, ASCII files are also useful when you are applying through a job board (for example, Monster.com, CareerBuilder.com, and HotJobs.com) or directly to a company's employment Website. In such cases, you may be asked to paste your cover letter and resume into an online job application. By having the ASCII text version of your documents ready to go, you can save a lot of time by not having to retype information into the boxes on the online form. Instead, you can simply cut and paste. It's quick and easy, and will save you a lot of time during your search.

To ensure that you create an ASCII file that is readable and correctly formatted, follow these simple steps (for Microsoft Word and similar word-processing programs):

➤ With your document open on the screen, choose "Save As" from the File menu.

➤ Select "text only," "ASCII," or "plain text" as your choice in the "Save As" option box. You may want to give the file a slightly different name (for example, Smith-textletter.txt) to differentiate it from your word-processed version (for example, Smith-ltr.doc). When you click "Save," you will get a message warning you about losing content or formatting by saving the file in ASCII format. Ignore the message and click on "Yes" or "OK" (whichever your computer displays).

➤ Close the file and then reopen it. You will see that your document has been stripped of all formatting and design enhancements, and appears as left-justified text in the Courier font.

➤ Now set both the left and right side margins at two inches. This will center the text on the screen and optimize its readability when the file is reopened at a later time. This will also allow you to recognize and fix any unusual line breaks that lead to awkward changes in format or spacing.

➤ Carefully proofread the document for any "glitches" that may have occurred during the file conversion. You may wish to print your letter and proofread from a "hard copy" at this point. You may see that many characters, such as quotation marks, dashes, or apostrophes, may now appear as question marks or some other characters. Simply replace these by typing in the appropriate character from your keyboard.

➤ Be sure to save the corrected version of your document.

➤ Proofread again, preferably after some time has passed, to ensure that you haven't missed anything.

On the following page is an example of a cover letter for Alan Johnson saved as an ASCII text file. Be sure to note that the letter is in the Courier font, has no type enhancements, and is clean and easy to read.

ALAN JOHNSON
847 Indian Landing Road
Rochester, New York 14699
585-555-1234
alanj@resumesos.com

November 20, 2006

Mr. John Joseph
Operations Manager
Citizens Communications
1234 Telephone Road
Rochester, New York 14688

Re: Call Center Director

Dear John,

After a successful 10-year track record with Finger Lakes Telecomm, I
am confidentially exploring new career possibilities that will
capitalize on my call center operations, account management, and sales
management capabilities. Your posting for Call Center Director appears
to be an excellent match for my existing skill sets. Accordingly, I
have enclosed for your reference a resume that outlines my
capabilities.

My key areas of expertise relevant to this position include:

* Managing call centers with up to 99 representatives and addressing
functions that include inbound and outbound telesales, lead
generation, order entry, and customer care.
* Assessing needs, defining project parameters, and developing
specifications for providing services to corporate clients.
* Recruiting, training, and developing high-performing call center
teams that have delivered multi-million dollar revenues with high-
profit margins to my employers.

I am convinced that I can contribute to Citizens' continuing success,
and would appreciate the opportunity to speak with you about this Call
Center Manager opportunity. I will call you early next week to arrange
a mutually convenient time for us to meet. Meanwhile, please feel free
to contact me sooner at my home phone or e-mail address shown above.

Thank you for your time. I look forward to speaking with you soon.

Sincerely,

Alan Johnson

Enclosure

Sending Your Cover Letter as an E-mail Attachment

Although anyone can read an ASCII text file, it's always to your advantage to send your cover letter and resume as e-mail attachments (Microsoft Word files) whenever possible. This means that your recipient will receive the nicely formatted, word-processed, print version of your letter rather than the bland ASCII version. This, in and of itself, can give you a distinctive edge over your competition. Remember, people are "meeting" a piece of paper; not you. Whatever you can do to distinguish yourself from the crowd and appear more professional will definitely serve to your advantage.

To improve the likelihood that your cover letter and resume documents arrive in an attractive and readable format, we strongly recommend that you prepare both documents in Microsoft Word, or a format compatible with it. Then, follow these guidelines:

▶ Use 0.75-inch margins on all four sides of the page.

▶ Choose a common font. Times New Roman and Arial are virtually universal to most versions of Microsoft Word currently in use. That doesn't mean that you can't use other typestyles for your *printed* documents, but for the best chance of compatibility with those reading your e-mailed cover letter and resume, use one of these two recommended fonts.

▶ If you use word-processing software other than Microsoft Word, consider saving the file in Rich Text Format (.rtf). In most word-processing applications, this is a choice in the "Save As" menu, and the .rtf suffix generally appears at the end of the file name when the document is saved. This more universally accepted file format is compatible with most word-processing software currently in use today.

▶ Send the e-mail attachment to yourself and to friends who are aware of your job search. This gives you the opportunity to see what your documents look like when downloaded and opened, and you can make adjustments to correct any problems prior to sending your resume and cover letter to employers or recruiters.

Preparing Your Files for Transmission

When preparing a cover letter to accompany your resume as an e-mail attachment, you have two distinct options for how to attach the document. The first—and the quickest and easiest—is to simply attach your cover letter to your e-mail message, just as you'll attach your resume. Then, you're all set to go.

However, we recommend a different strategy that ensures your cover letter and resume are transmitted as one complete package. Specifically, we suggest you save your cover letter as page one in your resume file. That way, the recipient has to click on only one document to get all of your information and, just as important, he or she only has to send one attachment in order to forward your complete information to someone else in the organization.

If you're not certain how to do this, just follow these easy instructions:

1. Open your cover letter document; go to "Edit"; "Select All"; and then "Copy." This will copy the entire text of your cover letter.

2. Open your resume document and make sure the cursor is at the very top of the first page, probably to the far left of the first letter of your first name in most instances.

3. Select the "Insert"; "Page Break" command in Microsoft Word; it will give you a blank page before the beginning of the resume.

4. Place the cursor at the top of this new, empty page and go to "Edit"; "Paste" to paste your letter into this document with your resume.

5. Save this new, combined document under a new name (for example, Smith-Resume & Letter—IBM, 11-15-06).

6. Adjust margins and eliminate any extra blank lines or page breaks that may appear, in order to make sure the format of the letter and resume are maintained. Don't forget to click on "Save" one more time to make sure any additional adjustments are captured.

Once your cover letter and resume have been prepared for electronic transmission, you can send them just as you would any other attachment. Simply open your e-mail program, create a message, attach your resume, and send the e-mail message with the document attached. It's that easy and only takes a minute. Remember, however, what we said about the importance of the subject line earlier in this chapter, and be sure to take the time to write a subject line that either states the name (and number) of the position for which you are applying or includes a brief statement identifying who you are. And because you've included a detailed cover letter in your attachment, your e-mail message can simply include a brief statement such as this example:

Senior Lab Technician (#A06-1234) – Resume of Randy Smith

"Please see the attached cover letter and resume detailing my 10+ years of experience as a Lab Technician for Dow Chemical Company."

Following on page 85 is an example of Alan Johnson's cover letter prepared in Microsoft Word for transmission as an attached file to his e-mail message.

ALAN JOHNSON

847 Indian Landing Road
Rochester, New York 14699

November 20, 2006

Mr. John Joseph
Operations Manager
Citizens Communications
1234 Telephone Road
Rochester, New York 14688

Re: Call Center Director

Dear John,

After a successful 10-year track record with Finger Lakes Telecomm, I am confidentially exploring new career possibilities that will capitalize on my call center operations, account management, and sales management capabilities. Your posting for a Call Center Director appears to be an excellent match for my existing skill sets. Accordingly, I have enclosed for your reference a resume that outlines my capabilities.

My key areas of expertise relevant to this position include:

* Managing call centers with up to 99 representatives and addressing functions that include inbound and outbound telesales, lead generation, order entry, and customer care.

* Assessing needs, defining project parameters, and developing specifications for providing services to corporate clients.

* Recruiting, training, and developing high-performing call center teams that have delivered multi-million dollar revenues with high-profit margins to my employers.

I am convinced that I can contribute to Citizens' continuing success, and would appreciate the opportunity to speak with you about this Call Center Manager opportunity. I will call you early next week to arrange a mutually convenient time for us to meet. Meanwhile, please feel free to contact me sooner at my home phone or e-mail address shown above.

Thank you for your time. I look forward to speaking with you soon.

Sincerely,

Alan Johnson

Enclosure

Scannable Cover Letters

If a prospective employer or recruiter asks you to provide a scannable resume, you may decide that it's to your advantage to also include a scannable copy of your cover letter. This way, it's more likely that both your resume and your cover letter will be scanned into the company's resume database.

As with a scannable resume, all of the fancy typestyles, use of **bold** and *italic* type enhancements, and any other graphics such as borders, underlining, or unique symbols, are stripped away to create a plain-Jane version of your letter. The goal is to make your letter easily read and interpreted by the scanning software many employers and recruiters use to upload and file your cover letter and resume in a database for later retrieval.

To maximize the likelihood that your cover letter will upload accurately, follow these guidelines to preparing a scannable version:

▸ Choose an easy-to-read font such as Times New Roman or Arial.

▸ Avoid using **bold,** *italic,* or underlined type.

▸ Stick to type sizes of 11-pt. or larger (12-pt. is optimal).

▸ Make sure that only your name appears on the top line of the letter, followed by your contact information.

▸ All of the text should be left-justified with a ragged-right margin.

▸ Be careful about using abbreviations and acronyms. B.A. for Bachelor of Arts or OSHA (Occupational Safety & Health Administration) are fine to include in your cover letter because they are so widely used. However, if you have any doubt about the proper interpretation of an abbreviation or acronym, be sure to spell it out in full.

▸ Eliminate borders or graphics, including horizontal or vertical lines, tables, and columns.

▸ Use common keyboard symbols (for example, *, -, and >) in places where you would use a bullet in your printed cover letter.

▸ Instead of using characters such as % or &, spell out the words ("percent" or "and").

▸ If slashes (/) are used, make sure you leave a space before and after each slash to ensure the scanner won't see it as a letter and misinterpret the word or phrase.

There may be situations in which you'll be e-mailing the scannable version of your cover letter and resume, and you'll simply attach the scannable documents to your e-mail messages. In other instances, you may be actually mailing the documents. If you are sending them via snail mail, be sure to:

▶ Use a laser printer and print your document on smooth, white paper, rather than paper with any kind of texture, color, or pattern. White photocopy paper that you can purchase at any office supply store is fine for this purpose.

▶ Always use a paper clip; never staple the pages together.

▶ Use a 9 × 12-inch envelope, so it won't be necessary to fold your documents.

Scannable cover letters and resumes are becoming less and less necessary as technology continues to evolve, but they are still requested by some recruiters and employers. As such, they are an important tool in your job search tool kit.

It is important to note that an ASCII text document can serve double duty as a scannable document. However, if you'd prefer to prepare a scannable version of your cover letter and resume in a font other than Courier (your only option in an ASCII file), you may wish to create a separate scannable document using Times New Roman, Arial, or one of the other common fonts available (for example, Tahoma, Verdana, Georgia, Bookman Old Style, or Garamond).

On the following page is an example of a scannable cover letter for Alan Johnson prepared in Arial. Note how different this scannable letter looks when compared to the ASCII text version of the same cover letter on page 82 and the Microsoft Word version of the letter on page 85 earlier in this chapter.

Avoid These Critical Mistakes When Preparing Your E-cover Letters

1. **Inappropriate e-mail subject lines.** In this context, the simplest is also the best. Stick with the formats recommended earlier in this chapter and don't write long, wordy subject lines that don't immediately communicate why you're contacting the recipient.

2. **Improperly formatted attachments.** If your attachments are not downloadable, or can't be easily read after they have been downloaded, a prospective employer or recruiter will most likely delete your e-mail message. That's it—you've lost that opportunity. Be sure to follow the formatting recommendations outlined throughout this chapter to be certain your documents transmit accurately.

3. **Getting caught by spam filters.** Be careful that your subject lines and e-mail messages don't contain information that the recipients' e-mail might misinterpret as a spam message (for example, words such as "free," "limited opportunity," or "call now").

ALAN JOHNSON
847 Indian Landing Road
Rochester, New York 14699
585-555-1234
alanj@resumesos.com

November 20, 2006

Mr. John Joseph
Operations Manager
Citizens Communications
1234 Telephone Road
Rochester, New York 14688

Re: Call Center Director

Dear John,

After a successful 10-year track record with Finger Lakes Telecomm, I am confidentially exploring new career possibilities that will capitalize on my call center operations, account management, and sales management capabilities. Your posting for a Call Center Director appears to be an excellent match for my existing skill sets. Accordingly, I have enclosed for your reference a resume that outlines my capabilities.

My key areas of expertise relevant to this position include:

*   Managing call centers with up to 99 representatives and addressing functions that include inbound and outbound telesales, lead generation, order entry, and customer care.

*   Assessing needs, defining project parameters, and developing specifications for providing services to corporate clients.

*   Recruiting, training, and developing high-performing call center teams that have delivered multi-million dollar revenues with high-profit margins to my employers.

I am convinced that I can contribute to Citizens' continuing success, and would appreciate the opportunity to speak with you about this Call Center Manager opportunity. I will call you early next week to arrange a mutually convenient time for us to meet. Meanwhile, please feel free to contact me sooner at my home phone or e-mail address shown above.

Thank you for your time. I look forward to speaking with you soon.

Sincerely,

Alan Johnson

Enclosure

4. **"Cute" e-mail addresses.** It may be fun to communicate with friends using "DrDoom@yahoo.com" or "CuteYoungThing@aol.com," but for your job search, try to stick with something more professional (and logical), such as a variation of your name: AJohnson@hotmail.com or SallySmith12@netzero.net. Also, be aware that an e-mail address such as zdv19456@domain.net might be filtered out as potential spam, because the characters before the @ symbol are not a recognizable word or name.

5. **Inappropriate auto signatures.** Many people enjoy using cute graphics (such as smiley faces) or including famous quotes in their auto signatures. Others get very creative with fonts and colors. The risk is that they won't transmit properly and will result in gibberish at the recipient's end, or that some quotation or citation that may be meaningful to you may be a turnoff for the recipient. Keep it simple and professional. If you use an auto signature for job search e-mails, simply include your name, phone number, and e-mail address.

6. **Patterned or colored backgrounds.** These can make the e-mail unreadable for the recipient or can take far too long to download when someone opens an e-mail message.

7. **Hard to read or colored fonts.** As with backgrounds and auto signatures, colors or unusual fonts may not transmit properly, leading to a completely unreadable e-mail message. Keep it simple—use Times New Roman or Arial, 10- or 12-pt., with judicious use of **bold** and *italics* for emphasis, as appropriate.

Electronic Cover Letters - Design Considerations

	Word-Processed Cover Letters	**ASCII Text Cover Letters**	**Scannable Cover Letters**
Font/ Typestyle	Crisp, clean, distinctive (See recommendations in Chapter 2).	Courier	Stick to the basics: Times New Roman, Arial.
Typestyle Effects	**Bold**, *italics*, and underlining are all acceptable and recommended.	CAPITALIZATION is the only enhancement available.	CAPITALIZATION is the only enhancement that will scan reliably.
Type Size	11-pt. or 12-pt. for body of the document. Use larger sizes (14, 16, 18) for name.	12-pt.	11-pt. or 12-pt. preferred.
White Space	Use to optimize readability.	Separate sections to enhance readability.	Use liberally to maximize scannability.

Electronic Cover Letters — Production Considerations

	Word-Processed Cover Letters	**ASCII Text Cover Letters**	**Scannable Cover Letters**
Text Format	Use centering, indents, and so on, to create an appealing presentation.	Everything strictly flush-left.	Everything strictly flush-left.
Preferred Length	Generally, one page.	Length doesn't matter. Converting the cover letter will undoubtedly make it longer than the printed version.	Length doesn't matter. Converting the cover letter will undoubtedly make it longer than the printed version.
Preferred Paper Color	White, ivory, or light gray are most preferred.	Not applicable.	Bright white or cream (natural). No patterns or shading that might interfere with scanning.

Chapter 5

▶ Cover Letters for
Accounting, Banking, and Finance Careers

Your cover letter presents an excellent opportunity to show prospective employers and recruiters how the skills and accomplishments documented on your resume relate to their specific hiring needs. Each industry and profession presents unique cover letter writing and design challenges. If you are interested in pursuing an accounting, banking, or finance career, be certain to include highlights of these important success factors in your cover letters:

Success Factor #1

Be as "quantitative" as possible when listing your accomplishments. Accounting and finance professionals understand and respect numbers, so whenever possible, integrate numbers, percentages, and statistics into your cover letters to support your achievements.

Success Factor #2

Highlight your specific accounting and financial management skills and competencies as they relate *directly* to the targeted position. Be specific and don't assume anything. If a company is looking for a candidate with experience in X, Y, and Z (and you have that specific experience), be sure to include it prominently in your cover letter.

Success Factor #3

Demonstrate your value by emphasizing your diverse portfolio of skills. Documenting these capabilities will illustrate the breadth and depth of your experience, and help to position you favorably against other qualified candidates.

🔖 **Success Factor #4**

Showcase your technical skills and qualifications. What accounting, financial analysis, mortgage processing, or budgeting software do you use? This expertise is essential in today's electronic information age, and it also shows your ability to adapt and learn new things.

Keywords and Keyword Phrases

Keywords and keyword phrases are critical components of every successful job seeker's cover letter. By using just one or two words, you're able to communicate a wealth of information about your skills, qualifications, and experience. What's more, keywords are the basis for scanning technology and are therefore critical to every job seeker's campaign in today's electronic-based job search market.

Following are the top 20 accounting, banking, and finance keywords, some of which may reflect your skills and some of which may not be appropriate for you at this time. Use these words as the foundation for developing your own list of keywords on the Professional Keyword List form in Appendix B.

Top 20 Keywords

Accounts Payable & Receivable	Financial Analysis & Reporting
Asset Management	Foreign Exchange
Auditing	Internal Accounting Controls
Budget Control & Administration	Investment Analysis & Management
Cash Management	Lending & Loan Administration
Consumer & Commercial Lending	Mergers & Acquisitions
Corporate Treasury	Profit & Loss Analysis
Cost Accounting	Project Accounting
Cost/Benefit Analysis	Risk Management
Credit & Collections	ROI & ROE Analysis

Following are some excellent examples of cover letters for careers in accounting, banking, and finance.

HARRY STRONG

900 Starling Lane
Indianapolis, IN 98019

harrystrong@yahoo.com

Cell: (505) 555–2837
Office: (505) 555–3399

January 25, 2007

Donna Parkerson
Recruiting Director – Accounting & Finance
Martin Shaw Recruiters
22 N. Ambrose Parkway, Suite 1190
Chicago, IL 60693

Dear Ms. Parkerson:

Like many recent graduates, I am eager to begin my career in finance. Unlike others, I realize that a new bachelor's degree is not enough to qualify in today's highly competitive market. As a result, I have worked diligently to supplement my college education with hands-on experience in financial environments, equipping me with a wide range of skills as a Financial Analyst. Through my employment and educational training, I have developed the qualifications that I'm sure will make me an asset to one of your client companies:

Financial Skills and Experience

More than two years of experience in a corporate environment as a financial advisor along with a solid background in financial analysis, reporting, budgeting, negotiating, and business/financial planning. Apply financial tools to identify, manage, and maximize investment funds.

Keen Research, Analytical, and Quantitative Skills

Adept in reviewing, analyzing and synthesizing financial data as well as viewing challenges from different perspectives to arrive at creative solutions.

Computer Software Tools

Demonstrated proficiency in learning new applications quickly; I am skilled in using Microsoft Word, Excel and Access database software. I also utilize Morningstar extensively to research data on mutual funds.

Proven Communications, Organization and Interpersonal Skills

My collective experiences have enabled me to hone both my interpersonal, written, and verbal communications skills, which include developing financial reports, interfacing with internal and external customers, and delivering presentations. Cultivating and maintaining positive relationships with a wide range of personalities have resulted in a large referral network from satisfied clients. Another strength is my ability to efficiently organize and manage my day-to-day responsibilities for maximum productivity.

I am open to relocation anywhere in the U.S. and am flexible in my salary requirements. I know that your recruiting practice specializes in placing recent graduates, so I'm hopeful you can be assistance to me. Thank you.

Sincerely,

Harry Strong

Enclosure

Written By: Louise Garver
Font: Tahoma

JANE BERG

702 Waukegan Rd., #102
Glenview, IL 60025
847-998-5823
berg@comcast.net

October 13, 2006

Dennis Custer
Hiring Manager
Cosmos Transportation Company
6633 Toastmasters Drive
Chicago, IL 60087

RE: Job Posting for Accountant (#928372)

Dear Mr. Custer:

I am a well-qualified Accounting Professional writing in response to your advertisement for an **Accountant.** Highlights of my professional career include:

- Considerable experience in Accounts Receivable, Billing, Credit/Collection, Accounts Payable, and Accounting/Financial Reporting.

- Introduction of PC applications to automate accounting functions and increase data accuracy for payment billings.

- Extensive qualifications in customer relationship management, communications, and negotiations.

- Excellent analytical, decision-making and problem-solving skills.

After you have the opportunity to review my resume, I would like to meet with you to discuss how I can effectively contribute to Cosmos Transportation. Should you have any questions before scheduling an appointment, I may be reached at the number listed above.

Thank you for your time and professional courtesy in reviewing the enclosed resume. I will call next week to schedule an interview.

Sincerely,

Jane Berg

Enclosure

Written By: Loretta Heck
Font: Bookman Old Style

SAVANNAH BUTLER

19 Lawnside Drive, Leichhardt NSW 2040
Home Ph: (02) 9999 0000 · savannahb@hotmail.com · Mobile: 0414 981 062

28th February, 2007

Mr. Gary H. Mulcahy
Senior Accountant
Bankers Trust
Level 32, 184 Clarence Street
SYDNEY NSW 2000

Dear Mr. Mulcahy:

It is with great interest that I am forwarding my resume for consideration as Systems Accountant within your organisation. With significant accounting experience and systems accounting exposure, I am confident that you will quickly recognise my ability to deliver immediate benefits to your organisation. Therefore, I ask that you consider the following in addition to my enclosed resume:

➤ Associate Member of the Chartered Institute of Management Accountants (CIMA) with nine years of accounting experience across diverse areas – systems accounting (Sun Systems & SAP), management accounting, financial accounting, and project accounting.

➤ Proven exposure to systems implementation, development, and maintenance. Played a pivotal role in the implementation of Sun Systems at AEC and Price Waterhouse, including testing, validating, and assisting in the transition from spreadsheet accounting to Sun Systems.

➤ Acknowledged by management for strong systems accounting knowledge. Selected to provide guidance and instruction to finance staff in system usage, provide systems support, and maintain and update the system as required.

➤ Proactive leader with proven experience in identifying organisational needs, analysing opportunities, developing reporting protocols, and implementing initiatives that improved financial operations. Thrive on challenges to overcome obstacles with solutions that are sound and financially feasible.

➤ Excellent written and verbal communication skills with demonstrated ability to develop relationships with senior members of staff. Aided in decision making by providing recommendations and solutions to management.

With a well-rounded background and a record of strong performance, I am well equipped and eager to handle diverse new challenges. Personally committed to continued growth and excellence, I have the drive, energy, vision, leadership and implementation skills to make a positive difference to your organisation.

My resume is enclosed to provide you with details of my skills and accomplishments, but I am certain that a personal interview would more fully reveal my desire and ability to contribute to your organisation. Thank you for your time and consideration, and do not hesitate to contact me if you have any questions. I look forward to speaking with you soon.

Yours sincerely,

Savannah Butler

Enclosure

Written By: Jennifer Rushton
Font: Georgia

Susan S. Walker

10999 Golden Gate Boulevard ◆ Chicago, IL 60222 ◆ (717) 558-1952 ◆ walkers@comcast.net

April 22, 2006

David R. Dutch
Recruiter
Bank of America
1000 Bank of America Plaza
Chicago, IL 60265

Dear Mr. Dutch:

If you are in need of a highly qualified Banking Professional, then we have good reason to meet. After researching your company, I believe my skills and experience may be of value to your team.

I offer more than 16 years of successful banking experience in positions of increasing responsibility and duties. With a broad-based understanding of financial / banking needs at all levels of business, I am skilled in account management, sales management, customer service, marketing, branch management, loan administration, regulatory compliance, quality control, and teller operations. Throughout my career, I have been recognized by management as a top performer for consistently achieving targeted sales goals and leading projects that have delivered profitable results and generated new business.

As a proven leader with excellent communication skills, I am proficient at motivating and training teams of professionals in meeting or exceeding identified company goals and customer expectations. With strong skills in customer service and relationship building, I possess the demonstrated ability to help clients select financial / banking options that meet their needs and expand / retain existing accounts. My unwavering commitment to high-quality service and customer satisfaction will be a valuable asset to your team. My resume provides further details of my skills and accomplishments.

I believe I can make an immediate and positive contribution to Bank of America. If it appears that my qualifications meet your current needs, I would like to further discuss my background in a meeting with you. Thank you for your time and consideration. I look forward to your reply.

Sincerely,

Susan S. Walker

Enc. resume

Written By: John Femia
Font: Times New Roman

ANGELO PALERMO

palermo@alum.calberkeley.org

115 Hardy Parkway
San Diego, CA 94888
Residence: (821) 663-6733
Cell: (821) 310-3446

June 22, 2006

John Macey
Stewart-Hess Recruiters
PO Box 10290
Los Angeles, CA 90087

Dear Mr. Macey:

I am responding to the **Senior Investment Representative** position advertised in the *LA Times*, and am certain that my skills and experience position me as an ideal candidate. What's more, I'm confident that your client company will be impressed by the strength and depth of my qualifications.

As a results-driven Licensed Investment Professional, I am experienced at educating individual clients and businesses on investments and insurance plans, and providing advice on options that achieve short-term and long-term goals. I am skilled in account management, portfolio management, estate planning, retirement planning, financial planning, investment planning, tax laws, and mutual funds. With strong organizational and analytical skills, I am proficient at managing multiple tasks and creating financial solutions that improve business operations.

With demonstrated communication and customer service skills, I am talented at presenting financial planning and investment products and solutions to individuals and group audiences. My professional credentials include a Bachelor's degree in Economics and Series 7, 66, and California Life and Health Insurance licenses. My proven ability to consistently build client relationships and develop new business will be a valuable asset to your team. My resume provides further details of my skills and accomplishments.

I feel confident I can make an immediate and positive contribution to your client company and would welcome the opportunity for an interview. Be advised that my salary requirements are $85,000+ and that I am open to relocation within California.

Thank you for your time and consideration. I look forward to your reply.

Sincerely,

Angelo Palermo

Enclosure: Resume

Written By: John Femia
Font: Arial

LISA HILLIARD

555 N. Windset Avenue   Chicago, IL 60605   708-555-2291   lhilliard@worldnet.att.net

February 21, 2007

The Community Foundation
P. O. Box 569
Chicago, IL 60605

Dear Hiring Professional:

In response to your search for a **Vice President of Finance and Administration,** I bring over 20 years of extensive experience in all areas of Finance and Administration, as well as Information Technology and Human Resources.

I am an extremely high-energy and innovative manager who leads by example. I consistently produce strong results with a high degree of integrity, dedication, and strong communication skills. My track record speaks for itself; I have been involved in virtually every area of an organization, and have made substantial contributions wherever I have been. One of my former bosses had this to say about me in a review:

> *Lisa is at the high end of the exceptional scale. She has top-flight management skills, intelligence, and people skills. She has done an exceptional job in a wide variety of areas. She is extremely capable as an individual and as a manager and leader. Her entire group exudes a "can-do" enthusiasm.*

I spoke with Jim Maynard, a Board Member Emeritus of The Community Foundation about the position and my interest and excitement about it. I know Jim from my volunteer work at the Unity Church, as he is President of the Church Board. He, too, was enthusiastic about my potential fit with your organization and thought that I could help you reach your goals.

My interest in moving to the non-profit world is genuine; I have spent years in corporate environments, and since I went back to school, have had a chance to better define where and how I want to contribute my talents. I have become very involved both in my church and as a volunteer in the bookstore, technology and fundraising committees, and on the technology and finance task forces of the organizing/steering committee for the Illinois Institute of Sciences.

My resume provides further details of my accomplishments. You will note that I have progressed in responsibility levels throughout my career. I look forward to discussing this exciting career opportunity with you, and will contact you next week to arrange a meeting so we may discuss the organization's needs in greater detail.

Sincerely,

Lisa Hilliard

Enclosure

cc: Jim Maynard

Written By: Gail Frank
Font: Times New Roman

ALFREDO BHONI
alfredo@aol.com

8292 West 104th Street, #202B
New York, NY 10001

Home: 212.555.1872
Work: 212.555.8212

October 10, 2006

Mr. Lester R. Maddox
Human Resources Manager
The Bank One Corporation
22 Wall Street
New York, NY 10022

Dear Mr. Maddox:

I have but one professional goal—to continue to build high-growth private banking programs targeted specifically to high net-worth Italian investors. It's where my career has focused for the past 10 years and where I have delivered outstanding performance results:

- Currently with Mellon Bank's International Division, I created an entirely new market segment of Italian investors that currently have more than $300 million in invested and deposited assets with Mellon.

- During my tenure with one of Italy's largest and most diversified financial institutions, I personally brought more than $100 million in assets to the bank over four years.

- While working with Barnes and Company, I was one of only three finance professionals responsible for establishing the company's initial market presence throughout Italy. First-year results exceeded expectations by over 120%.

I bring to the Bank One Corporation a strong blend of business development, marketing, sales and customer management expertise. Combine that with my solid financial, investment, portfolio management, asset management and analytical skills, and I guarantee my ability to produce. My only interest in leaving Mellon (it's been a great experience for five years!) is that I am ready for new responsibilities, challenges and opportunities.

If you are interested in a candidate with my qualifications and objectives, I would welcome a personal interview at your earliest convenience. Be advised that I am open to relocation and extensive travel as may be required.

Thank you.

Sincerely,

Alfredo Bhoni

Enclosure

Written By: Wendy Enelow
Font: Times New Roman

DAN DULANEY

909 Smith Lake Road
Moneta, VA 24877

Home (540) 555-2765
drdulaney@msn.com

November 19, 2006

Andrew McCartney
President
Dial Corporation
One Dial Boulevard
San Simeon, FL 39093

Dear Mr. McCartney:

I am submitting my name as a candidate for your advertised CFO position. Briefly summarized, my qualifications include:

- Twenty years of senior-level financial leadership experience with Donnelly Corporation and several of its largest operating companies.
- Expert qualifications across all core accounting and financial practices, including financial planning and reporting, tax, treasury, cash management, general and cost accounting, internal audit, credit, budgeting, forecasting, and internal controls.
- Negotiation of more than $19 million in corporate financing transactions and participation in over 10 mergers and acquisitions.
- Extensive qualifications in the strategic design and implementation of advanced information systems.
- Management of corporate facilities, real estate, leasing and a massive purchasing program.
- Pioneer in innovative business practices (e.g., outsourcing, workflow and performance efficiencies and corporate ethics).

As the Senior Financial Advisor to top executive and operating management teams, I have provided both the strategic and operating leadership critical to improving financial results, strengthening market position, enhancing product quality and manufacturability, and upgrading our organizational structure. Further, I have delivered more than **$20 million in cost savings** through the introduction of improved business processes, best practices and standards for financial management, along with a portfolio of advanced technology tools.

Characterized by others as creative, intuitive, flexible and decisive, I believe my greatest value is my broad operational and business perspective. Donnelly has been an outstanding organization with which to grow and demonstrate my capabilities. Now, however, I am ready for new challenges and new opportunities.

I look forward to speaking with you regarding the referenced position, and thank you for your consideration.

Sincerely,

Dan Dulaney

Enclosure

Written By: Wendy Enelow
Font: Arial

ANDREW M. LAWSON
aml222@gmail.com
6226 Mellon Run Lane
Toledo, Ohio 44902
Home (416) 555-9028   Office (416) 555-6802

September 12, 2000

Leslie R. Morrow
President & CEO
Insurance Recruiters of America
22 Gateway Drive
Pittsburgh, PA 15909

Dear Ms. Morrow:

I am currently the General Auditor for Life & Home Insurance Company. After eight years with the organization, I have decided to confidentially explore new opportunities and am contacting a select group of executive recruiters specializing in Corporate Audit and Finance. My resume is enclosed for your review.

Highlights of my career include:

- Progressive management career as the Senior Audit Executive for three Fortune 500 corporations, each in vastly differing industries and customer markets.

- Consistent record of achievement in improving bottom-line financial results by introducing improved audit strategies, processes, controls and technologies. Key contributor to several successful start-up ventures and large-scale corporate turnarounds.

- Success in positioning Audit as a business partner, not an adversary, with both internal and external audiences. These efforts have been vital to restoring corporate credibility.

- Strong general management qualifications in strategic planning, finance, budgeting, professional staffing, organizational development, quality and performance improvement.

My leadership style is direct and decisive, yet flexible in responding to constantly changing demands. I work well in high-pressure and demanding positions with my objective always focused on creating synergy and consensus to achieve common goals. My background also includes extensive training experience and active leadership in several professional organizations.

If you are working with a client corporation seeking a candidate with my qualifications, I would welcome the opportunity to speak with you. Be advised that I am open to relocation. Thank you.

Sincerely,

Andrew M. Lawson

Enclosure

Written By: Wendy Enelow
Font: Tahoma

Chapter 6

▶ Cover Letters for
Administrative and Clerical Careers

Your cover letter presents an excellent opportunity to show prospective employers and recruiters how the skills and accomplishments documented on your resume relate to their specific hiring needs. Each industry and profession presents unique cover letter writing and design challenges. If you are interested in pursuing an administrative or clerical career, be certain to include highlights of these important success factors in your cover letters:

Success Factor #1

Focus on the contributions you have made to the overall success of your employers (for example, increasing revenues, reducing costs, upgrading technologies, managing key projects, or improving productivity and efficiency).

Success Factor #2

Highlight the vast array of skills, qualifications, competencies, and talents that you offer which, for most administrative professionals, is quite extensive due to the varied nature of the work you perform.

Success Factor #3

Demonstrate your value by emphasizing the number and types of people and organizations you have supported to give further "depth" to your experience. And don't forget your "customer service" skills, even if your "customers" are internal.

Success Factor #4

Showcase all of your technical skills and qualifications. Word processing, spreadsheets, accounting software, and customer databases all can be important. They are essential in today's electronic world of work!

Keywords and Keyword Phrases

Keywords and keyword phrases are critical components of every successful job seeker's cover letter. By using just one or two words, you're able to communicate a wealth of information about your skills, qualifications, and experience. What's more, keywords are the basis for scanning technology and are therefore critical to every job seeker's campaign in today's electronic-based job search market.

Following are the top 20 administrative and clerical keywords, some of which may reflect your skills and some of which may not be appropriate for you at this time. Use these words as the foundation for developing your own list of keywords on the Professional Keyword List form in Appendix B.

Top 20 Keywords

Budget Administration	Meeting Planning
Business Administration	Office Management
Clerical Support	Policy & Procedure
Client Communications	Productivity Improvement
Confidential Correspondence	Project Management
Contract Administration	Records Management
Corporate Recordkeeping	Regulatory Reporting
Document Management	Resource Management
Efficiency Improvement	Time Management
Liaison Affairs	Workflow Planning/Prioritization

Following are some excellent examples of cover letters for administrative and clerical careers.

CINDY DUNLOP

3000 Mountain View
Weston, WA 98000-4444
(333) 555-7790
email: Cindy@yahoo.com

October 14, 2006

Jonathan Ramos
Director of Administration & Finance
Kellogg Corporation
100 Kellogg Boulevard, Suite 200
Seattle, WA 90988

RE: Appointments Coordinator

Dear Mr. Ramos:

Am I able to leap tall buildings in a single bound? Stop bullets with the flick of a wrist? Move at the speed of light? Well, perhaps not. But I have been observed moving at Wonder Woman speed in carrying out multitudinous duties, thus giving the appearance of having six hands and four legs! I am an accomplished juggler of schedules, phones, people, and coffee pots, and am very excited about the potential for employment with a progressive and fun team.

I enclose my resume summarizing my experience. You will note that I possess excellent organizational, communication, and computer skills. I am an energetic, creative, cheerful individual who enjoys people, does not shy away from hard work, and I am ready for a change.

Maybe you won't actually be adding Wonder Woman to your team, but you will be adding a fun-loving, qualified, and dependable Front Desk Goddess. Your decision to interview me will be enthusiastically received, and I do look forward to hearing from you. I can be reached at (333) 555-7790 to schedule a mutually convenient date and time.

Sincerely,

Cindy Dunlop

Enclosure

Written By: Janice Shepherd
Font: Bookman Old Style

(416) 555 - 1212   **Caitlin Arnold**   2245 Jane Street
carnold@gmail.com   Toronto, ON   M9P 2X4

February 21, 2006

Ms. Amanda Smith
Manager, Administrative Services
Cadzee Consulting LLB
223 Bay Street
Toronto, ON
M2N 6Y2

Dear Ms. Smith:

I am a highly trained, knowledgeable Administrative Assistant with a strong background in my chosen profession and am now seeking a full-time position.

Please consider my credentials:

- Five years as Executive Assistant to senior managers in an HR consulting firm
- Two years as Office Administrator for a non-profit organization
- Four years as Departmental Administrator at a private school
- Extensive working knowledge of the MS Office suite
- Certificate in Travel and Tourism

As you can see, I have a diverse background in the administrative field. My employment experience is broad, covering a wide range of office functions including reception, customer service, travel, HR, and education.

I have always enjoyed a strong reputation as a highly professional and innovative individual who knows the daily functions of the office environment at many levels. I am confident that I can make similar contributions to Cadzee Consulting and would welcome the opportunity to meet with you. I will call your office next week to discuss the potential for a mutually beneficial relationship.

Sincerely,

Caitlin Arnold

Enclosure

Written By: Anne Brunelle
Font: Times New Roman

ROSEMARY REILLY

1954 West Highland Avenue • Elmwood Park, IL 66666
Home (847) 987-6543 • Cell (847) 234-5678 • rr1954@aol.com

July 13, 2006

Hiring Committee
Jones Manufacturing, Inc.
9087 Walker Road
Franklin Park, IL 66903

Dear Hiring Committee:

With a diverse background that encompasses office management, process improvement, benefits administration, and facilities management, I am currently seeking a challenging and rewarding position where I can continue to contribute to office efficiency and productivity. I would welcome an opportunity to discuss the mutual benefits of an employment partnership at your earliest convenience.

For the past 20 years, I have worked for Casman Incorporated and have grown professionally during this period as the company expanded and launched new ventures and limited partnership organizations. Originally, my role was managing a one-person office, and has now evolved into managing all office operations with five back-office employees and 140 commodities traders.

My responsibilities encompass a wide range of functions, including systems development, process improvement, facilities management, human resource and benefits administration, regulatory compliance, and staff training and development. Among my strengths are meticulous organization, attentive listening, articulate communication, diplomacy, and level-headedness under the most stressful situations.

After reviewing my attached resume, please contact me to discuss opportunities with your firm. I look forward to speaking with you soon, and thank you for your consideration.

Sincerely,

Rosemary Reilly

Enclosure

Written By: Rosemary Fish Justen
Font: Times

LOUISE E. APPLETON

#404 - 6382 EASTPOINT DRIVE, VANCOUVER, BC V6N 4H8

(H) 604.491.9172   (W) 604.685.1967   (C) 604.278.9336   (F) 604.685.1962   LAPPLE@TELUS.NET

January 12, 2007

Progressive Law Corporation
Suite 200—1927 Williams Avenue
Toronto, Ontario M5C 3K8

Attention: Mr. Rick Callaway, Director of Administrative Services
Re: **Office Administrator/Bookkeeper** employment opportunity (#2005-OA2)

Dear Mr. Callaway:

I am a proactive, dedicated Office Administrator/Bookkeeper who knows the job, requires minimal training, and would be quick to assist with other areas of your business. People describe me as well-organized, effective, comfortable with others, and having a great sense of humor. My highly professional manner, positive attitude, and enjoyment for administrative work really help me to consistently deliver quality results.

As a highly experienced Office Administrator with approximately 20 successful years working in a legal environment, I have the skills required to meet the needs of your practice in a very short time. I perform well for my current employer and have also found numerous ways to improve operations. Here are a few reasons why I would make a good addition to the Progressive team:

- My *experience in both legal and administrative activities* began as a legal secretary and later continued on in office administration, making me very familiar with the activities of both jobs. My administrative work has encompassed both financial/accounting and human resources aspects, and this has given me a strong grasp of current methods and guidelines.

- My *extensive people skills* have come from years of working with a wide variety of different people, including lawyers, clients, support staff, and suppliers. Besides frequently supervising others, I make it my business to both humor and motivate them. A dedicated team player, I enjoy working with my colleagues to create order out of chaos.

- Finally, my *solid personal work ethic* enables me to stay punctual, focused, organized, reliable, and able to handle whatever tasks come my way.

Thank you for reading my resume. I will follow up with you in two weeks to set up a meeting to discuss the fine details of what you seek in an Office Administrator and how I might help you streamline your operations. Please contact me at anytime if I can provide you with any additional information. I look forward to talking with you soon!

Sincerely,

Louise E. Appleton

Enclosure

Written By: Paul Bennett
Font: Times New Roman

ELAINE BROOKS

23 Mountain Road ◆ Monsey, NY 10952 ◆ (914) 237-1883 ◆ ebrooks@earthlink.net

May 6, 2006

Ms. Laurie Dern, Principal
Ringwood Township School
200 Main Street
Ringwood, NJ 08825

Dear Ms. Dern:

Your opening for a secretary captured my interest as it seems an ideal match for my experience, talents, and interests. As a highly regarded administrative assistant with excellent interpersonal skills, a lifelong love of working with students, and a demonstrated commitment to service, I would like to explore the possibility of putting my talents to work for you.

As you can see from the enclosed resume, my background includes a wealth of administrative experience, 20 years of which were spent in school settings. Conscientious, organized, and effective, I established a long-standing reputation as a productive and effective staff member during my career. Perhaps more important, though, is my devotion to the students. I take pleasure in my ability to build rapport with students, and treasure the special bonds I enjoy with them. Of particular note, I am proud to say that I was honored by the Kingwood Place School's graduating class of 2005 with a yearbook dedication, marking the first time in the school's 70-year history that a staff member was so honored.

Among my other strengths, you will find that I am a resourceful individual and a fast learner who is always quick to become the office go-to person. I am friendly and easygoing with outstanding interpersonal skills, so students, parents, and faculty members alike find me to be approachable and accommodating. With a passion for providing top-notch service, I have proven to be a valued employee in every position I have held. With a record of success behind me, I am confident that I will be an asset to your staff as well.

I would be pleased to have the opportunity to discuss future employment, and look forward to speaking with you. Please feel free to contact me at the address and phone number listed above to arrange a meeting.

Thank you for your consideration.

Sincerely,

Elaine Brooks

Enclosure

Written By: Carol Altomare
Font: Garamond

SUSAN SORENSON
43 Beacon Court, Robbinsville, NJ 08691
Tel: 609.371.4444 ▪ Email: susansorenson27@btp.net

October 21, 2006

Mr. Tom O'Kane
Human Resources Manager
Firmenich Incorporated
P.O. Box 5880
Princeton, NJ 08543

Dear Mr. O'Kane:

Kirsten Alexander of Human Resources suggested that I contact you regarding the open position of **Administrative Manager.** If you have need of a well-qualified professional with **German and French language skills** as well as experience in office administration, customer service, sales, training, and marketing, then we should meet. My resume is enclosed for your review. Highlights include:

☑ Over **eight years of experience** in organization, coordination, communication, and customer service with Charmareaux, an international exporter of consumer goods. Consistent focus on creating and maintaining profitable client relationships. Supervised and trained 15 administrative assistants and customer service representatives in stellar client communications.

☑ A resourceful **problem-solver** with a track record of getting positive results, including a record-setting 75% collection rate on accounts 90 days past due.

☑ Ability to **build confidence and trust** at all levels with domestic and international customers, and demonstrated experience in promoting results-oriented environments. Achieved lowest turnover rate for administrative assistants and customer service representatives in company's history.

☑ **Proven communication skills,** including fluency in **French and German.** Up-to-date technology skills in **MS Office Suite** (Word, Excel, Access, PowerPoint, and Outlook), Internet, email, and multiple peripherals (fax machines, scanners, digital cameras, and printers).

My career success has been due in large part to building supportive relationships, and tackling persistent problem areas with creative approaches. I am seeking the opportunity to transition my experience, skills, and enthusiasm into a new organization where I can have an impact on company growth.

I will call your office next week to answer any initial questions you may have, and to set up a mutually convenient appointment. Thank you for your consideration.

Sincerely,

Susan Sorenson

Enclosure: RESUME

"Susan's concern for the customer and her organizational strengths have sustained our confidence in Charmareaux's commitment to quality service AND delivery. We simply would not use another source."
– Georges Damieau, VP of Operations, Marketplace Francais

Written By: Susan Guameri
Font: Tahoma

Chapter **7**

▶ Cover Letters for
Government Careers

Your cover letter presents an excellent opportunity to show prospective employers and recruiters how the skills and accomplishments documented on your resume relate to their specific hiring needs. Each industry and profession presents unique cover letter writing and design challenges. If you are interested in pursuing a career in government, be certain to include highlights of these important success factors in your cover letters:

Success Factor #1

Often when applying for a government position, you will be requested to submit a resume along with other documentation. This might include statements of Key Skill Areas (KSAs), responses to specific questions, information about your particular competencies, and more. If this is the situation, the best advice for writing your cover letter is to include information that is unique to you and your experience, and that makes you stand out from other applicants.

Success Factor #2

Some postings will use the term "Letter of Interest" instead of "Cover Letter." Show your *interest* in the position by showcasing how you will use your skills and experience to address the challenges of that particular position.

Success Factor #3

Use your cover letter to explain any special circumstances that aren't covered in the resume. These might include your desire to relocate (and why), reasons for a career change, or special accommodations for a disability. (Note that a candidate with a disability may be sought after by hiring officials, due to the government's desire to fulfill EOE/Affirmative Action goals and objectives.)

⚑ Success Factor #4

Some agencies offer the choice of submitting a paper application or an electronic application. In many instances, the electronic application process does *not* allow you to include a cover letter. For this reason, consider using the paper application process, whenever possible, to take advantage of the opportunity to sell yourself with a powerful cover letter targeted for that specific position.

Keywords and Keyword Phrases

Keywords and keyword phrases are critical components of every successful job seeker's cover letter. By using just one or two words, you're able to communicate a wealth of information about your skills, qualifications, and experience. What's more, keywords are the basis for scanning technology and are therefore critical to every job seeker's campaign in today's electronic-based job search market.

Following are the top 20 government keywords, some of which may reflect your skills and some of which may not be appropriate for you at this time. Use these words as the foundation for developing your own list of keywords on the Professional Keyword List form in Appendix B.

Top 20 Keywords

Briefings & Trainings

Budget Planning & Allocation

Congressional Affairs

Cross-Cultural Communications

Cultural Diversity

Foreign Government Relations

Governmental Affairs

Inter-Agency Relations

International Trade & Commerce

Legislative Affairs

Liaison Affairs

Lobbying

Press Relations & Media Affairs

Procurement & Acquisitions

Program Design & Management

Public Advocacy

Public Works

Regulatory Reporting

SEC Affairs

Zoning & Compliance

Following are some excellent examples of cover letters for government careers.

ADELAIDE SPECLEMAN
(416) 555-1212
specleman@sympatico.ca

123 WOODBINE AVENUE
SCARBOROUGH, ONTARIO
M1B 2A3

June 21, 2006

Ms. Lucy Mak
Human Resources
Ministry of Community and Social Services
246 College Street
Toronto, ON   M4G 2X5

Dear Ms. Mak:

Re: Posting #GO06-135 Administrative Director

When I read the posting for an Administrative Director on the GOjobs website, I could not help but notice how well your requirements align with my experience, education, skills, and background.

While my enclosed resume provides a good overview of my strengths and achievements, I have also listed some of your specific requirements for the position and my applicable skills:

You require:	I offer:
Ability to coordinate and oversee the work of administrative assistants	Experience in supervising 25 office employees and ensuring staff efficiency as the manager of administrative services in a large downtown hospital
Ability to strategically plan, develop, and implement programs and operations toward achievement of team's mission, goals, and objectives	Experience developing and implementing operations programs designed to strengthen the efficiency of the administrative support team
Financial and personnel management expertise	Expertise in both areas, through accounting and office management background
Interpersonal and communication skills that promote ability to serve as a liaison and resource	Significant experience giving presentations, speaking persuasively, and interacting successfully with diverse individuals

Since my experience and expertise fit your requirements so closely, I look forward to meeting with you and the Ministry of Community and Social Services management team.

Sincerely,

Adelaide Specleman

Enclosure

Written By: Anne Brunelle
Font: Times New Roman

Keith Grassing
1247 Carmon Boulevard Boston, Massachusetts 02101
✉ cityproman22@bellsouth.net – ☎ 339.555.8655 (home) – 339.555.3429 (cell)

July 27, 2006

Mr. Jack Kleinst
City Manager
City of Punta Dorada
City Hall Annex, 3rd Floor
4444 Conch Avenue
Punta Dorada, FL 33000

Dear Mr. Kleinst:

If you could design the perfect Assistant City Manager for Punta Dorada, would the following meet the most demanding requirements of your broadest constituency?

- ❑ A passionate team player who doesn't care who gets the credit as long as the job is done with excellence,

- ❑ A manager who knows how to get things done so well that people think his suggestions are their own good ideas, and

- ❑ A leader who uses his own professional development programs to help others.

You have just read the 54-word version of my resume. You'll find the full document on the following pages. It probably doesn't look like other applications you have seen. I thought you deserved to see, right at the top of the first page, capabilities that citizens associate with the best in municipal government. Backing them up are 17 examples of programs moved forward, teamwork improved, and performance enhanced.

If my approach and track record appeal to you, I'd like to suggest a logical next step. I want to explore Punta Dorada's most pressing municipal problems, hearing the priorities in your own words, so I can begin to think about how I can serve you best. May I call in a few days to set aside time to do that?

Sincerely,

Keith Grassing

Enclosure: Resume

Written By: Don Orlando
Font: Book Antiqua

PETER LAWRENCE

67 Downey Street ■ West Milton, CT 08875 ■ 203.788.2133 ■ peterlawr@aol.com

September 2, 2006

Mayor John R. Grossman
Town of West Milton
100 Main Street
West Milton, CT 08876

Dear Mayor Grossman:

During my 10-year career as a public official, I have acquired broad experience and honed diverse skills that I believe will be of interest to the Town of West Milton. My background, highlighted in the enclosed resume, demonstrates that I possess the necessary strategic planning and financial, project, and people management capabilities that would qualify me to serve as your community's Town Administrator.

What do I offer?

- More than 10 years of municipal government experience as a Selectman and Chair governing the Town of Southington, which is complemented by private sector management experience.
- Proactive leadership with proven ability to inspire cooperation, communication, and consensus among personnel and other groups.
- Development and administration of $10 million budget as well as planning and overseeing multiple projects to meet community needs.
- Contributing to economic development by building strong public/private partnerships and negotiating agreements.

Examples of my accomplishments:

- Leadership of several town revitalization projects providing key services.
- Negotiating Tax Incentive Financing Agreements for retaining and attracting employers.
- Sound fiscal management that includes improved benefit programs without cost increases.
- Fostering a work environment that builds team spirit and energizes employees to perform at their best. As a result, our staff is recognized for exceptional responsiveness and positive community relations.

This position as Town Administrator is particularly exciting to me for several reasons. As a native of the community, I am familiar with the area's demographics and general issues facing West Milton. In addition, I still consider the community my "home" as I have extended family living in the area, am a property owner, and would love to be a resident of the community once again.

I have always had a passion for municipal government service and would enjoy making it my full-time career. Therefore, I welcome the opportunity to discuss my qualifications and the contributions I would make as your community's Town Administrator. Thank you for your consideration.

Sincerely,

Peter Lawrence

Enclosure

Written By: Louise Garver
Font: Book Antiqua

JOSEPH T. FAIRNESS

1881 Main Street
Alexandria, VA 22209
Home: 703-555-0001 Cell: 703-555-0002
Email: fairjo24@gmail.com

July 12, 2006

Alexandria City Government
Office of Judicial Support Services
1720 Bay Street, 23rd Floor
Alexandria, VA 22220

Dear Hiring Committee:

JUSTICE OF THE PEACE – DISTRICT COURT OF ALEXANDRIA

As indicated in Ms. Lalane's letter to me of July 8, 2006:

> *"Justices of the Peace appointments require a responsible individual with integrity and the ability to interpret relevant legislation and bylaws, knowledge and understanding of Virginia's judicial system and process, excellent oral and written communication skills, sound interpersonal skills, good administrative skills, and superior analytical ability combined with sound judgement."*

I have carefully considered the requirements and believe I have the necessary qualifications and experience to succeed as a Justice of the Peace for the District Court of Alexandria. I am, therefore, offering myself as a candidate.

As a **Case Worker** for more than 10 years with the Department of Community and Social Services, I have encountered many challenges and have had to make tough decisions, but the positive outcomes speak to my commitment to fairness, integrity, and due process. I have a solid record of community involvement, which is one of your prerequisites, and through this involvement and my dedication to the pursuit of justice for youths, I have been honored with a number of federal, state, and local awards. I have a sound knowledge of related legislation and bylaws and a very good understanding of Alexandria's judicial system through my employment in social services and my work as a volunteer probation officer.

My paid and volunteer experiences all entail working collaboratively with people and employing sound interpersonal skills, excellent analytical ability, and success in making decisions in a timely manner. I have exceptional oral and written communication skills and can clearly articulate my position on issues in a professional and understandable manner.

I am confident that my background and diverse experiences could make a difference in the administration of justice in the District Court of Alexandria. Please review the attached resume and give me a call to set up a time for us to meet.

Sincerely,

Joseph T. Fairness

Enclosure

Written By: Daisy Wright
Font: Arial

JAMES BURROWS
35-15 36th Avenue ▪ Astoria, NY 11102 USA ▪ Cell: 917-852-4411 ▪ jburrows@gmail.com

January 21, 2006

Ms. Marilyn Pratt
HR Manager
Counter Terrorist Coordination Command (CTCC)
PO Box 1322
Washington, DC 20090

Dear Ms. Pratt:

Investigating and analyzing disparate and sometimes conflicting sources of information and synthesizing data to make all the pieces of the puzzle fit is what I do best. It is with great interest that I submit my candidacy for your agency's open position for a Senior Intelligence Analyst. My value proposition, as it relates to your selection criteria, is detailed below.

Your Selection Criteria
Demonstrated high-level research, analytical, oral, and written communication skills; experience preparing intelligence reports and delivering briefings.

My Value-Added
- **Uncovered over US$270M in fraudulent banking transactions** and analyzed all related financial documentation in conjunction with my investigative role for the Independent Inquiry Committee into the United Nations Oil-for-Food Program. Documented and briefed the findings to the editorial panel for the Committee's reports on program infractions to the UN Security Council.

Your Selection Criteria
A high working knowledge of tactical and strategic intelligence and the ability to apply intelligence concepts. High level of ability to use computerized information management systems.

My Value-Added
- **Contributed geo-political and socio-economic knowledge of Middle Eastern business practices and culture** to expose illicit commercial activities, and maximized efficiency of evidence collection for the Independent Inquiry Committee. Leveraged experience in proven data mining abilities to "connect the dots" concerning entity affiliations to uncover improprieties.
- **Implemented a new process to reduce time spent in responding to police inquiries, resulting in significant improvement in data accuracy, integrity, and relevancy** for Interpol. Sourced alternative methods for collecting and analyzing incoming information expeditiously by identifying patterns and establishing and streamlining distinct search and extrapolation criteria. Procedure was developed and implemented in the immediate aftermath of the March 11th, 2004 terrorist bombing in Madrid and proved crucial in providing time-sensitive analyses.

Ms. Marilyn Pratt
January 21, 2006
Page 2

<u>Your Selection Criteria</u>
Tertiary qualifications in intelligence or research-related area. Broad knowledge of global and domestic terrorism issues. Must be suitable to obtain a secret-level national security clearance. Experience in the management, supervision, and development of staff.

<u>My Value-Added</u>
- **Comprehensive investigative / counter-terrorist experience with two global institutions (The United Nations and Interpol)** and significant exposure to intelligence issues through global and regional channels.
- **Extensive and established network of worldwide contacts ranging from local-specific to global expertise encompassing multi-level sources of information and assessment abilities**. Network includes a very diverse knowledge base ranging from security officials and academics, to local craftsmen and merchants.
- **Mentored staff** on the implementation of the new analysis and search procedure (stated above), and advised analysts on the intricacies of Middle Eastern culture, business, and politics.

I appreciate your consideration and would welcome the chance to explore this opportunity in a personal interview. Be assured that my skills in investigative research and data collection / analysis will add measurable value to your organization.

Sincerely,

James Burrows

Enclosure

Written By: Barbara Safani
Font: Book Antiqua

Abygael Aleksandra, BS, MBA
19 Lawnside Drive
Dover, NJ 09903

Home: (201) 555-3827
Mobile: (201) 555-8273
Email: abygaela@optusnet.com

October 11, 2006

HR Director
City of Newark
9000 City Boulevard
Newark, NJ 09088

Dear Sir/Madam:

Throughout my career, I have not only displayed strong business management expertise, but also the unique ability to build consensus among diverse political and special interest groups to work cooperatively towards common goals. With extensive experience working for the highest levels of government and on high-profile cross-agency projects, I have demonstrated outstanding leadership skills and the ability to manage extensive, diverse responsibilities that have been of high value to organizations.

Leading by example, I plan strategies to help facilitate departmental vision by committing to action and achieving goals in the most efficient and effective manner. Through cognitive thinking, I am able to understand and respond methodically to the complexities inherent in project management, protecting departmental interests through the development of long and short-term strategies that will identify, analyze, and solve problems.

My greatest strength lies in my ability to build high-performance, cross-disciplinary teams vital to overall project management and product delivery. Recognizing that a diversity of experience and knowledge can only enhance the quality of the team's work, I contribute actively to team projects by working with peers and colleagues collaboratively toward consensual solutions. Projecting an air of assurance that encourages confidence in others, I am able to maintain productive working conditions and promote employee loyalty and involvement.

With an excellent mix of skills, experience, and knowledge that delivers results, I bring to your organization proven project management skills, combined with an in-depth knowledge of many facets of government operations and management. Communicating in a compelling and articulate manner that instills commitment, and adapting communication to ensure that different audiences understand key message, allows me to negotiate and maintain relationships that produce "win-win" results.

My resume is enclosed to provide you with details of my skills and accomplishments, but I am certain that a personal interview would more fully reveal my desire and ability to contribute to your organization. Thank you for your time and consideration, and do not hesitate to contact me if you have any questions. I look forward to speaking with you soon.

Yours sincerely,

Abygael Aleksandra

Enclosure

Written By: Jennifer Rushton
Font: Georgia

Chapter 8

▶ Cover Letters for
Healthcare and Social Service Careers

Your cover letter presents an excellent opportunity to show prospective employers and recruiters how the skills and accomplishments documented on your resume relate to their specific hiring needs. Each industry and profession presents unique cover letter writing and design challenges. If you are interested in pursuing a career in healthcare or social services, be certain to include highlights of these important success factors in your cover letters:

🎗 Success Factor #1

Show your diverse experience by including the different types of patients/consumers you have treated or served. Including this information demonstrates your versatility and sensitivity to individuals with varying needs.

🎗 Success Factor #2

Be sure to mention relevant healthcare procedures you can perform or equipment you can operate. Don't assume your current job title equates to the same job duties in a new organization. By documenting your skills, you ensure that your next employer will see what you can do and how you add value.

🎗 Success Factor #3

List your credentials at the top of your letter. Include either the appropriate initials after your name, or spell out your licenses or certifications and place them near the top of your letter. This is critical information and immediately communicates that you have the *right* qualifications for a particular position.

Success Factor #4

Highlight your participation in any research projects or in the development and/or introduction of new procedures or techniques. Even though you may believe your role was relatively minor, your exposure to leading-edge treatments and protocols could be a point of interest for a new employer.

Keywords and Keyword Phrases

Keywords and keyword phrases are critical components of every successful job seeker's cover letter. By using just one or two words, you're able to communicate a wealth of information about your skills, qualifications, and experience. What's more, keywords are the basis for scanning technology and are therefore critical to every job seeker's campaign in today's electronic-based job search market.

Following are the top 20 healthcare and social service keywords, some of which may reflect your skills and some of which may not be appropriate for you at this time. Use these words as the foundation for developing your own list of keywords on the Professional Keyword List form in Appendix B.

Top 20 Keywords

Ambulatory Care

Behavior Modification

Case Management

Chronic Care

Client Advocacy

Community Outreach

Crisis Intervention

Diagnostic Evaluation & Intervention

Healthcare Administration

Healthcare Delivery

Human Services

Inpatient & Outpatient Care

Insurance Administration

Integrated Service Delivery

Patient/Client Relations

Practice Management

Protective Services

Regulatory Affairs & Reporting

Risk Management

Vocational Rehabilitation

Following are some excellent examples of cover letters for healthcare and social services careers.

FRED ADAMS
316 Old Milford Road
Milford, KS 66514
Home: 785-237-1548
Work: 785-235-7200
adamsf@hotmail.com

August 19, 2006

Mr. Arnold Swartz
Gold's Gym
1016 Cole Avenue
Los Angeles, CA 90046

Dear Mr. Swartz:

I am enclosing my resume in response to your ad for a **Physical Fitness Trainer** that was listed in last Sunday's *Los Angeles Times.*

In addition to the skills as reflected on my resume, I won first place in the Lightweight classification for body building while assigned to military service in Korea. Additionally, I placed in the top 10 in the Osan, Korea All-Services competition. While assigned to Fort Hood, Texas, I held the Lightweight wrestling title and was undefeated for three years. I exceeded annual Army requirements for physical fitness testing by scoring at least 290 out of 300 on each test.

In addition to the resume, I have included a recent photo of myself that will attest to my personal physical condition. I am confident that I can help your clients who desire to improve their physical fitness and appearance.

I will call you within the next two weeks to follow up on my resume, answer any questions you may have, and set a date and time for an interview.

Thank you.

Sincerely,

Fred Adams

Enclosure

Written By: James Walker
Font: Times New Roman

MARGARET J. WILTON

163 Crescent Drive ▪ Baldwin, NY 11510 ▪ mjwilton@yahoo.com ▪ 631-898-0543

May 12, 2006

Ms. Cynthia Patell, Supervisor
South Shore Healthcare
245 West Merrick Road
Baldwin, NY 11510

Dear Ms. Patell,

Hospitals and medical centers spend thousands of dollars each year to manage their medical records backlog. Many employ interim staffing agencies with costly fees and an employee base that requires considerable training. But what if a facility could hire an exceptional transcriptionist on a short-term basis at a fraction of the cost?

Throughout my 18 years as a medical transcriptionist, I have impressed my employers with my extensive knowledge of medical terminology, ability to quickly learn medical systems, extraordinary speed, and impeccable accuracy. With experience in over 20 hospitals, medical centers, and radiology centers across the country, I possess multiple references that can vouch for my outstanding record of service. My value-added skills include:

Speed	Consistently exceed industry standards for records completion as much as 200%; average 1,800 - 2,000 lines daily.
Accuracy	Produce quality document transcription with virtually no errors.
Efficiency	Eliminate significant document backlog well ahead of projected time frames.
Training	Master medical software programs in a fraction of the time typically required; to date have learned all systems in less than one hour.
Software	Proficient in multiple medical software packages including Lanier, Meditech, Softmed, and Chartscript.
Flexibility	Three years of experience as a traveling MT with success assimilating into diverse work environments as an independent contractor and employee of Medi-Temp and Temp-Force.

I am confident that I can deliver results similar to those described above for your organization and would welcome the opportunity to discuss my qualifications in more detail. I'll follow up later this week to schedule an interview. Thank you for your consideration.

Sincerely,

Margaret J. Wilton

Enclosure

Written By: Barbara Safani
Font: Times New Roman

Rosita Lopez, M.S.W.

9438 11th Avenue
Santa Fe, NM 87501

(505) 555-5872
rosylopez@dot.net

December 3, 2006

Ms. Margaret McLean, M.S.W.
Director of Social Services
St. Francis Hospital
2000 Harcourt Parkway
Santa Fe, NM 87501

Dear Ms. McLean:

My recent internship in the Social Services Department at Danforth Memorial Hospital, working with cancer patients and their families, has convinced me that this is truly my career goal. I derive my greatest satisfaction from responding to patients' emotional and social needs, ensuring they receive quality care while coping with their devastating illnesses.

My role within the radiation oncology program included:

* ❖ Providing short-term patient counseling, concrete services, and agency referrals, as well as addressing bereavement issues and intervening in crisis situations.

* ❖ Assessing patients for substance abuse, nutrition status, support systems, physical functioning, financial situation, and other factors.

* ❖ Screening and assessing patients to determine their eligibility for nursing home acceptance or alternative care options based on their economic situation.

* ❖ Coordinating patients' discharge, transportation, and ongoing therapy with nurses and other social and medical professionals following their release from the hospital.

In performing these tasks, I feel I have developed the capabilities you are looking for in a candidate for your open position. In addition, I am fluent in both English and Spanish, and function well within an interdisciplinary team.

If we have the opportunity to meet in person, you would find me to be a personable and compassionate individual who relates well to people and adapts easily to new environments.

Thank you in advance for your time. I hope to speak with you soon.

Sincerely,

Rosita Lopez

Enclosure: Resume

Written By: Melanie Noonan
Font: Lucida Sans

SHAWN CORTES, LSCW-R

.n Street
.efferson, NY 11777

(631) 555-8921
scortes@email.com

July 21, 2006

John J. Martinez
Long Island Mental Health Services
47 Fifth Avenue
Bay Shore, NY 11706

Dear Mr. Martinez:

Working collaboratively with clients, I offer an approachable, compassionate, and adaptable therapeutic style that meets each client's unique and individual needs. Through my ability to draw upon client strengths to explore and develop strategies, I am confident I can help your clients address areas of growth.

Interacting with clients suffering from various illnesses and conditions, I have gained the experience needed to provide them with ongoing support to overcome self-limiting beliefs. I find that individuals seek counseling for various reasons, including stress, depression, anxiety, family and relationship issues, physical and sexual abuse, and substance dependence. Although different reasons drive them to seek assistance, they all want the same result—the ability to lead fulfilling and rewarding lives.

At this time, I am open to fee-for-service or a full-time social work position in which I can create an environment allowing clients to get a deeper and broader understanding of their behavior. My resume is enclosed to provide you with additional details concerning my background and qualifications for this position. I am certain an interview would fully reveal my abilities and enthusiasm for the opportunity to contribute to your facility.

Thank you for your time and consideration. Please do not hesitate to contact me if you have any questions. I look forward to meeting with you.

Sincerely,

Shawn Cortes, LCSW-R

Enclosure

KATE PAYTON

15 Whitehouse Drive ◆ **Yardley, PA 19067** ◆ **(215) 353-6677** ◆ **kpays@msn.com**

September 13, 2006

Ms. Jeanne Oscarson
HR Director
Comfort Care Learning Center
7700 Greene Boulevard
Pittsburgh, PA 19093

Dear Ms. Oscarson:

As a competent occupational therapist with extensive experience working with children in school settings, I believe I am someone who will be an asset to your staff. With solid skills and a proven record of success in assessing children's OT needs and developing and executing targeted treatment plans, I would like to consider putting my talents and experience to work for you.

As you can see from my enclosed resume, my background includes more than eight years of experience as an occupational therapist. For the last six years, however, my work has been exclusively with students from ages three and up. Providing services in both public school districts and special needs schools during this time, I have addressed and treated a broad range of needs while accumulating a wealth of knowledge and expertise. Indicative of my success, I have received frequent praise from teachers and parents alike for both my therapeutic skills and my cooperative approach. As a result, I have enjoyed the benefit of repeat, long-term assignments.

Among the keys to my success, my strengths include solid training and up-to-date therapeutic skills. In addition, I offer an independent nature, exceptional creativity in adapting equipment and modifying environmental factors, and excellent communication skills. Known for the ability to build an easy rapport with others, I work exceptionally well with teachers and am valued for my flexible, accommodating style. However, I believe the trait that sets me apart is my unsurpassed commitment to service. Truly motivated to help students reach goals and objectives, I am relentless in my approach and quick to do what I think best serves students' needs.

With the track record I offer, you can be confident that I will be an asset to your organization and your students. As such, I would be pleased to have the opportunity to discuss future employment and look forward to speaking with you. Please contact me at the address and phone number listed above to arrange an interview.

Thank you for your consideration.

Sincerely,

Kate Payton

Enclosure

Written By: Carol Altomare
Font: Times New Roman

ELIZABETH CARNEY, RN, BSN, PHRN, CN III

23701 Oviatt Road
Northridge, California 91312

818 -733-3611
ecarney@msn.com

February 25, 2006

Leo Constanza
Neuroscience-Orthopedic Nurse Manager
UCLA Medical Center
10833 Le Conte Avenue
Los Angeles, California 90095

RE: New Lead Nurse Position

Dear Mr. Constanza:

Are you looking for an enthusiastic, energetic leader? Someone to promote UCLA's spirit while upholding UCLA's mission to provide the best in healthcare? A lead nurse with a partnering philosophy?

If so, please consider my candidacy. With 12 years of experience at UCLA Medical Center, 10 as a charge nurse and the last 6 as a CN III, as well as being a UCLA alumna, I would embody all that UCLA could wish for in a Lead Nurse. As an instructor and presenter at the UCLA Medical Center, I am constantly striving to stay on the cutting edge of technology and healthcare by continuously educating myself beyond the required ongoing training.

This new position offers many challenges and opportunities for professional growth and would allow me to contribute to my journey toward nursing excellence. I have created harmonious work teams and don't ask anything of my staff that I wouldn't do myself. I lead by example and have precepted RNs in specialty and float teams, as well as both novice and experienced RNs. I am always willing to help and pitch in where needed.

My strengths lie in my clinical expertise, neuroscience knowledge, analytical thinking, outstanding leadership skills, patient care competencies, and teaching style. I am able to convey complex information in meaningful terms.

You also acquire a well-rounded individual with a strong work ethic and high standards. I have several outside interests which allow me to be a better nurse and leader. As my resume shows, I am a support group leader for Resolve of Greater Los Angeles (a National Infertility Organization), a classroom volunteer at Pico Canyon Elementary School, and an active participant in PTA activities.

I would very much like to be a part of this new and exciting venture. As such, I look forward to a personal interview.

Respectfully submitted,

Elizabeth Carney

Enclosure

Written By: Myriam-Rose Kohn
Font: Arial

JULES BERNQUIST

Licensed Nursing Home Administrator

555 Spring Hill Drive   Evanston, IL   773.455.1299

julesbernquist@brx.com

September 29, 2006

Lauren J. Jones, MD, JD
President & CEO
Deerwood Place
45 Deerwood Drive
Aurora, IL 60512

Dear Dr. Jones:

Jennifer Logan asked that I forward my resume to you in consideration for the Executive Director position with Deerwood. She indicated that she had visited with you about my qualifications and that you would be expecting my letter. It is with great interest and enthusiasm that I submit the enclosed information.

Briefly stated, my credentials include:

- Current licensure in the states of Illinois and Indiana as a Nursing Home Administrator, Registered Nurse, and Registered Dietician.
- 12 years of Continuing Care Retirement Community (CCRC) experience in managerial, administrative, and leadership roles, guiding a talented team of 150+ staff members.
- Candidate for MBA degree with completion slated for June 2007.
- Registered Nurse with extensive background in Emergency Room, Outpatient Surgery, and Surgical Units; prior career as a Registered Dietician.
- Lifelong interest, involvement, and commitment to serving the elderly population; reared in a family of physicians.

The attached resume outlines in greater detail my background and experience in the nursing home administration profession. I'd be happy to share more details in a private meeting and once again, please know how much I appreciate your consideration. Feel free to contact me at the above-referenced cellular number. I look forward to continued conversation at your earliest convenience.

Sincerely,

Jules Bernquist

Enclosures

Written By: Billie Ruth Sucher
Font: Trebuchet MS

RONALD N. DOVER

101 Williams Drive ▪ Ludlow, MA 01056 ▪ H: (413) 589-4040-1787 C: (413) 542-6816 ▪ rndover@comcast.net

March 28, 2006

PO Box 1088
Boston, MA 02209

Dear Human Resources Representative:

Developing solid provider networks that offer "the deepest discounts and the best providers" is just one accomplishment that I am proud of during the course of my career in health care. After 20 years in management and executive roles for leading HMOs in New England, I find myself looking forward to new challenges and growth opportunities. I'm one of those rare people who really enjoys his job 99% of the time and loves being in a position to make decisions that directly contribute to the company's success.

After seeing your posting for a Vice President of Provider Relations, I was convinced that my qualifications are an ideal fit with your needs. Briefly, my skills and expertise encompass the following:

➤ **Recruitment and Contract Negotiations** – Possess a philosophy that the process has to be bipartisan and all involved parties must feel as though it is a winning situation. Negotiated an exclusive agreement with a 15-physician primary care practice that saved the HMO a projected $500,000 in annual claims by replacing a traditional fee-for-service (FFS) arrangement with a capitation model to help practice curb unneeded costs.

➤ **Network Development and Management** – Savvy at assessing all components in order to create and operate a strong provider network with reimbursement methodologies that are cost effective, but fair to all parties. For a newly formed HMO, built up a network of 6,000 providers that included a tertiary care center, three hospitals, 3000 physicians, and several ancillary providers, all within only eight months.

➤ **Managed Care Operations** – As a pivotal member of two start-up healthcare companies, was directly involved in functional areas that included claims, accounting, client services, and information systems, all of which helped to build thriving managed care organizations with 350,000 members in total.

➤ **Client Relationship Management** – Established long-lasting and meaningful relationships with physicians, hospitals, and ancillary providers that have resulted in provider-friendly networks and very satisfied clients. Recognized and well respected within healthcare communities throughout the Northeast.

➤ **Data Management and Reporting** – Began earlier career in healthcare statistics and then transitioned into developing information systems to support managed and healthcare reporting. Amassed concrete knowledge of the data required to demonstrate cost savings and make meaningful financial decisions at the managerial and executive levels.

I welcome the opportunity to discuss how my contributions would positively impact your providers, clients, and bottom line. Thank you for your consideration. I look forward to hearing from you shortly.

Sincerely,

Ronald N. Dover

Enclosure

Written By: Jill Grindle
Font: Garamond

Chapter 9

▶ Cover Letters for
Hospitality and Food Service
Careers

Your cover letter presents an excellent opportunity to show prospective employers and recruiters how the skills and accomplishments documented on your resume relate to their specific hiring needs. Each industry and profession presents unique cover letter writing and design challenges. If you are interested in pursuing a hotel or food service career, be certain to include highlights of these important success factors in your cover letters:

Success Factor #1

If you're in the food service industry, mention the types of cuisine with which you are familiar. If you worked at a restaurant, was it a four-star establishment? If you worked at a hotel, what kind of guests did you cater to and what types of facilities did you have (for example, spa, golf course, or tennis club)?

Success Factor #2

Do you plan, prepare food, or set up for banquets or large-scale receptions and parties? How many people attend these events? As you well know, a banquet for 500 people is an entirely different function than the day-to-day operations of a medium-sized restaurant.

Success Factor #3

If you have studied or worked under a famous chef or at a renowned restaurant, hotel, or resort, be sure to mention it prominently, including any training or apprenticeship programs that were involved.

🔑 **Success Factor #4**

Include any administrative functions for which you have been responsible, such as purchasing, inventory control, food and labor cost controls, sales, customer service, or facilities. Don't forget to include these important roles and the contribution they represent to your employer's success.

Keywords and Keyword Phrases

Keywords and keyword phrases are critical components of every successful job seeker's cover letter. By using just one or two words, you're able to communicate a wealth of information about your skills, qualifications, and experience. What's more, keywords are the basis for scanning technology and are therefore critical to every job seeker's campaign in today's electronic-based job search market.

Following are the top 20 hotel and food service keywords, some of which may reflect your skills and some of which may not be appropriate for you at this time. Use these words as the foundation for developing your own list of keywords on the Professional Keyword List form in Appendix B.

Top 20 Keywords

Back-of-the-House Operations	Inventory Planning & Control
Catering Services	Labor Cost Controls
Conference & Meeting Planning	Menu Planning & Pricing
Corporate Dining Room Operations	Multi-Unit Operations
Customer Service Management	Occupancy Management
Food & Beverage Operations	Portion Control
Front-of-the-House Operations	Property Development
Guest Service & Satisfaction	Resort Management
Hospitality Management	Revenue Planning & Reporting
Housekeeping Operations	Special Events Planning

Following are some excellent examples of cover letters for hospitality and food service careers.

PAM CHARLES

7 Titus Road ◆ Pennington, NJ 08543 ◆ (609) 466-2222 ◆ pamcharles@aol.com

October 31, 2006

John Rodgers, Partner
Rodgers, Stein & Goldman
12 Arnold Avenue, 19th Floor
Newark, NJ 02902

Dear Mr. Rodgers:

As an accomplished sales coordinator with a demonstrated commitment to service excellence and a proven drive to succeed, I believe I offer a set of skills that will be of benefit to one of your client companies. With outstanding organizational abilities, a talent for building productive business relationships, and exceptional customer service skills, I would like to explore the possibility of putting my talents to work at an organization in need of strong and decisive sales leadership.

As you can see from my enclosed resume, I am currently employed as a Sales Coordinator at the Holiday Inn in Pennington. Promoted to this position at a time when revenues from meeting room bookings and other group services were in decline, I pride myself on the new life I brought to the business. Among my accomplishments: I lured back the business of Pharmacia, a key client, attracted significant repeat and referral business, and rebuilt customer loyalty through the implementation of new service standards.

Key to my success, you will find that I am passionate about customer service and will do whatever I can to ensure customer satisfaction. Organized and efficient, I easily handle multiple tasks and am successful in balancing the competing demands of a busy hotel. Valued for strong communication skills and responsive problem-solving capabilities, I am also a polished presenter who inspires confidence and trust which translates into success in marketing products and closing sales.

With this combination of skills and traits, I have proven to be a valued employee in the past, and with the track record I offer, you can be confident that I will be an asset any one of your client companies. I am open to relocation and anticipate a salary between $75,000 and $85,000 annually. Please feel free to contact me at the address and phone number listed above to arrange a meeting.

Thank you for your consideration.

Sincerely,

Pam Charles

Enclosure

Written By: Carol Altomare
Font: Georgia

Allyson Green

5415 N. Clark Street
Chicago, Illinois 60640
(773) 907-8660
allygreen@acme.com

September 1, 2006

Ms. Wendy Lewis
General Manager
Marriott Food Services Corporation
1 Marriott Plaza
Vienna, VA 22090

Dear Ms. Lewis:

I am interested in joining Marriott Food Services Corporation in a managerial position. The enclosed resume outlines my experience and achievements. I will be happy to provide references or further information at your request.

As my resume indicates, I have broad experience in the hospitality industry having worked as a Manager in Corporate Sales, Conference Services, and Catering Sales. In all of these positions, I have met and exceeded goals for sales and guest service. At the same time, I have worked with other departments to find new ways to improve relationships with corporate clients and expand product offerings. My priority is always to listen carefully and understand what each client expects. Then I work hard to satisfy that person and their guests in a way that exceeds initial expectations. I am confident that this combination of skills and experience will make me a valuable member of your team.

I offer you the following qualities:

- **Organization:** *Establish goals and consistently meet or exceed them by setting priorities and managing time effectively.*

- **Self-motivation:** *Approach all tasks with a sense of ownership, responsibility, and a dedication to doing quality work.*

- **Personality:** *Disciplined performer who focuses on results.*

Realizing that this summary cannot fully communicate my potential contribution, I would appreciate the opportunity to speak with you personally. I'll follow up next Thursday to schedule an interview.

Thank you for your consideration.

Sincerely,

Allyson Green

Enclosure

Written By: Clay Cerny
Font: Georgia

ROGER PATEL

444 Hunters Glen Road ◆ Amarillo, TX 12168 ◆ (518) 482-9813 ◆ rogerpatel@hotmail.com

July 23, 2006

Martin R. Reiss
Hiring Director
Smith-Brown Enterprises, Inc.
9800 Rocky Gorge Road
Dallas, TX 77809

Dear Mr. Reiss:

If you are in need of a highly qualified Hotel Management Professional, then we have good reason to meet. After researching your firm and your needs, I believe my skills and experience may be of value to your team.

I offer 16 years of successful experience in the hospitality industry at various hotels, serving in positions of progressive responsibility at the corporate and hotel level. I offer broad-based skills as a Controller and Hotel Accountant, including budgeting, forecasting, auditing, account management, financial statements, accounts payable, accounts receivable, taxes, general ledger, cash flow, profit and loss, and asset management. Throughout my career, I have been recognized by upper management as a top performer for consistently meeting or exceeding company goals, and always achieving commendable scores on SOX and internal audits.

With a keen eye for detail and strong organizational skills, I am known for always meeting deadlines and handling multiple projects, tasks, and priorities effectively. As a skilled communicator, I am proficient at training and motivating teams of professionals in meeting goals and challenges. My dedication to high-quality work and commitment to organizational goals will be a valuable asset to your team. My educational background includes an Associate's degree in Hotel / Motel Management. My resume provides further details of my skills and accomplishments.

I feel confident I can make an immediate and positive contribution to your organization. If it appears that my qualifications meet your current needs, I would like to further discuss my background in a meeting with you. Thank you for your time and consideration. I look forward to your reply.

Sincerely,

Roger Patel

Enclosure: Resume

Written By: John Femia
Font: Times New Roman

COURTNEY GIBBS
cgibbs@yahoo.com

20588 Marciano Lane
Chatsworth, California 91331

Residence: 818 882-8354
Cellular: 310 548-7057

October 17, 2006

The Mediterranean
4824 Olive Way
Burbank, California 91502

"Treat employees like partners and they act like partners."
Fred Allen, CEO, Pitney Bowes

As a business operations manager, I strongly believe in giving employees ownership of their work. This empowerment has been key to my success as a **Food Service Director and Manager**. Just as significant are my strengths in personnel, management development, budgeting, financial management, quality assurance, and purchasing.

The enclosed resume shows what I bring to you and your team:

- Over 20 years of experience in the food and hospitality industry.
- A dynamic career of consistently increasing sales and improving customer service and quality.
- Energy, enthusiasm, perseverance, and motivation.
- A proven record in sales, leadership, and management that shines with superior achievements.

My key strength is initiating and implementing changes to turn restaurants and hotels around into profit machines. This process starts with building rapport with my employees and colleagues, motivating others to exceed expectations, and then delivering the extra effort necessary to achieve the goals of The Mediterranean.

You will note that my work history ends in 2004. Unfortunately, illness prevented me from returning to work; however, I am back 100% now and you need not worry about absenteeism. I possess a strong work ethic and would not be applying to work at The Mediterranean if I didn't feel I could completely commit to the job.

At this point in my career, I am seeking new professional challenges and opportunities. An extremely good fit exists between your requirements and my background. I look forward to discussing how I might contribute to your company's growth and increased profitability through excellence in customer service. As such, I will call you next week to set up an appointment for a personal meeting.

Thank you for your time and consideration.

Sincerely,

Courtney Gibbs

Enclosure

Written By: Myriam-Rose Kohn
Font: Arial

Jason VanDeveer
8123 Jackson Boulevard
Bridgeport, CT 06604

jayvee@cyberspace.com   (203) 555-9825

October 17, 2006

Mr. Eugene Baumann
Director of Food and Beverage Operations
Arlington Hotel Group
5009 Madison Avenue
New York, NY 10001

Dear Mr. Baumann:

I am enclosing a copy of my resume for your review with the thought that the kitchen operations of one of your metropolitan area hotels could be greatly enhanced by my skills as an **award-winning Executive Chef**. For the past nine years, my culinary talents were demonstrated in food preparation from a la carte to large-scale banquets, with particular expertise in design and presentation. I have broad knowledge of all current trends in fine cuisine. As a back-of-house manager, I have an astute awareness of business finances and am successful at directing a productive staff with low turnover in an industry notorious for personnel problems.

To give you an example of some of my achievements:

> **Created distinctive signature dishes named for the various rooms at the Crystal Manor, and oversaw preparation of all foods made on premises, including wedding cakes, pastries, hors d'oeuvres, patés, and hot dishes.**

> **Managed a $1.5 million dollar purchasing budget (90% food), keeping costs well below industry standards through accurate inventory control, competitive bidding with over 30 purveyors, and stewardship of provisions and stables to avoid spoilage and waste.**

> **Won 10 gold medals, 5 silver medals, and 4 bronze medals conferred by prestigious organizations in various culinary competitions since 2001.**

> **Featured as "Chef of the Week" in** The News Courier **, May 2004**

Based on my background and skills, I feel confident I can handle the responsibilities of executive chef at one of your fine hotels. I would appreciate an opportunity to discuss with your regional management team how I may contribute my expertise.

I am looking forward to a positive response.

Sincerely,

Jason VanDeveer

Enclosure: Resume

Written By: Melanie Noonan
Font: Tahoma

Matthew P. Hashimoto

801 – 708 Mainland Boulevard, Vancouver, BC V9E 5L7   matthashimoto@hotmail.com   (604)694-1062

September 14, 2006

Ms. Elizabeth Sweet, General Manager
Diamond Hotels and Resorts
Suite 2700, 1200 West Georgia Street
Vancouver, BC   V8H 3B7

Re: **Executive Chef opportunity – Diamond "Crown Plaza Vancouver"**

Dear Ms. Sweet:

I have long admired the professionalism with which Diamond properties are managed, and I was excited to hear from Jerry Richardson of Jerry's Hospitality Consulting about a possible opening for an Executive Chef at your Crown Plaza facility. As a hospitality and food services specialist with over twenty years of experience, in-depth culinary knowledge, and extensive hands-on experience in all areas of high-end food service preparation and management, I could efficiently and cost effectively handle your Crown Plaza operations.

Here are a few reasons why I would make an excellent addition to the Crown Plaza team:

> **Substantial cooking experience:** I have loved to cook since the age of sixteen. "Passionate" is merely an adequate description of my love for the craft. My years in kitchens have afforded me the opportunity to work with many different cuisines and for a wide variety of clientele.

> **Restaurant management expertise:** Almost since I first graduated with my Commercial Cookery Certificate in 1987, business management has been a central part of many of the positions that I have held. I have plenty of experience with hiring, scheduling, training, mentoring, and supervising. Additionally, I am highly skilled at menu planning, purchasing, inventory management, and many of the financial activities associated with running a food service establishment.

> **Extensive training and education:** My education at TAFE (New South Wales, Australia) includes extensive training in commercial cooking as well as advanced specializations in chocolate, confectionaries, culinary art, and vegetable carving. Also, my five years of apprenticeships were with two businesses known for having top-notch standards in all aspects of their operations.

> **A success-oriented personality:** In my case, "a hard worker" would be an understatement. I *thrive* on situations involving pressure, deadlines, and new challenges. My aim is to deliver a dining experience above expectations, every time, and to promote a harmonious, efficient, environment for my team, which enables their success.

Thank you for reviewing the attached resume. I would like to meet with you within the next few weeks to review, in detail, the challenges and opportunities facing the Crown Plaza operations. Please don't hesitate to get in touch with me if I can provide any further information.

Sincerely,

Matthew P. Hashimoto

Enclosure (resume)

Written By: Paul Bennett
Font: Times New Roman

Chapter 10

▶ Cover Letters for

Human Resources and Training Careers

Your cover letter presents an excellent opportunity to show prospective employers and recruiters how the skills and accomplishments documented on your resume relate to their specific hiring needs. Each industry and profession presents unique cover letter writing and design challenges. If you are interested in pursuing a career in human resources or training, be certain to include highlights of these important success factors in your cover letters:

Success Factor #1

Show your diverse skills by mentioning the different aspects of human resource management with which you have experience (for example, benefits administration, recruiting, payroll, employee relations, and training).

Success Factor #2

Mention initiatives you have developed or implemented to improve employee satisfaction and retention. This might include counseling individual employees on professional development or introducing employee incentive programs recognizing peak performance.

Success Factor #3

For trainers, include activities such as needs assessment, curriculum planning, course design, online instruction, classroom training, and instructional materials design.

Success Factor #4

Include detailed information about your familiarity with technology-based human resource management systems (for example, timekeeping, payroll, benefits administration, and manpower planning). These technical skills are critical in today's tech-based HR environment.

Keywords and Keyword Phrases

Keywords and keyword phrases are critical components of every successful job seeker's cover letter. By using just one or two words, you're able to communicate a wealth of information about your skills, qualifications, and experience. What's more, keywords are the basis for scanning technology and are therefore critical to every job seeker's campaign in today's electronic-based job search market.

Following are the top 20 human resources and training keywords, some of which may reflect your skills and some of which may not be appropriate for you at this time. Use these words as the foundation for developing your own list of keywords on the Professional Keyword List form in Appendix B.

Top 20 Keywords

Benefits Design & Administration	Manpower Planning
Change Management	Organizational Development
Employee Assistance Programs	Performance Incentives
Employee Communications	Performance Reviews & Appraisals
Employee Relations	Recruitment & Selection
Employee Retention	Staffing
Grievance Proceedings & Arbitration	Succession Planning
Human Resources Administration	Training & Development
Labor Contract Negotiations	Union Relations
Leadership Development	Wage Administration

Following are some excellent examples of cover letters for human resources and training careers.

Deborah Torney

248 South Maple Avenue, Livingston, NJ 07039 • (973) 402-8890

October 12, 2006

Mr. Thomas Smith
Director of Training
Brilliant Toys, Inc.
101 Eisenhower Parkway
Roseland, NJ 07068

Dear Mr. Smith,

You recently advertised in *The Star-Ledger* for a Corporate Trainer. I feel my background and expertise are a strong match with your needs.

Highlights of my background include:

- **Proven ability to train and mentor employees** (in both group and one-on-one settings) for increased performance and greater customer satisfaction.

- **Quality control background** provides the ability to offer effective suggestions with a focus on enhanced productivity and process flow.

- **Dedicated, loyal employee** with a successful track record in both large and small corporate environments.

- **Bachelor's degree in education** as well as teaching certificates in both New Jersey and New York.

My resume is enclosed for your review. I moved back to New Jersey earlier this year to be closer to family and am now looking to secure employment. Should you want to discuss my qualifications in further detail, you may reach me at the above telephone number.

Thank you for your time and thoughtful consideration.

Sincerely yours,

Deborah Torney

Enclosure

Written By: Laurie Berenson
Font: Book Antiqua

Daniel Wallace

5415 N. Clark Street
Chicago, Illinois 60640
(773) 907-8660
dwall@acme.com

August 11, 2006

Dan Gordon
Gordon Recruiting Agency
12 Elm Street
Chicago, IL 60662

Dear Mr. Gordon:

I am seeking a position (full time or consulting) in benefits administration, human resources, or a related area, and have enclosed my resume for your review. I will be happy to provide references or further information at your request.

Throughout my career, I have helped large and mid-sized companies streamline benefits operations, so employees are given excellent service and administrative costs are controlled. I have broad expertise in areas that are vital to effective benefits administration:

- **Section 125 of the IRS code**
- **ERISA**
- **Public Plan Policies**
- **Taft-Hartley Act**
- **PPO/HMO coding**

This background has allowed me to address specific employee needs while also protecting the company from overcharges by insurance companies and other vendors.

I can also contribute if your client's benefits are outsourced. My experience managing phone centers has taught me how to evaluate the performance of those important partners and ensure that they are providing the level of service they promise. I approach outsourced vendors and insurance companies knowing that their interests are not the same as yours. By setting clear expectations and tracking performance, I can keep costs down without diminishing service.

Character is an intangible value I offer any prospective employer. I pride myself on solving problems and putting systems in place so those problems do not arise in the future. Moreover, I lead in a way that sets an example for my staff of someone who is honest, hard working, and dedicated. My mission is to inspire each employee to work with the goal of total client satisfaction in mind.

Realizing that this summary cannot fully communicate my potential contribution, I would appreciate the opportunity to speak with you personally about any current search assignments you may have for a candidate with my qualifications. My salary requirements are $75,000+, but are negotiable. Thank you for your consideration.

Sincerely,

Daniel Wallace

Enclosure

Written By: Clay Cerny
Font: Georgia

SHARON NOWICKI

75223 W. Georgia Place • Miami Beach, FL 77101 • 717-555-8425 • nowickisk@yahoo.com

May 17, 2006

Martin Beck, Recruiter
Fields Bakery Corporation
9008 Fields Boulevard
Boca Raton, FL 33982

Dear Mr. Beck:

As a highly qualified Human Resources Analyst with an MBA in Human Resources Management
and Organizational Development, and seven years of related professional experience, I offer
expertise in streamlining HR departments, motivating employees, and driving process improvement
programs. Highlights of my qualifications include:

- *Resolving key issues, facilitating business integration and transition, and
  promoting positive culture change.*
- *Creating winning employee incentives / packages that spur increased
  productivity and enhanced employee morale.*
- *Developing easy-to-understand training manuals for new hires where there
  formerly were none.*
- *Restructuring the interview / hiring process from hiring "off the street" to
  recruiting from professional employment agencies, resulting in reduced training
  time and costs.*

Through key management roles, focused on driving both internal and external objectives, I have
exhibited a consistent track record of strong performance results. My innate understanding of
organizational development and the role it plays from both business and financial perspectives is
crucial in helping companies develop real-world business strategies and shape performance
improvements.

The enclosed resume briefly outlines my experience and accomplishments. If it appears that my
qualifications meet your current needs, I would be happy to further discuss my background. I'll
follow up with a phone call next Tuesday, or please feel free to contact me at the above telephone
number at your convenience. Thank you.

Sincerely,

Sharon Nowicki

Enclosure

Written By: Erin Kennedy
Font: Times New Roman

KELLI KUPER, PHR
3000 Mountain View
Weston, WA 98000-4444
(333) 555-7777
email: Kelli@yahoo.com

April 14, 2006

Employee/Labor Relations
Generalist Search Committee
Compton University
200 Grover Garden
Weston, WA 98000

Dear Committee Members:

My resume summarizes a professional background featuring 15 years of progressively responsible HR experience that I believe closely matches the requirements for the **Employee/Labor Relations Generalist** position you seek to fill. Highlights of my career include the following:

- Strong generalist qualifications in all core HR functions, with particular strengths in labor relations and employee relations. This collective experience also enhances my comprehensive knowledge of state and federal personnel regulations, and ability to interpret complex guidelines, codes, regulations, policies, and procedures.

- A track record of building cooperative relationships with employees, management teams, and union representatives. This approach has fostered high levels of employee retention and attest to my ability to respond to employee issues, identify potential HR problems, and create solutions.

In addition to the above qualifications, I possess a B.S. from Compton University and earned my PHR certification two years ago. I am confident that my experience, dedication to excellence, and ability to interact effectively and professionally with all levels of personnel make me an excellent candidate. I understand you will be receiving applications until April 20. After that, I look forward to an opportunity to discuss your needs and my qualifications in greater detail. Thank you.

Sincerely,

Kelli Kuper

Enclosure: Resume
               References

Written By: Janice Shepherd
Font: Lucida Sans

CARLOS RAMIREZ _____

86 1
(610) 4

146

820

November 14, 2006

Mr. David Lewis
Human Resources Manager
Textron Business Services, Inc.
1200 Arch Street, 4th Floor
Philadelphia, PA 19103

Dear Mr. Lewis:

The posted opportunity for an Assistant Manager of Corporate Training is an excellent match with my experience. My career includes more than eight years of progressive responsibility in training, marketing, and customer service.

Highlights of my strengths include:

> **Program Development.** *Design and deliver training materials for technical and business skill development, including a creative—and successful—plan to increase training opportunities for customer service reps in a call center environment, without taking away from their phone time.*

> **Skills Assessment.** *Analyze and interpret quality-monitoring data to best enhance workplace productivity, office functionality, and employee performance. Proposed and facilitated peer feedback sessions in which employees with varying strengths were grouped so that participants benefited by learning from each other.*

> **Coaching Techniques.** *Develop and utilize effective one-on-one coaching methods. Co-created a thriving in-house model for coaching customer service reps on results of their monitoring. Easily remembered acronym identifies the stages of a session in which the coach guides the employee in identifying his/her own strengths and areas for further development. Created related training module and employed technique in actual coaching sessions.*

Currently exploring new opportunities, I am confident in my ability to make an immediate and lasting contribution to your organization and would welcome an interview at your earliest convenience.

I look forward to speaking with you soon.

Sincerely,

Carlos Ramirez

Enclosure

Written By: Laurie Berenson
Font: Garamond

DALE GROSSMAN, SPHR

◆◆◆

Bella Vista Lane
Bella Vista, AR 72717

E-mail: dgrossman@hotmail.com

Cellular: (479) 640-3265
Home: (479) 235-7332

October 20, 2006

Daniel Lorenson, President
Springdale Manufacturing
5300 Bryant Boulevard
Springdale, AR 72764

Dear Mr. Lorenson:

Your recent advertisement at Monster.com for a Director of Human Resources captured my interest because your needs and my background are a close match.

A Human Resources Director with more than 20 years of experience, I am known for creating HR organizations that are innovative, customer-service oriented, and focused on bottom-line results. My career accomplishments include successful re-engineering initiatives, as well as corporate-wide recruitment, staffing, and employee development programs. In addition to performance improvements, my efforts have contributed to the overall long-term stability of my employers.

Please note that while directing the overall HR function, I have also remained an extremely strong generalist in all core HR functions. Major projects have included benefits/compensation design, HRIS selection/implementation, and large-scale recruitment activities in business pre-opening situations (more than 2,000 employees recruited).

I would welcome the opportunity to speak with you about your needs and how I can contribute to your success. I will follow up in the next few days to ensure you've received my materials and answer any preliminary questions you may have. Thank you for your consideration.

Sincerely,

Dale Grossman

Enclosure: Resume

Written By: Michelle Haffner
Font: Tahoma

ARNOLD COLLINS
3219 Eisenhower Avenue   Junction City, KS 66441
Home: 785-278-6220   Work: 785-329-7800
arnold.collins@yahoo.com

November 20, 2006

Mr. William Black
City Manager
Municipal Building
900 N. Washington
Junction City, KS 66441

Dear Mr. Black:

It is with considerable interest that I enclose my application and resume in response to your recent advertisement in the *Junction City Daily Union* for a **Human Resource Director.** This appears to be an exciting career opportunity, and I would welcome the chance to meet with you personally to discuss the contributions I could make to your organization. I believe that my resume will attest to my strong credentials for this position.

I have more than 20 years of human resource management training and experience. As the head publisher for the Air Force, I maintained an excellent relationship with labor union officials at the publications distribution facilities located in Baltimore, Maryland and St. Louis, Missouri. I had formal and informal visits with these officials and actively participated in union contract negotiations.

My experience also includes a heavy emphasis on organizational performance, employee incentives, executive HR briefings, recruitment planning / analysis, and performance appraisals. In addition, I have testified at EEOC proceedings.

I currently reside in Geary County and serve as a member of the Parks and Recreation Board for the City of Milford. My other local activities include serving as the Assistant Director for Girl Scouts at Fort Riley and as a patron of the Junction City Little Theater and the Geary County Historical Society. I can be reached at my home number listed above after 6 p.m. or during the day at 785-329-7800. I will call you in the near future to follow up, and thank you for your consideration.

Sincerely,

Arnold Collins

Enclosure

Written By: James Walker
Font: Times New Roman

Chapter 11

▶ Cover Letters for Law Enforcement and Legal Careers

Your cover letter presents an excellent opportunity to show prospective employers and recruiters how the skills and accomplishments documented on your resume relate to their specific hiring needs. Each industry and profession presents unique cover letter writing and design challenges. If you are interested in pursuing a law enforcement or legal career, be certain to include highlights of these important success factors in your cover letters:

Success Factor #1

Credentials and certifications are key. Prominently mention firearms, special tactics, or special investigative credentials. For attorneys, list the courts and states in which you are admitted to practice.

Success Factor #2

In addition to credentials, include other professional training in areas relevant to the position you are pursuing. Law enforcement and legal professions place a heavy emphasis on professional development, so be sure to include yours.

Success Factor #3

Be sure to mention any measures of performance. What's your success rate in cases you've tried as an attorney? As a police officer, how many arrests have you made or how has the crime rate been reduced because of your actions?

Success Factor #4

Remember to include information about the administrative aspects of your job, especially if you're interested in advancing into supervisory or management positions. This may include personnel training and supervision, record-keeping, report preparation, regulatory review and compliance, and a host of other functions.

Keywords and Keyword Phrases

Keywords and keyword phrases are critical components of every successful job seeker's cover letter. By using just one or two words, you're able to communicate a wealth of information about your skills, qualifications, and experience. What's more, keywords are the basis for scanning technology and are therefore critical to every job seeker's campaign in today's electronic-based job search market.

Following are the top 20 law enforcement and legal keywords, some of which may reflect your skills and some of which may not be appropriate for you at this time. Use these words as the foundation for developing your own list of keywords on the Professional Keyword List form in Appendix B.

Top 20 Keywords

Arbitration

Arrest & Prosecution

Civil Law Proceedings

Corporate Law & Representation

Courtroom Proceedings

Criminal Investigations

Depositions & Discovery

Due Diligence

Intellectual Property

Interrogations

Judicial Affairs

Legal Research & Analysis

Legislative Review & Analysis

Litigation

Public Safety & Administration

Regulatory Affairs

Risk Management

Search & Seizure

Trademark & Copyright Law

Workers' Compensation

Following are some excellent examples of cover letters for law enforcement and legal careers.

Edward Sean Quinn

635 Elmer Lane, Long Island, NY 10997 ◆ 898.433.4102 ◆ edwardsquinn@comcast.net

September 12, 2006

Roger P. Wilkinson, Supervisor
Personnel Development
Executive Security, Inc.
4736 Eighth Avenue
New York, NY 10227

Dear Mr. Wilkinson:

In searching career opportunities within your organization for openings in the senior investigative division, I identified several opportunities and, as such, have enclosed my resume for your review. Currently a New York City Detective with 24 years of distinguished experience in law enforcement, I am proud to be a member of the police department responsible for the largest crime reduction in the history of the City of New York. I will retire from the force in six months, but am available for a job interview at your convenience. Allow me to illustrate my extensive qualifications.

Highlights and accomplishments of my professional background include numerous notable arrests, several NYPD awards, and the coveted certification in Specialized Surveillance Training. In addition, I believe my genuine drive and determination make me an excellent candidate for an investigative position within your organization. Able to effectively conduct analysis of evidence with physical and electronic surveillance, I possess the perseverance necessary to locate offenders when all avenues appear exhausted. My experience has made me fully aware of how crucial seconds are in emergencies. I cope well in high-stress situations and have won three prestigious High Departmental Recognition awards for honorable and courageous service.

In conclusion, I am seeking a position that offers challenge, responsibility, and renewed opportunity to help in maintaining the public's trust in our criminal justice system. I would welcome a personal interview to demonstrate how my firmly established credentials and strong experience in law enforcement can be utilized for our mutual benefit. If I do not hear from you within the next 10 days, I will call in the hope of arranging a suitable time for an appointment.

Thank you for your time and consideration.

Sincerely,

Edward Sean Quinn

Enclosure: Resume

Written By: Edward Turilli
Font: Book Antiqua

CLANCY THOMAS

1088 Franklin Street, Vancouver, BC V6A 4H2 / (h) 604 926 0029 / (f) 604 592 2627   thomasc@canadaweb.ca

September 13, 2006

City of Rutherford
3000 Derwent Way
Rutherford, BC   V7R 7J9

Attention: Human Resources Division
Re: **Employment Competition #VS2004-36 (Bylaw and Animal Control Inspector)**

Dear Selection Committee:

When a community expands as rapidly as the City of Rutherford has over the last few years - with surging numbers of domestic animals and a mushrooming growth in local business activity - the need for effective bylaw enforcement becomes an urgent concern. Many communities in this part of BC are suffering from an acute shortage of bylaw officers; as a case in point, the City of Vancouver has often just *one* full-time animal control officer on staff. The pressing need for qualified officers will only continue to grow.

I am a senior Detective with the Vancouver City Police who will soon retire at a young age after over 30 years of service. Now I am seeking new career opportunities in investigations and enforcement, and the Bylaw and Animal Control Inspector position is *precisely* the kind of job that I am looking for. My career has involved a great deal of this type of work; as a result, I would come quickly up to speed with very little training required. Here are a few examples why I am particularly well qualified for this position:

> ➤ *Investigative and enforcement experience:* Early in my career (as a Constable), I became an expert in gathering and preparing forensic evidence. More recently, during the last seven years (as a Detective), I have gathered and processed intelligence in a number of different areas, and have become skilled at managing complex investigations.

> ➤ *Administrative and courtroom expertise:* Having spent plenty of time in the office as well as "on the beat," I am no stranger to administrative activities. My written and oral communication skills are excellent, and I enjoy collaborating on projects. Also, I have given many evidence presentations in court, and have been certified as an expert witness regarding forensic evidence.

> ➤ *Solid work ethic:* My peers and supervisors describe me as hardworking, proactive, organized, dedicated, self-motivated, knowledgeable, and a great team player. A fast learner, I would quickly develop an inside-out knowledge of the bylaws of the City of Rutherford.

Thank you for reading my resume. I am very keen to discuss the Bylaw and Animal Control Inspector position in greater detail. Please don't hesitate to get in touch with me if I may provide any further information. I look forward to talking with you soon!

Sincerely,

Clancy Thomas

Enclosure (resume)

Written By: Paul Bennett
Font: Times New Roman

CURTIS J. MERICA

N88 W16226 Park Boulevard   cjmerica@wi.rr.com   Residence: (262) 375-3498
Cedarburg, WI 53012   Mobile: (262) 803-4534   Office: (262) 377-1700

September 13, 2006

City of Cedarburg
Attn: Human Resources
W61 N567 Washington Avenue
Cedarburg, WI 53012

To the Human Resources Director and the Search Committee:

As your advertisement indicated, the position of Chief of Police requires an individual with a strong law enforcement leadership background, as well as a complete understanding of the many unique challenges facing the City of Cedarburg. A lifelong resident with more than 20 years as a certified law enforcement professional, I am the best-qualified candidate to continue the effective police leadership the city has received under Chief Roska.

- **You require 10 years of law enforcement experience with at least five years at the administrative and command level. Additionally, you require a proven record of leadership including successful labor management experience.** I have a 16-year record of effective leadership and management that has included (1) command-level planning and organizing; (2) supervision of 40 employees and delegation of authority; (3) efficient administration of resources; (4) communication and successful relations with union-represented and non-represented employees, staff, and constituents; and (5) the involvement of others in consensus building and decision making. My experience covers several functional and specialty areas including patrol, detective bureau / investigation, court services, tactical enforcement, school / police liaison efforts, and search / rescue.

- **You require a demonstration of community-oriented policing experience.** Throughout my tenure with the City of Cedarburg, I have directed and / or served in community policing initiatives including command of the school / police liaison program, direction of law enforcement service contracts, and command of the search and rescue team.

- **You require a demonstration of budgeting experience.** Over the last 15 years, I have assisted with the development of operational and capital budgets, as well as examining and re-allocating resources to achieve higher return on investment.

I would appreciate the opportunity to interview for this position. My salary and benefits requirements are negotiable. As you begin the screening process, should you have any additional questions, please feel free to contact me at (262) 377-1700.

Sincerely,

Curtis J. Merica

Enclosure: Resume
                Letter of Recommendation

Reynaldo T. Martinez

145 West 67th Street, Apt 21C • New York, NY 10023 • 212-531-0731
RTMartin@nyc.rr.com

December 15, 2006

Mr. Michael Gray, Esq.
Associate General Counsel
Early Dispute Resolution Group
Lehman Brothers
3 World Financial Center
New York, NY 10080

Dear Mr. Gray:

Recently, I met with Peter Morris of Lehman Brothers' legal department, whom I have known for several years. He suggested contacting you about a possible position with Lehman Brothers, and I have enclosed my resume for your review. After meeting with Mr. Morris, I am very interested in working for your firm.

With over five years of experience in corporate and securities law, I am well-versed in drafting and reviewing contracts in such areas as corporate finance, employment, real estate, and commercial and intellectual property. I am also knowledgeable in the registration and reporting requirements under the Securities Exchange Act of 1934.

Particularly relevant experience from my background includes working as an attorney in the Alternative Dispute Resolution Unit for New York Life Insurance Company, analyzing complaints made by policy owners against their agents, concerning agents' sales tactics to determine compliance with company guidelines and state insurance department regulations. I reviewed allegations, interviewed agents, and made determinations of liability and relief.

My skills and experience will make a valuable contribution to your legal department. I would be pleased to meet with you to discuss further how my qualifications may lead to a career with Lehman Brothers.

Please contact me at (212) 531-0731 to set up an interview at your earliest convenience.

Very truly yours,

Reynaldo T. Martinez

Enclosure

Written By: Laurie Berenson
Font: Garamond

Gabriel Connor
22 Greene Corner Cove
Albuquerque, NM 55938

Mobile: (505) 555-3928
Home: (505) 555-0028
Email: gc@optusnet.com

September 30, 2006

David Smith, Esq.
HR Director
Mallesons Stephen Jacques
12 Monet Boulevard, 23rd Floor
Taos, NM 55823

Dear Mr. Smith:

It is with great interest that I am forwarding my resume for consideration as an Article Clerk with your law firm. With a sound understanding of law practices gained through academic and volunteer experience, combined with outstanding communication, research, and analytical skills, I am confident you will quickly realize my ability to make major contributions to your firm.

My experience demonstrates attributes that make me a valuable candidate:

- **Transferable skills** gained through extensive volunteer experience that would be an asset to any organization – leadership qualities, creative and analytical thinking, training and presentation skills, communication, negotiation, and problem solving.

- **Discipline to handle complex challenges well.** This is evidenced through my volunteer experience as a board member at the Community Services Group for the last 4 years. This position requires that I listen attentively, assess situations, question assumptions, and propose well-considered solutions. I thrive on opportunities to deliver results that address challenging problems.

- **Excellent communicator** capable of working effectively with a diverse group of individuals from all levels, and maintaining an excellent rapport with peers and interdisciplinary staff. Communication is critical in my volunteer roles as a tennis coach and as a board member of the Community Services Group.

- **Highly organized with the ability to set priorities** and manage multiple projects. This is demonstrated by my ability to successfully balance my university studies, part-time work experience and volunteer experience as a management board member at the Community Services Group.

As my ultimate career goal is to become an attorney, I believe the opportunity to work with your firm presents me with a great learning experience and start to my legal career. Working with some of the leading corporate lawyers in the country and observing the handling of complex matters would be a tremendously valuable way to launch my career.

The key qualities that outline my relevant capability for your firm include a great passion for the law, commitment to excellence, strong logical and reasoning skills, and attention to detail. I enjoy the hands-on experience and interaction with people and believe I have the skills and enthusiasm to tackle any task set before me.

Thank you for your time and consideration of my application. I look forward to discussing the significant value I bring to your firm and invite you to contact me, at your convenience, at any of the above numbers.

Yours sincerely,

Gabriel Connor

Enclosure

Written By: Jennifer Rushton
Font: Georgia

LIN KIM PARK

10 Olden Drive
Bridgewater, NJ 08807
908-725-0001 • lkpark@optonline.net

September 13, 2006

Ms. Linda Pearl
Uptown Legal Partners
150 Riverside Drive
Newark, NJ 07102

Dear Ms. Pearl:

As a recently certified paralegal with a diverse professional background and a strong work ethic, I believe I am someone who would be a welcome addition to your staff. Knowing that your firm is recommended by the career center at Fairleigh Dickinson, I would like to explore the possibility of putting my skills and experience to work for you. Among my strengths, I offer excellent administrative skills, a love of learning, a passion for the law, and an unrelenting commitment to achieving goals.

As you can see from my resume, I earned my paralegal certification from Fairleigh Dickinson in May 2005, and have experience as a paralegal for a title company, as well as an intern for the Superior Court of New Jersey. In a short time, I have established a reputation as a hard-working individual who effectively manages the demands of working in busy environments. In fact, while with the title company, even though the newest paralegal, I was entrusted with handling transactions for real estate cases that were deemed the most challenging. Prior to entering the paralegal field, I enjoyed a challenging and rewarding career in high-level administrative roles for Johnson & Johnson, providing a backdrop for my developing paralegal career. I believe my breadth of practical knowledge, strong skills, and the wealth of administrative experience that I have accumulated will make me an asset to your office.

Throughout my career, I have achieved success through my resourcefulness, persistence, and ability to communicate effectively with people at all levels. Among my other strengths, you will find that I am organized and thorough and show good judgment in making decisions. Service-oriented, I consider myself a team player who is willing to do whatever is necessary to get the job done, and I pride myself on my ability to take on challenging assignments and see them through to completion.

This combination of skills has served me well in the past, allowing me to make significant contributions while establishing a reputation as an efficient and effective employee. With this solid record of accomplishment as the basis, you can be confident that I will do the same for you.

I would be pleased to have the opportunity to discuss your needs and how I might be able to meet them. Please feel free to contact me by phone or e-mail to arrange a meeting. I look forward to speaking with you soon and will follow up with you next week.

Sincerely,

Lin Kim Park

Enclosure

Written By: Carol Altomare
Font: Garamond

Chapter **12**

▶ Cover Letters for

Manufacturing and Operations Careers

Your cover letter presents an excellent opportunity to show prospective employers and recruiters how the skills and accomplishments documented on your resume relate to their specific hiring needs. Each industry and profession presents unique cover letter writing and design challenges. If you are interested in pursuing a career in manufacturing or operations, be certain to include highlights of these important success factors in your cover letters:

Success Factor #1

Highlight your experience and training in principles and methods such as Lean Manufacturing, Six Sigma, Just-In-Time inventory, TQM, SAP, and ISO standards.

Success Factor #2

Showcase information about your contributions to process improvements, scrap reduction, or other innovations that increase operating efficiency or reduce production costs. Use dollar figures or percentages to quantify results, and, when possible, relate these results to the prospective employer's needs.

Success Factor #3

Demonstrate the diversity of your skillset by mentioning the various operations and processes with which you have experience (for example, cell manufacturing, assembly line, fabrication, stamping/molding, or clean-room operations). Emphasize those experiences that are most relevant to the needs of the targeted employer.

** ⚑ Success Factor #4**

Include statistics about quality and customer interactions. As domestic manufacturers compete in the global market, delivering defect-free products and being attentive to customers are critical for success.

Keywords and Keyword Phrases

Keywords and keyword phrases are critical components of every successful job seeker's cover letter. By using just one or two words, you're able to communicate a wealth of information about your skills, qualifications, and experience. What's more, keywords are the basis for scanning technology and are therefore critical to every job seeker's campaign in today's electronic-based job search market.

Following are the top 20 manufacturing and operations keywords, some of which may reflect your skills and some of which may not be appropriate for you at this time. Use these words as the foundation for developing your own list of keywords on the Professional Keyword List form in Appendix B.

Top 20 Keywords

Budget Planning & Administration	Operations Re-engineering
Continuous Process Improvement	Plant Management
Cost Reduction & Avoidance	Process Automation
Efficiency Improvement	Productivity Improvement
Facilities Engineering	Quality Assurance & Control
Inventory Planning & Control	Resource Planning & Management
Logistics	Supply Chain Management
Manufacturing Technology	Technology Integration
Multi-Site Operations Management	Workflow Optimization
Occupational Health & Safety	Workforce Planning & Management

Following are some excellent examples of cover letters for manufacturing and operations careers.

ALEX R. TRETIAK

3456 John Avenue • Roselle, IL 60475 • (708) 567-2345 • altretiak@netzero.com

October 10, 2006

Josh Barnes
Chief Operating Officer
Lyne Brothers Manufacturing
PO Box 7760
Ames, IA 79087

Dear Mr. Barnes:

Are you contemplating **initiating or redesigning a safety and health program, implementing organizational change initiatives,** or **reengineering inefficient processes,** but lack the resources to successfully achieve these objectives? If so, I suggest we schedule a meeting to discuss the mutual benefits of an employment partnership at your earliest convenience.

As Manager of Safety and Health for a mid-size manufacturing firm, I introduced a highly effective safety program that has dramatically reduced workers' compensation incidents and significantly lowered insurance premiums over a seven-year period. Educating supervisors and employees on safety procedures, empowering staff and line workers with responsibility for each other, and achieving safety goals have resulted in minimal accidents and injuries.

My objective is to take this expertise, combined with 10 years of production and operations experience (I established two pharmaceutical plants for Grayson Pharmaceuticals), to a company positioned for growth. My background in staff development, strategic planning, and program design makes me a valuable addition to most any senior management team. As my attached resume details, I have the ability to make the hard decisions that **improve profit margins**, **reduce overhead expenses, and increase employee productivity**.

I will contact you by the end of next week to discuss prospects and opportunities with your client companies. Thank you for your consideration.

Sincerely,

Alex R. Tretiak

Enclosure

Written By: Rosemary Fish Justen
Font: Arial

MARTIN BUTLER

2222 Desert View Street Reno, Nevada 89501

✉ martin.butler@aol.com ☎775.567.8901 (Home) – 775.678.9012 (Cell)

June 28, 2006

Mr. Mark Broome
Central Control, Inc.
4444 Industrial Boulevard
Kansas City, MO 64101

Dear Mr. Broome:

I want to join the Central Control's team as a "productivity multiplier." I believe your firm calls this position a Production Manager.

My resume shows many job titles; all of them were related to production. I was never officially called "The Productivity Multiplier," but that's the outlook I bring to every problem I solve. My resume includes a half dozen selected examples of my solutions in action. All of them came from setting the standards for my team, getting my hands dirty, and asking others to work as hard as I do. Each time, the outcome contributed right to our bottom line.

My company has promoted me four times, but I feel I am approaching the limit of what I can expect to achieve and am, therefore, looking for new challenges. That's why I am sending this confidential application.

If Central Control can use my energy and expertise, we should meet so I can hear about your production needs. I would like to call in a few days to set up an appointment. I appreciate your discretion, as my current employer is unaware of my job search.

Sincerely,

Martin Butler

Enclosure: Resume

Written By: Don Orlando
Font: Arial

ZACHARY MONTANA

2346 Clearwater Way, Kitimat, BC V9R 6T1   zackmontana@telus.net

(home) 271.684.2853
(mobile) 406.883.2974

September 13, 2006

Forestall Wood Products
Suite 2200—1575 Chamberlain Street
Nanaimo, BC V7L 4C6

Attention: Mr. Larry Cuthbertson (Vice President—Sawmill Operations)
Re: **Sawmill Manager**—Nanaimo Operations

Dear Mr. Cuthbertson:

I am a 28-year veteran of the coastal BC sawmilling industry and have spent over 24 of those years handling steadily increasing supervisory and management responsibilities. Most of my career has been on Vancouver Island, and for the last nine years I have been employed in Kitimat as a Plant Superintendent. Now I would like to move back to Central Vancouver Island and manage a sawmill there.

With my lengthy experience as a mill worker, supervisor, manager, and superintendent, I have "worn all of the hats" and have a solid set of skills to meet the challenges of a fast-paced Sawmill Manager position:

➢ **Health and safety focus:** This is an area in which I am most proud of my achievements. Through my initiatives as the Safety Prevention Officer for my current employer, I have turned around what was once a terrible safety and absenteeism record to one that is exemplary for the sawmilling industry.

➢ **Experience in mill planning and upgrading:** Over the years, I have led several projects to plan new mills and upgrade existing facilities. From a hands-on perspective, I have worked with practically all of the machinery and tools used in sawmills.

➢ **Operations expertise:** Regardless of whether I'm dealing with a production, personnel, safety, organizational, or any other issue, my ability to quickly size up situations and gather information enables me to make timely, effective decisions.

➢ **Proven talent in marketing and sales:** Frequently, I have had the opportunity to market my employers' wares and work with clients to learn their requirements, help them discover profitable opportunities involving our products, and provide them with exemplary customer service. I am particularly experienced in working with Asian and American clients.

Thank you for reviewing my resume. I am very keen to share with you my ideas about how I could efficiently, safely, and profitably lead your Nanaimo operations. I will contact you in two weeks to arrange a meeting; in the meantime, please don't hesitate to get in touch with me if I can provide any further information. I look forward to talking with you soon.

Sincerely,

Zachary Montana

Enclosure (resume)

Written By: Paul Bennett
Font: Times New Roman

Jeffrey Coates

1300 Ridge Street
Evanston, IL 60201

(847) 448-5658
jcoates@chicago.rr.com

November 30, 2006

Mr. Scott Dailey
Archer Outdoors
2000 Wacker Drive
Chicago, IL 60606

Dear Mr. Dailey:

I am an accomplished leader with successful management experience that could be of significant benefit to Archer Outdoors. My background makes me an excellent candidate for senior-level positions in operations requiring skills in production, planning, sourcing, purchasing, and administration.

Throughout my career, I have demonstrated the natural ability to quickly assess organizations, identify key opportunities for improvement, and execute strategies to build performance-driven business environments and significantly enhance bottom-line results. My track record includes the successful introduction of leading-edge manufacturing processes, technologies, and methodologies to create cost-effective, world-class operations. In nearly all of my positions, intense sourcing and negotiation skills have been instrumental in expanding capacities while achieving quality, cost, and delivery objectives.

My management roles have been in varied environments including start-up, turnaround, and high-growth operations. Effective leadership has required strengths in communicating with all levels of an organization to include owners, executive managers, line managers, and associates as well as material vendors, manufacturing contractors, and government agencies.

Enclosed is my resume. I would like to be considered for the Director of Operations position with Archer Outdoors and look forward to speaking with you soon. I'll follow up with you next Tuesday to schedule a personal interview.

Sincerely,

Jeffrey Coates

Enclosure

Written By: Julie Rains
Font: Tahoma

Mark Forbart, Operations Manager

555 Frank Road, Winthrop, MA 02152 (617) 555-2084
mforbart@yahoo.com

July 15, 2006

ATTN: Human Resource Department
GENCO Manufacturing
451 Andover Street
Lowell, MA 01852

Dear Hiring Professional:

In response to your search for a quality Manufacturing Management professional, I bring eight years of extensive, hands-on experience in Operations. This includes project and facility management, people development, quality procedures, and new product development.

I am an extremely high-energy and innovative engineer who leads by example. I consistently produce strong results with a high degree of integrity, dedication, and problem-solving skills.

Many of my achievements are due to my ability to create and maintain rapport with individuals within the organization. This quality, coupled with a drive to think analytically and manage deadlines, has given me a track record of success. Some highlights include:

- Promotions from Process Engineer to Manufacturing Supervisor to Productions Engineer to Manufacturing Manager to my current Operations Manager position within an eight-year span.
- Success with both ISO 9001 and ISO 9002 programs.
- Led new product launch, pilot plant production, and nationwide rollout.
- Set up new facilities in record time.
- Made several process improvements, inventory level improvements, and reductions in standard product costs.
- Hired, trained, and developed a team of 38 employees with 21 direct reports.

My resume and a summary page provide further details of my accomplishments. You will note that I have progressed in responsibility levels throughout my career. I look forward to discussing a challenging new opportunity with you, and will contact you next week to arrange a meeting so we may discuss your company's needs in greater detail.

Sincerely,

Mark Forbart

Enclosure

Written By: Gail Frank
Font: Palatino Linotype

THEODORE MOSCOWITZ

100 Scarborough Drive ·· Fullerton, California 97886
966.446.9822 ·· tedmosc@cox.net

July 21, 2006

James Bolton
Bolton-Dutch Recruitment, Inc.
1000 Marshall Boulevard
Los Angeles, CA 90093

Dear Mr. Bolton:

As Director of Operations for a nationwide retail organization, I successfully innovated and introduced operational, merchandising, customer service, and employee training programs.

- **Bottom-Line: Sales climbed $25 million annually and the gross profit margin increased by 13 full points within the first year of my tenure.**

As Regional Manager, I reversed a store-closing trend and turned a non-producing region into a highly profitable operation.

- **Bottom-Line: Under my management, the region achieved the highest sales volume throughout the entire company comprised of 52 regions.**

As Store Manager, I provided superior customer service, increasing the average sale by 50%.

- **Bottom-Line: Recognized for significantly increasing store sales, margins, and profits to record heights.**

Equally important has been my success in recruiting, developing, and directing teams of well-qualified management and sales personnel. By creating proactive business cultures encouraging employee participation in the decision-making process and rewarding individual contributions, I have built profitable business operations.

I am now exploring new opportunities that will offer new challenges. If you are working with a client company seeking a candidate with my qualifications, I would welcome a personal interview to discuss the opportunity. At that point, I'll also share specifics about my compensation requirements, relocation capabilities, and other relevant personal information.

Very truly yours,

Theodore Moscowitz

Enclosure

Written By: Louise Garver
Font: Times New Roman

GORDON JIMENEZ
5251 North Decorah Road
West Bend, WI 53095

E-mail: gjimenez@wi.rr.com
Residence: (262) 334-4078
Mobile: (414) 313-8365

September 21, 2006

Clifford Johnson, President
Manufacturing Recruiters
600 Ventura Boulevard
Inglewood, CA 90301

Dear Mr. Johnson:

Building organizational value and profitability is my expertise. Throughout my tenure with Midwest Manufacturing, currently as **National Director of Operations,** we have pioneered innovative solutions to improve installation cycle times, reduce operating costs, enhance customer satisfaction, and accelerate top-line revenue.

With more than 15 years of leadership experience in operations and production, I bring a strong track record of performance:

- *Strategic vision and leadership of a manufacturing division that we grew from $460 million to $550 million in less than four years with a 50% cycle time reduction, a 50% improvement in forecasting, and a five-point increase in our customer satisfaction index.*

- *Training, development, and leadership of high-performing, multi-discipline professionals in Production Operations, Logistics / Supply Chain, Engineering Project Management, and Installation Service.*

- *Direct P&L accountability for multi-million dollar operations: $5 million to $550 million, with teams ranging from seven to 650.*

- *Demonstrated ability to impact positive change and strengthen profitability as a change agent.*

My goal is another senior-level position with an organization in need of strong, decisive, and visionary leadership. For the right opportunity, I am open to relocation and am anticipating a compensation package well into the six figures.

Thank you for your time and your consideration. I look forward to meeting with you to discuss specific opportunities with your client companies.

Sincerely,

Gordon Jimenez

Written By: Michele Haffner
Font: Century Schoolbook

MARTIN R. REEDSON
12 Grove Run Road
Lancaster, PA 19087
(707) 555-2873
mrreedson@aol.com

April 12, 2006

Joyce Barnes
President
DYK Manufacturing, Inc.
9000 Bland Boulevard
Philadelphia, PA 19023

Dear Ms. Barnes:

Building high-profit, high-end consumer products manufacturing operations is my expertise. Whether launching a new multi-site manufacturing organization, developing private label and branded products, or coordinating international product distribution, I have consistently delivered strong and sustainable financial results. Most notably, I:

- Founded and built a new venture from concept to **$120 million in annual sales** with distribution centers in 10 countries and contract manufacturing partnerships with 20 companies throughout Asia.

- Launched a product development company that introduced state-of-the-art fabrics to the global garment industry and generated over **$70 million in profitable annual sales**.

- Currently, as Director of Manufacturing for an apparel design company, I've built a new market niche, established a firm market hold and am currently generating **double-digit profits**.

Each of these companies has catered to an exclusive and upscale clientele, discriminating in their tastes, and willing to spend significant dollars for the "right" image, the "right" look and the "right" label.

The greatest value I bring to DYK is the depth and diversity of my management talent—from strategic planning, marketing and new business development to product design, manufacturing and distribution. What's more, I have strong financial, analytical, negotiation and team-building skills. I am never satisfied with the status quo, but constantly working to enhance performance, strengthen quality of operations and service, and improve bottom-line profitability.

At this point in my career, I am seeking a top leadership opportunity with a well-established and prominent manufacturer who understands the value of the customer relationship and the innovation it takes to win in today's marketplace. What's more, I am interested in a company with an intense commitment to growth. As such, there is no organization I would rather be associated with than DYK and would welcome a personal interview at your earliest convenience.

Thank you.

Sincerely,

Martin R. Reedson

Enclosure

Written By: Wendy Enelow
Font: Times New Roman

DARREN A. SIMPSON

9701 Holmes Road
Stockton, CA 90872

das999@earthlink.net
Home: (909) 555-6548

August 15, 2006

Spencer Greenwald
Executive Vice President
Meyerson Manufacturing Industries, Inc.
133 Main Street
Dallas, TX 77802

Dear Mr. Greenwald:

Building top-performing manufacturing organizations is my expertise. Whether launching a start-up venture, spearheading a turnaround or leading a company through accelerated growth, I have consistently delivered strong financial results:

- Currently on target to deliver 30% revenue growth and 400% income growth to Diers Mill in 2006.

- Achieved 50% revenue growth and 544% profit growth for Comet Industries, Inc., an industrial equipment manufacturer.

- Built revenues from $18 million to $35 million with a $5 million increase in EBIT for Lewiston Industries, an international industrial manufacturer.

These achievements are indicative of the quality and caliber of my professional career—eliminating organizational weaknesses and optimizing product, technology and market advantages. My teams and I have repeatedly demonstrated our ability to produce and outperform major competition.

My strengths span the entire spectrum of general management with particular emphasis on manufacturing operations, sales/marketing, finance, product development and information technology. In addition, I have solid skills in strategic planning and organizational development in tandem with outstanding performance in team-building and group leadership.

Currently I am confidentially exploring new executive opportunities and would welcome a personal interview at your convenience. I guarantee that the combination of my entrepreneurial drive and solid management skills will add value to your operations.

Thank you.

Sincerely,

Darren A. Simpson

Enclosure

Written By: Wendy Enelow
Font: Verdana

Chapter 13

___

▶ Cover Letters for
Sales, Marketing, and Customer Service Careers

Your cover letter presents an excellent opportunity to show prospective employers and recruiters how the skills and accomplishments documented on your resume relate to their specific hiring needs. Each industry and profession presents unique cover letter writing and design challenges. If you are interested in pursuing a career in sales, marketing, or customer service management, be certain to include highlights of these important success factors in your cover letters:

Success Factor #1

Use statistics to quantify your achievements whenever possible. Show percentage increases in revenues, your top ranking among other sales associates, or the number of new accounts you've closed to demonstrate how you've added value. If you're a marketing professional, how much was market share or sales volume increased based on the campaign(s) you recommended?

Success Factor #2

Demonstrate how your work history has prepared you to meet the specific needs of the prospective employer at this time. Show your versatility in representing different product categories or serving various types of customers (for example, business-to-business and business-to-consumer).

Success Factor #3

Highlight consultative selling and relationship-building skills. In today's environment, connecting well with customers, expertly assessing their needs, and recommending the right solutions are highly valued qualities in sales and customer service professionals.

☦ Success Factor #4

Mention your technology skills, especially presentation software or contact management applications that help sales professionals do their jobs more efficiently. For customer service people, experience with various order entry/tracking software is important.

Keywords and Keyword Phrases

Keywords and keyword phrases are critical components of every successful job seeker's cover letter. By using just one or two words, you're able to communicate a wealth of information about your skills, qualifications, and experience. What's more, keywords are the basis for scanning technology and are therefore critical to every job seeker's campaign in today's electronic-based job search market.

Following are the top 20 sales, marketing, and customer service keywords, some of which may reflect your skills and some of which may not be appropriate for you at this time. Use these words as the foundation for developing your own list of keywords on the Professional Keyword List form in Appendix B.

Top 20 Keywords

Brand Development & Launch	Multi-Channel Marketing
Competitive Market Intelligence	Multimedia Marketing & Promotion
Contract Negotiations	Product & Market Positioning
Corporate Communications	Product Lifecycle Management
Customer Relationship Management	Public Relations
Customer Service & Retention	Sales Administration
E-Commerce	Sales Presentations
International Trade	Sales Training
Key Account Management	Solutions Selling
Media Affairs & Press Relations	Time & Territory Management

Following are some excellent examples of cover letters for sales, marketing, and customer service careers.

Louise B. Shannon, LPN

95 Ellery Road, Sexton, WA 02842 (H) 455-947-6533 (C) 455-833-2161 shan22@aol.com

November 24, 2006

Frieda M. Roderick
Regional Trainer/Recruiter
Smith Kline Beecham Pharmaceuticals
Harbor Place Two, Suite 444
Spokane, WA 88801

Dear Ms. Roderick:

Please accept this letter as my application for a pharmaceutical sales position with Smith Kline Beecham. I had spoken with Carlene Bennett, your office Administrative Assistant, regarding the exciting opportunities for pharmaceutical sales consultants and have enclosed my resume for your consideration.

My extensive employment experience, along with my background in sales in both the travel and real estate industries, coupled with excellent educational qualifications, provide me with ideal credentials for a position in pharmaceutical sales. In addition, my LPN training has served to refocus my own professional objective toward sales in this important, rapidly expanding, and fascinating arena of the health services field.

Perceptive to the needs of clients and resolute in securing all potential sales, I have built a solid reputation with employers and customers for being trustworthy, dependable, and dedicated in my responsibilities. A self-starter willing to take on significant responsibilities, I have worked competently on independent projects and often as a contributing team member.

I hope to share my qualifications with you and /or another representative of Smith Kline Beecham in a personal interview, and will follow up next Wednesday to set a date and time convenient for your schedule.

Thank you for considering my application for employment.

Sincerely,

Louise B. Shannon, LPN

Enclosure

Written By: Edward Turilli
Font: Bookman Old Style

Job ID: 447

Beverly Parks
4100 Rice Circle Montgomery, Alabama 36100
✉ beverly_parks@knology.net   ☎ 334.555.3827 (Home) /334.555.4330 (Cell)

15 July, 2006

Ms. Kathleen Harris, Sales Manager
TopLine, Inc.
500 Northridge Parkway, Suite 400
Montgomery, Alabama 36100

Dear Ms. Harris:

Could TopLine use a sales representative who can persuade customers to champion your products to their bosses? That's the kind of powerful sales for which I'm known.

What I do isn't magic. I know how to find and win over the *real* decision makers and the gatekeepers who guard them. And I've applied that knowledge energetically to sell everything from insurance to cell phones to lawnmowers. I've sold business-to-business and business-to-consumer. But, what I *really* do is find a way for our customers to see a return on their investment each time they pay us.

You'll see my track record starting on the next page. No buzzwords or lists of traits there. In their places are four profit-building capabilities I want to put at your disposal at once. You'll also read 11 examples of new markets penetrated, accounts (even hard to close accounts) captured, and sales grown.

If what I do appeals to TopLine, perhaps a good next step is for me to hear about your special sales needs in your own words. May I call in a few days to set an appointment?

Sincerely,

Beverly Parks

Enclosure: Resume

Written By: Don Orlando
Font: Book Antiqua

JOSHUA K. SKITTLE

1082 Katie Lane • Cincinnati, OH 45211 • (513) 598-9100 • skittle@hotmail.net

October 21, 2006

Mr. Michael Vash
Sports Network, Inc./SNI
1082 Dory Corporate Center
Claire, NY 11020

Dear Mr. Vash:

Your SNI website posting for the "dream job" of Marketing Manager, is right on target … it IS my dream job. I have <u>exactly</u> the qualifications you are seeking, including significant marketing and advertising experience with a leading retailer of consumer products. While the enclosed resume illustrates more fully how my background is suited to your needs, please consider the following:

Your Needs	My Qualifications
* Bachelor's degree plus 3-5 years of marketing experience with the marketing department of a consumer packaged goods/retail company.	* Bachelor's degrees in Marketing and Finance, enhanced by over 5 years of experience in the marketing department with Procter & Gamble.
* Solid understanding of marketing fundamentals, qualitative / quantitative research, marketing strategies, and ability to manage budgets.	* Education and experience have provided solid understanding of marketing fundamentals. Work with qualitative and quantitative research methods on a daily basis. Have written and directed the writing of ad copy for print, radio, and TV. Managed budgets up to $5.2 million.
* Passion for sports.	* Currently enjoy golf, running, weightlifting, softball, flag football, and basketball. College sports included varsity softball, intramural basketball, and coaching Little League. High School: football, basketball, and track.
* PC proficiency with Word / Excel / PowerPoint.	* I am proficient with Word, Excel, and PowerPoint.
* Excellent oral / written communication skills.	* My current position requires excellent communication skills, including the ability to speak effectively before groups, as well as the ability to ensure instructions and expectations are clearly outlined for everyone involved in a given project. I also have excellent follow-through skills.

As my resume indicates, my current position involves working with ad agencies, coordinating both creative and production processes, and handling timetables and media budgets. I work with our market research partners on a daily basis and understand the importance of obtaining legal approvals. Finally, I have played a key role in helping my current employer to leverage their full complement of corporate assets to get the most value for every marketing dollar we spend. I am now ready to do the same for SNI.

I can make myself available for an interview at your convenience. Thank you for your consideration.

Sincerely,

Joshua K. Skittle

Enclosure

Written By: Michelle Mastruserio Reitz
Font: Times New Roman

JOHN J. SCHMIDT
7758 Royal Oak Drive
West Chester, PA 19508
414-729-8853

Business Philosophy: *"You can't build a reputation on what you are _going_ to do."* -Henry Ford

January 4, 2007

Mr. Dale Rastetter, CEO
Camden Controls Inc.
8554 Camden Parkway
Philadelphia, PA 19521

Dear Mr. Rastetter:

John Rand, our mutual friend, suggested I contact you to let you know of my intent to search for a challenging, executive-level position in the Philadelphia market. John speaks quite highly of you and Camden Controls, and mentioned several of the most critical projects that you're currently launching. It certainly sounds as though you have a dynamic organization that is poised for remarkable growth over the next few years.

Corporate profitability and sales depend on continual innovation and excellence in the area of customer service. The customers of Camden Controls are entitled to the best customer service possible. To this end, my plan for attaining the highest level of service can be stated this way:

Dedication to Excellence in Employee Training and Development — **Will Ultimately Result In** → **World-Class Customer Service and Increased Profitability**

Implementation of targeted employee training has been the biggest reason for my success as Vice President of Sales with Roth Industries. When I accepted this turnaround position five years ago, the customer service departments in all twenty locations focused on sales, not customers!

My own research showed that our former customers were purchasing from companies that actually charged slightly higher prices, but gave the customers the world-class service they expected and deserved. Predictably, the result was decreased sales (with a real potential for layoffs), and an increasingly negative reputation in the marketplace. Through direct observation, I realized that my staff was woefully inept at problem-solving and articulating viable solutions to customers to capture and maintain their business.

JOHN J. SCHMIDT
7758 Royal Oak Drive
West Chester, PA 19508
414-729-8853

Business Philosophy: *"You can't build a reputation on what you are going to do."* -Henry Ford

Mr. Dale Rastetter, CEO
January 4, 2007
Page 2

The correlation between lack of training and low levels of customer satisfaction became clear. In response to this finding, funds were reallocated to provide employees with customized training programs with specific, measurable objectives. A series of intensive, hands-on, team-training workshops (which included positive reinforcement and rewards) were conducted with amazing results. In under six months' time, the staff *transformed itself* into a highly focused, results-driven, solution-seeking machine! Sales increased by 48% within one year. New, existing, and a growing number of former customers have expressed satisfaction with our commitment to service and our genuine desire to earn their business!

I look forward to the opportunity to discuss the position of Vice President of Customer Service with you personally, and to outline a few of the proven strategies that will work for Camden Controls. I will call you in the next two weeks as a follow-up to this letter.

Best Regards,

John J. Schmidt

Enclosure

cc: John Rand

Written By: Susan Hoopes
Font: Arial

Diana Lynn Harrison
37384 South 39th Street, Appleton, WI 54912
920-832-4444 Home • DiLHarrison@ptd.net

October 29, 2006

Morgan Lewis
Hiring Manager
Federated Stores
11 Albany Lane
Beaverton, OR 90873

Dear Mr. Lewis:

Are you looking for a take-charge, customer-focused Retail Store Manager, Department Manager or Director of Retail Operations? Someone with a strong track record of success in sales management, store operations, buying, and merchandising to build retail store teams that achieve multi-million-dollar sales?

If so, we should meet. My career history has included producing consistently strong sales and profits while cutting costs, creating more efficient systems and procedures, and motivating team members to excel. My resume details the successes I have had in the retail home furnishings and floral/gift industries, starting out in interior design, merchandising and buying, and progressing to multi-store retail management. Here are a few selected highlights:

⇒ **Peak Sales Performance.** On-target to reach 2006 sales quota of $1.7 million for upscale home furnishings destination store, turning around previous sales decline.

⇒ **Competitive Market Positioning.** Instituted adjusted retail store hours of operation and introduced TV advertising to reach target market, resulting in immediate increases in customer traffic by 6% in slow winter season.

⇒ **Multi-Site Management.** Managed up to 9 retail stores, directly supervising 8 store managers, with dotted-line responsibility for 65-70 full-time and part-time staff. Brought in up to $1.9 million in annual sales. Oversaw new concept launch of floral-and-gift stores within grocery store locations.

⇒ **Change Management and Turnaround.** Delivered highest-ranking sales performance for individual store (out of 9 retail locations) after temporarily managing it for only 4 months. Outstripped nearest competition by more than 50%.

My background of progressive retail sales and store management experience has allowed me to grow my consumer sales, merchandising, team building, financial (P&L) management, and operations management skills. I am eager to put that experience to work in another organization where I can continue to expand my capabilities.

May we talk soon? It would be a pleasure to arrange a telephone meeting with you at your convenience to discuss your needs and answer your questions. I will contact you next week to see when we could arrange such a meeting. Thank you for your consideration and interest.

Sincerely,

Diana Lynn Harrison

Enclosure: Resume

Written By: Susan Guarneri
Font: Georgia

Jane A. Simmons
9007 Rainor Road ▪ Chapel Hill, NC 65540 ▪ Home: 436-.997.0668 ▪ Mobile: 436.997.3378 ▪ janeasimmons@aol.com

"Having worked with Jane in a very dynamic and fast-paced environment, I was always impressed with her ability to look straight at the goal and help guide the team to the objectives. This ability was invaluable to the group when working with various organizations, people, and processes, to build cohesive business and marketing plans spanning the entire worldwide organization. Jane has the leadership to build a common understanding of the customers and the marketing organization, as well as to assist the organization in defining strategies and programs to address this market."

Fred Jones, VP—Marketing Center Technology, Inc.

"Jane could be counted on to take an assignment, project, or complex problem and pull the right resources together (people and funding) to drive to success. She works to understand the customer needs, requirements and pain points, and then addresses those in creative new ways. She drives her team and her projects with great independence and with an eye for quality, ultimately delivering exceptional results on behalf of the end-user customer and our company. She is an extraordinary team player and one of the most talented individuals I have had the pleasure to work with in my 18 years."

Ellen Lawrence, Worldwide VP—Marketing Center Technology, Inc.

May 1, 2006

Joe Albertson
President & CEO
Armada Technologies, Inc.
PO Box 1109
Raleigh, NC 22093-1109

Dear Mr. Albertson:

As a business and marketing leader in program management and process improvements that result in increased revenues and reduced costs, I can offer a wealth of knowledge to Armada Technologies. My expertise in leading companies through periods of growth and change has prepared me for any number of challenges that Armada may be facing.

Highlights of my achievements during my rapid growth at Center Technology, Inc. include:

As Marketing Manager for the global business unit:

- Led a global team of marketing and product managers to redefine the program scope, which increased revenue by more than $50 million incrementally in 6 months.

As Marketing Manager for the hardware program:

- Directed the reduction of over 120 marketing programs with a $13 million quarterly budget down to eight marketing programs with an $8 million budget.
- Implemented promotions and extensive training programs to increase cross-sell of PCs and support services by over 25% annually.

As Business Planning Manager:

- Leveraged the company's global account organization and sales force to increase global accounts revenue by more than 12%.
- Improved relationships between the Americas' regional business and marketing teams through the implementation of best practices.

If you need a strategic marketing executive with strong business acumen and out-of-the-box problem-solving talent blended with extraordinary team leadership and the ability to execute tactically, then I am your candidate. I would welcome the opportunity to discuss how my vision, creativity and skillsets could benefit your organization. May we meet?

Sincerely,

Jane A. Simmons

Written By: Louise Garver
Font: Garamond

GEORGE B. HEIDEN

516 Flatbush Avenue • Brooklyn, NY 11225
718-748-5112 • gbheiden@comcast.net

February 14, 2007

Jackson Lamar, VP, Business Development
B&R Technologies
420 Park Avenue South
New York, NY 10016

Dear Mr. Lamar:

Creating marketing campaigns that build brand identity and new revenue centers is my strength and my passion. During my 12+ year career in sales and marketing, I have launched multiple product initiatives for the wireless, home center, computer, electronic, retail, and supermarket industries resulting in billions of dollars in revenue. A partial listing of my key accomplishments is detailed below:

- **Catapulted revenue from $400M to $1.3B** in four years for leading insurance company and third-party marketer.

- **Created and patented a $400M portfolio of products** for the wireless, home center, computer, and electronic industries.

- **Bolstered revenues by 45%** by compiling competitive market intelligence, utilizing multi-channel distribution systems, and instituting a formal brand management process.

- **Reduced time spent on sales process exponentially** by systematizing procedures for sales delivery and developing improved marketing collaterals.

In addition, I have an MBA and was selected to participate in a 12-month marketing program at Columbia University.

Impressed by your company's steady expansion in recent years, as well as the positive press you've received from *The Wall Street Journal* and *Fast Company* magazine, I would welcome the chance to meet with you to discuss my qualifications in more detail. I am confident that I can contribute to the growth of your organization and look forward to a personal interview.

Sincerely,

George B. Heiden

Enclosure

Written By: Barbara Safani
Font: Book Antiqua

GREG PEARL

91 Mill Street • Mississauga, Ontario • L8R 1Z1
Telephone: 905.699.0100 • Cellular: 416.410.8309 • Email: gpearl@gmail.com

December 15, 2006

Mr. Christopher Robbins
Vice President, Strategic Sales Opportunities
Strathcona Direct Marketing
880 Bay Street, Suite 100
Toronto, Ontario M4R 2J9

RE: Director, Business Development

Dear Mr. Robbins:

Sales and marketing is about developing and implementing an innovative and tactical vision that will generate outstanding sales results and profitability for an organization. My leadership abilities and extensive hands-on experience create a synergy between ideas and people that will not only meet, but exceed, your expectations. Promoted to progressively more challenging and responsible positions, I have had the opportunity to excel in the areas of business development, channel management, and operations.

My strengths are as follows:

- **Leadership** – Outstanding record in the recruitment, motivation, and performance of sales teams. Currently manage a team of eight that has exceeded their margin target in Q3 of the current fiscal year.

- **Business Development** – Demonstrated ability to assess the marketplace and uncover new clients, coupled with strengths in growing market share and sales with existing clients.

- **Relationship Management** – Solid skills in forging and solidifying client, partner, and vendor relationships. Proven ability to negotiate fair and reasonable expectations and deliver an exemplary return on investment to all parties involved.

- **Operations Management** – Ability to function as the focal point of contact for project implementations and enable organizations to transform ideas into reality.

My skills at leading sales teams to conceptualize, build, and implement ground-breaking marketing strategies will bring Strathcona Direct Marketing to the forefront of the industry.

I am excited by the potential challenges and growth your position offers and I would welcome a personal interview to explore our mutual interests. I look forward to your call.

Sincerely,

Greg Pearl

Enclosure

Written By: Denyse Cowling
Font: Trebuchet MS

DAVID MADISON, LUTCF, CLTC, CFA

Cell: 203-599-0308 | Office: 203-981-2213 | dmadison@yahoo.com

May 16, 2006

George Ramey, Partner
Ramey, Rather and Smyth Partners
1000 Chimney Branch Road
Boston, MA 01909

Dear Mr. Ramey:

Delivering stakeholder value through effective leadership, marketing and business development is my forte. For the past 20 years, I have played a pivotal role in creating and managing successful financial operations for two industry giants—MassMutual and MetLife. During this time, I've not only been recognized as a top performer, honored with numerous industry and corporate awards, but I have also been a catalyst in helping to ignite the careers of many other top-flight sales professionals. I'm hoping that you can help me find a new and equally challenging executive assignment.

I am at my best when I face a new set of challenges and am known for my ability to shatter corporate sales records through both my own initiatives and by developing high-octane teams of sales professionals. The opportunity you have right now seems to present a win-win situation for both of us. Highlights of what I can offer include:

- **Expertise in developing and overseeing highly successful operations.** Created a robust financial services practice from the ground floor up that, within two years, ranked in the top 10 out of 350 in sales, profitability and customer satisfaction.

- **Unique ability to distill corporate barriers, cut through red tape, and effectively manage systems and resources to achieve an organization's mission.** Track record of consistently outperforming sales goals by executing practical and appealing sales strategies and kindling a strong team spirit.

- **One-of-a-kind marketing campaigns that deliver highly profitable results.** Piloted an outreach initiative that was the first of its kind in the financial services industry. Developed a "storefront" marketing program to attract Hispanic clients that was endorsed by community leaders in Hartford, CT. Resulted in a 40% revenue increase within that market segment.

- **Magnetic networking, client relationship and customer retention abilities.** Headed up a retention program at MetLife with brokers and affiliates that curbed the loss of clients and protected over $5.6 million in assets under management.

- **Innate ability to champion professional excellence through staff recruiting, training and mentoring.** Pioneered a new financial services sales training "Boot Camp" program that increased the revenue performance of sales representatives by 39% in just eight months.

I would welcome the opportunity to speak with you about your current search assignments appropriate for an individual with my qualifications. I am open to relocation and would anticipate a total compensation package well over $200,000 annually. Thank you for your time. I'll follow up with you in a few days.

Sincerely,

Dave Madison

1 Montgomery Place ◆ West Hartford, CT 06117

Written By: Jill Grindle
Font: Garamond

EMILY G. GARDNER

6556 Ascot Run Lane
Dover, Delaware 19081

Residence (302) 555-7265
eggardner425@aol.com

May 27, 2006

Norman Greenley
President/CEO
Phillips Broadband Networks, Inc.
100 Minuteman Boulevard
Providence, RI 09276

RE: Vice President—Worldwide Sales

Dear Mr. Greenley:

As a follow-up to my recent conversation with Tom Reynolds of Reynolds & Smith Executive Recruiters, I am forwarding highlights of my career that may be of particular interest to you for your VP Worldwide Sales position. Please note that my career includes extensive experience in start-up, early-stage and high-growth technology companies, each requiring the ability to architect a plan of action to build sales, drive revenues and deliver solid bottom-line profits.

Specifically, my career includes:

International Sales Management Experience

I bring to Phillips Broadband more than 10 years of international sales and marketing management experience that has taken me around the globe, with a particular focus in both emerging and mature markets in Europe, Asia, South America and Africa. My expertise includes developing multinational and cross-cultural business relationships to accelerate revenue and profit growth, while establishing a dominant position of market leadership in more than 30 different countries. Further, I have outstanding cross-cultural communications skills and an in-depth knowledge of the business cultures and norms of each country.

Most notably, I have personally negotiated and closed over $50 million in total sales over the past 10 years within intensely competitive global markets. This includes, but is not limited to, technology licensing, partnerships, OEM sales, consultant sales and end-user sales programs.

Technology Experience

My entire career has focused on the sale/marketing of advanced technology software, hardware and solutions. Although not a hands-on "techie," I am extremely well versed in the applications of technology, and am able to quickly and accurately identify customer needs and respond with the appropriate technology solutions. This extensive knowledge has been vital to my success in new customer and new market development.

Norman Greenley
May 27, 2006
Page Two

Organizational & Team Leadership Experience

Without a strong team and decisive leadership, no organization will thrive. This is perhaps the greatest contribution of my career. In each and every organization, I have provided the strategic and tactical leadership critical to profitable revenue and market growth. My efforts have ranged from the recruitment, training and development of other sales professionals to active participation in long-range product R&D efforts. In addition, I have built entire field sales organizations and created effective sales processes to manage entire global sales organizations, structured by region and by product line.

Business Leadership

In addition to my portfolio of qualifications in sales, marketing and business development, I bring to Phillips solid experience in strategic planning, corporate finance, budgeting, business systems design and corporate administration. Further, I have held direct P&L responsibility for more than five years. These skills allow me the opportunity to actively participate in the overall planning and leadership of an entire business unit, division and/or company.

Relationship Management

Building and managing formidable customer relationships, partnerships and alliances is another one of my strongest suits. I have personally built and nurtured relationships with companies around the world, including Fortune 500 firms as well as major multinationals. In addition, I have structured and negotiated alliances with major consulting firms and with government officials around the world. Perhaps most significantly, I have the contacts within local markets worldwide so that Phillips' efforts can be set in motion virtually immediately.

Michael Dell, of Dell Computers, is one of today's greatest business leaders and an individual whose work I follow closely. I have read many of his articles and appreciate his insights, convictions and vision for our industry. His commitment to hiring the "right" people and not accepting the status quo is just one of the underlying keys to Dell's phenomenal success. Bringing it closer to home, I am also aware of the strong reputation and technical competencies of the entire Phillips family of companies, and would welcome the opportunity to work under your leadership and direction as Phillips Broadband continues to build and strengthen its global market presence. I believe that you and I will find a good fit with one another, and will share many common visions and action goals.

Thank you for your time and consideration. I look forward to meeting with you to demonstrate my qualifications for your VP of Worldwide Sales position.

Sincerely,

Emily G. Gardner

THAN KYUNGHO
tkyungho@aol.com

2040 Kennedy Boulevard ... Fresno, CA 90872 ... (909) 555-2736

September 13, 2006

Tony Andrews, President & CEO
First-Time Technology Ventures, Inc.
100 Main Street, Suite 11-B
San Diego, CA 98720

Dear Mr. Andrews:

Twenty years ago, technology innovations virtually sold themselves. With a bit of advertising here and there, a company was set to launch a new product. Today, however, things have changed dramatically and marketing has become one of the most vital components to any technology venture. With both global competition and new product rollouts at an all-time high, it is no longer enough to just develop a product. What is required is an astute marketer with technological expertise. And that is precisely who I am.

Working with some of the world's leading technology companies (e.g., Dell, Emerson, AMERIA), I have led innovative technology R&D programs with complete responsibility for product marketing, commercialization, joint ventures, partnerships, licensing and related business development functions. Most significant have been my financial results:

- For Emerson, I drove development of six new products generating total revenues of $35 million annually.
- For Morcom, a Swiss-based company, I increased European market sales from $2 million to $10 million.
- For AMERIA, I developed and commercialized 20 products with a 70% win rate on competitive contracts.
- For Dell, I reengineered existing product technology and saved over $1.5 million in company operating costs.

These achievements are indicative of the quality and caliber of my entire professional career—identifying market opportunities, driving technology development, and creating profitable sales and marketing programs. The strength of my hands-on technology skills has been vital to my success in business development and revenue generation. Further, my ability to build cooperative client relationships and deliver what we have promised, has accelerated our growth and market dominance.

Since leaving Emerson last year, I have continued to focus my efforts on technology development and global marketing, and would be pleased to share specific engagements with you during an interview. Currently, I am exploring new career opportunities in technology marketing and would be delighted to meet with you. Thank you.

Sincerely,

Than Kyungho

Enclosure

Written By: Wendy Enelow
Font: Times New Roman

HARRIS R. MORGAN
hrmme@msn.com

8901 Martin Road   *   Lewiston, ME 02001   *   (381) 555-8712

May 17, 2006

Allen R. Mendelsohn
Managing Director
ALCO Sports Products, Inc.
11211 Beechwood Boulevard
Raines, WI 78309

Dear Mr. Mendelsohn:

I started out as a baseball player in 9th grade, and played all through high school and college. At the same time, I was fortunate to become involved with the Charlotte Cavaliers, a AAA baseball club. Eventually, I became Clubhouse Manager, coordinating all equipment, facilities, personnel and more for over 60 games each season. It was great experience!

In the meantime, I graduated from college and "fell" into a job with a major insurance agency that was actively recruiting on campus. I quickly learned two important things about myself —I had a natural talent for sales and customer relationship management, and I had strong analytical, deductive reasoning and financial skills. The combination of both was the foundation for what has been a strong sales career within the insurance industry.

Now I want to go back to where I belong—the sports industry. Open to a number of different types of sales, marketing and account management positions, I'm looking for the opportunity to use my professional qualifications wherever they may be of most value to you.

On more a personal note, I guarantee you that I am intensely hard working and driven to deliver strong results. What's more, I have extensive public speaking, community relations and leadership experience that is of significant value in any situation.

I appreciate your time and consideration, and look forward to speaking with you. If I do not hear from you in two weeks, I'll follow up with a phone call.

Sincerely,

Harris R. Morgan

Enclosure

Written By: Wendy Enelow
Font: Bookman Old Style

Chapter 14

▶ Cover Letters for
Skilled Trades Careers

Your cover letter presents an excellent opportunity to show prospective employers and recruiters how the skills and accomplishments documented on your resume relate to their specific hiring needs. Each industry and profession presents unique cover letter writing and design challenges. If you are interested in pursuing a career in the skilled trades, be certain to include highlights of these important success factors in your cover letters:

Success Factor #1

Be sure to highlight specific training programs, internships, or apprenticeships you've completed that relate directly to the position for which you are applying. Then, be sure to highlight any additional certifications or licenses you have earned (for example, welding, HVAC, and so on).

Success Factor #2

Show your range of experience. For example: framing, roofing, finish cabinet work (carpenter); 120-volts, 480-volts, network cabling (electrician); pneumatics, hydraulics, and high-pressure lines (plumber).

Success Factor #3

Remember to mention special skills that set you apart and that directly relate to the stated needs of the prospective employer (for example, conduit bending, fiber optic installation, EDM processes, or compound and progressive die building/repair).

Success Factor #4

Highlight your familiarity with the latest technology. Do you use CAD/CAM software, CNC programming, or other technology tools and aids? If so, be sure to include them. They're a great asset for you in your job search.

Keywords and Keyword Phrases

Keywords and keyword phrases are critical components of every successful job seeker's cover letter. By using just one or two words, you're able to communicate a wealth of information about your skills, qualifications, and experience. What's more, keywords are the basis for scanning technology and are therefore critical to every job seeker's campaign in today's electronic-based job search market.

Following are the top 20 keywords for careers in the skilled trades, some of which may reflect your skills and some of which may not be appropriate for you at this time. Use these words as the foundation for developing your own list of keywords on the Professional Keyword List form in Appendix B.

Top 20 Keywords

Blueprints & Drawings

Contract Administration

Crew Supervision

Customer Relations

Electrical, Plumbing & HVAC

Fault Isolation & Analysis

Maintenance & Repair

Material Management

Preventative Maintenance

Project Management

Project Scheduling & Documentation

Project Specifications

Regulatory Compliance

Residential & Commercial Projects

Scope-of-Work Documents

Security Systems Installation

Testing & Troubleshooting

Tools & Equipment Control

Training & Apprenticeships

Work Site Safety

Following are some excellent examples of cover letters for skilled trades careers.

GERRY RADCLIFF

1195 Calkins Road
Rochester, New York 14623
(585) 334-9999
cliff@resumesos.com

March 10, 2006

Archer Equipment & Moving
109 Coleman Boulevard
Rochester, NY 14620

Dear Hiring Manager:

   With more than 18 years of experience as a **Forklift & Heavy Equipment Operator**, I am seeking employment opportunities in the construction industry or with a manufacturing firm. Please accept the enclosed resume as evidence of my interest in a position compatible with my background.

   I am proficient in the operation of:

- **Case W26-B Lift Truck**
- **Backhoe / Front-End Loader**
- **Skid Loader**
- **Lift-All Telescopic Lift**
- **Forklift (Standing, Walk-Behind, Articulating)**

   My experience has included **industrial equipment rigging, forklift operation, materials handling**, and **delivery of construction materials.**

   I am a hard working, reliable, and knowledgeable individual with a stable work history and adaptability to changing environments. I would appreciate the opportunity to speak with you about job openings with your company. Thank you.

Sincerely,

Gerry Radcliff

Enclosure

Written By: Christine Robinson
Font: Bookman Old Style

16 Banner Crescent
Oxford Gardens
Brisbane, Queensland 7049
Mobile: 0417 885 000

26th March 2006

Mr. Douglas Cooper
Queensland Electric Company Ltd.
PO Box 7908
BRISBANE
Queensland 7000

Dear Mr. Cooper:

I am applying for the position of **Pole Surveyor** advertised in the *Brisbane Courier Mail* on 24th March 2006.

My Electrical Linesman First Class certification, plus more than 10 years of experience in the full range of underground and overhead installations, includes work for the Department of Commerce in Queensland, South Australia and the Northern Territory. My current position is with Peterson International, which is contracted to install lighting towers at all federal airports throughout Australia.

In addition, I have repaired and maintained electrical systems, as well as constructing new systems. I worked for a number of years at various Commerce Department bases on the replacement of electrical transmission systems and the construction of new systems. Much of this work has involved the inspection of wooden and metal poles for physical condition and earthing.

My technical expertise includes using the national standards to ascertain tension in high- and low-voltage live conductors, and using a Newton meter in conjunction with appropriate tools to physically tension or re-tension conductors to required specifications. I am particularly experienced and skilled in determining the residual weight and strain capacity of poles, and am familiar with the national standards for the replacement of poles.

Enclosed is my current resume and I look forward to meeting you to discuss my application in person.

Yours sincerely,

Daley Waters

Enclosure

Written By: Brian Leeson
Font: Verdana

GARRETT FREDERICKS
7178 Holly-Byron Road
Byron, New York 14422
(585) 548-9786

April 14, 2006

Greenbrier Tooling & Machining
6332 Route 237
Byron, NY 14420

Dear Sir/Madam:

As an experienced **Journeyman Tool & Die Maker** with a 17-year background in the aerospace industry, I am exploring employment opportunities that will capitalize on my skills and training. I have enjoyed a rewarding career with ITT Government Systems—an ISO-9002 manufacturing environment—and have made consistent contributions using strong troubleshooting skills and innovative thinking to overcome complex machine maintenance issues.

The enclosed resume highlights my experience, training, and professional assets which include:

- **Licensed Tool & Die Maker with proficiency in troubleshooting and maintaining dies for high-volume production; and experience operating and maintaining high-speed presses and dies that produce close tolerance parts.**

- **Strong technical skills with solid ability to work with CAD technology, CNC machine tools, and computerized measuring devices.**

- **In-depth understanding of machining tools and principles.**

- **Skills in metalworking processes, such as chrome plating and heat treating.**

- **High integrity, work ethic, and professionalism.**

I would appreciate the chance to speak with you in person about potential opportunities with your company. After reviewing my resume, I hope you will contact me to arrange an interview so that we may discuss the criteria you seek in a candidate and how I can best fulfill your needs.

Thank you for your consideration.

Sincerely,

Garrett Fredericks

Enclosure

Written By: Christine Robinson
Font: Tahoma

Mackenzie "Mac" Michaels

515 Brandywine Drive   (585) 383-4321
Pittsford, New York 14534   mmichaels@resumesos.com

December 2, 2006

Seneca Nation Casinos, LLC
jobs@cascadecasino.com

Dear Hiring Authority:

Your recent posting for a Stationary Engineer is an excellent match for my existing skills, and I believe I can be an asset to your organization in this role. Therefore, I have enclosed a resume outlining my qualifications.

Considering your requirements, the following points may be of particular interest:

➢ *As a licensed Stationary Engineer (City of Rochester, New York), I have qualifications and experience operating steam boilers, turbines, and steam generators.*

➢ *As an Operating Engineer for a 26-story office building, I have experience maintaining and operating a wide array of electrical, plumbing, and fire control systems.*

➢ *In my current position, I am accountable for purchasing parts and supplies, and maintaining parts/supplies inventory.*

➢ *I have experience operating computerized environmental controls, including Johnson Controls— Metasys.*

In addition, I believe that my 10 years of experience at Mapledale Party House gives me special insights into the unique challenges faced by large facilities hosting special events on a routine basis.

I would welcome an opportunity to meet and discuss how my capabilities can address your needs. Please contact me to arrange a mutually convenient time for an initial interview.

Thank you for your time and consideration. I look forward to speaking with you soon.

Sincerely,

Mackenzie Michaels

Enclosure

Written By: Arnie Boldt
Font: Times New Roman

CALVIN JAMES
8676 Townline Road
Oakfield, New York 14135
calj@resumesos.com

(H) 585-344-9876   (C) 585-820-9876

November 2, 2006

Ms. Brenda Johnson
Batavia City School District
1000 Commerce Drive
Batavia, NY 14128

Dear Ms. Johnson:

I am writing to inquire about employment opportunities within your transportation / equipment maintenance department that would utilize my extensive mechanical experience and training. As a previous employee of Batavia City School District, I performed a wide array of mechanical repairs on a fleet of 37 buses and district vehicles, most with diesel engines.

The enclosed resume outlines some of my qualifications which include:

- ✓ Masterful mechanical ability with more than 15 years of combined experience providing mechanical repair and maintenance to trucks, heavy equipment, and buses; plus eight years of experience as a Journeyman Maintenance Mechanic for Eastman Kodak responding to maintenance and repair calls on industrial machinery.

- ✓ Comprehensive training that ranges from diagnostics and repair of air brakes, transmissions, and automotive charging systems, to the millwright, tinsmith, and plumbing trades.

- ✓ Journeyman Automotive Mechanic, previously licensed to perform automobile inspections. During my work with LeRoy Motors, I received the GM Mark of Excellence Quality Service Award. In addition, I have been certified to inspect and repair overhead industrial cranes.

- ✓ Strong leadership ability and motivation. In addition to previously owning and operating my own towing business, I have been elected by coworkers to several two-year terms as a Group Leader at Kodak.

- ✓ Class B CDL with Passenger and Towing endorsements; certified to operate forklifts.

I would appreciate the opportunity to speak with you about my qualifications and how they might best serve the needs of your organization. Please contact me to schedule an interview at a mutually convenient time. I look forward to speaking with you soon. Thank you for your time and consideration.

Sincerely,

Calvin James

Enclosure

Written By: Christine Robinson
Font: Tahoma

ALLEN T. BORNEO
8001 Satchel Drive
Greenfield, MA 98554
Home: (413) 559-6643 • Cell: (413) 559-7799
E-mail: allentb@aol.com

July 24, 2006

Mr. John Deering
Director of Facility Maintenance
Marietta Manufacturing
Marietta Plaza
Greenfield, MA 98554

Dear Mr. Deering:

Although circumstances allowed me to retire at a young age, I have come to realize that I have too much energy and many skills that I still enjoy using. Therefore, your ad for a **Maintenance Specialist** caught my attention, as I offer the key qualifications your company needs.

Specifically, I have an excellent performance record in the operation and maintenance of building systems and equipment, including electrical, HVAC, telecommunications, pneumatic, electro-mechanical, and hydraulics. I also have in-depth knowledge of state building codes, safety, and other regulatory guidelines.

My expertise encompasses multi-site facilities oversight, staff supervision, project management, and vendor relations. Examples of relevant accomplishments include reducing annual maintenance costs and improving functional capabilities while consistently delivering quality service.

Equally important are my planning, organization, and communication strengths. Despite the challenges that can often be encountered, I have completed projects on time and under budget on a consistent basis.

I would welcome a personal interview to discuss the value I would add to your company and look forward to speaking with you.

Sincerely,

Allen T. Borneo

Enclosure

Written By: Louise Garver
Font: Bookman Old Style

FREDERICK VINCENT

999 Ridge Road
Webster, New York 14580

(585) 872-9999
fredv@resumesos.com

February 19, 2007

Human Resources Department
Delphi Fuel Systems
PO Box 1009
Honeoye Falls, NY 14472

Dear Hiring Authority:

As an experienced Plant Maintenance Mechanic with 10+ years of experience in an ISO-9002 manufacturing facility, as well as years of experience in successful entrepreneurial pursuits, I can offer your company a well-rounded background defined by drive and integrity. My resume is enclosed for your consideration.

Some of the key qualifications I can bring to a position with your firm include:

❖ **Trained and experienced NYS Journeyman Maintenance Mechanic. Over the last 15 years, I have advanced both my knowledge and responsibility in a role that encompasses installation, repair, preventive maintenance, and relocation of large industrial machinery and equipment. I was elected by my peers to serve as a Group Leader with oversight of 17 employees. Additionally, I am routinely called upon to assist with hoist relocation projects, based on my expertise in that area.**

❖ **Hands-on experience operating, rebuilding, and maintaining heavy equipment. Over the years, I have purchased and refurbished numerous pieces of construction equipment for resale or personal use.**

❖ **Successful 12-year ownership of a retail business, as well as 11 years as a landlord of residential rental properties, all of which demonstrate strong business sense, professionalism, and a firm commitment to succeed.**

I am open to both supervisory and hands-on opportunities that will capitalize on my project management, team leadership, and technical skills. I would be pleased to speak with you in person about what I can contribute to the future success of your organization. Please feel free to telephone me to arrange an interview.

Thank you.

Sincerely,

Frederick Vincent

Enclosure

Written By: Christine Robinson
Font: Garamond

Chapter 15

▶ Cover Letters for
Teaching and Education Careers

Your cover letter presents an excellent opportunity to show prospective employers and recruiters how the skills and accomplishments documented on your resume relate to their specific hiring needs. Each industry and profession presents unique cover letter writing and design challenges. If you are interested in pursuing a career in teaching and education, be certain to include highlights of these important success factors in your cover letters:

Success Factor #1

List your credentials/certifications prominently, possibly right after your contact information. Principals and administrators want to see right away what subject areas or grade levels you are qualified to teach and/or administer.

Success Factor #2

Mention the classes you have taught, including grade levels and subjects. Include any information about special lesson plans or field trips related to a particular subject area to illustrate your ingenuity and creativity in bringing the subject matter alive for your students. Relate these activities to the particular needs of the school or school district to which you are applying.

Success Factor #3

Highlight any committees you have been a member of or student activities for which you have served as an advisor (for example, Science Curriculum Committee or Olympics of the Mind Advisor).

⚱ **Success Factor #4**

Include travel or other enriching activities that contribute to your ability to bring additional value to the classroom. A social studies teacher who has spent extensive time exploring Europe or Native American cultures in the Southwest can be a much more fascinating candidate than someone who hasn't had similar experiences.

Keywords and Keyword Phrases

Keywords and keyword phrases are critical components of every successful job seeker's cover letter. By using just one or two words, you're able to communicate a wealth of information about your skills, qualifications, and experience. What's more, keywords are the basis for scanning technology and are therefore critical to every job seeker's campaign in today's electronic-based job search market.

Following are the top 20 teaching and education keywords, some of which may reflect your skills and some of which may not be appropriate for you at this time. Use these words as the foundation for developing your own list of keywords on the Professional Keyword List form in Appendix B.

Top 20 Keywords

Accreditation	Parent-Teacher Relations
Academic Advising	Research & Publishing
Academic Standards	School Administration
Classroom Management	Student Advisement
Course Design	Student Placement
Curriculum Development	Student Recruitment
Educational Services Administration	Student Relations
Higher Education	Teacher Training & Instruction
Instructional Materials	Testing & Evaluation
Multimedia Learning Methodologies	Textbook Review & Selection

Following are some excellent examples of cover letters for teaching and education careers.

MATTHEW R. JONES

4315 East Elizabeth Street • Tampa, FL 33607
Phone (813) 934-7362 • mrjones@hotmail.com

June 7, 2006

Mr. Albert Heinz
Principal
Baxter Elementary School
250 Sampson Road
Tampa, FL 33629

Dear Mr. Heinz:

This letter is to express my strong interest in joining your elementary school as a Physical Education teacher. With specific skills in student instruction, athletic conditioning, and team sports, I feel I can provide your Physical Education department with a high degree of professionalism and excellence.

Highlights of my strengths include:

- **Student Instruction** – Assisted in coordinating summer baseball camps for 5-13 year olds (averaging 50 campers per week) for the past four years. Also served as Head Coach for the Junior Varsity Baseball Team at The University of South Florida for the past four years. Relevant experience also includes working as a Summer Camp Instructor for six summers for 5-13 year olds.

- **Well-versed in Conditioning & Weight Training** – Currently, a YMCA Fitness Assistant and previously the Conditioning Coordinator for The University of South Florida's baseball team.

- **Strong Background in Baseball; Overall Love of Sports** – Presently, the Assistant Pitching Coach for the University of South Florida. Responsible for 21 JV players moving up to Varsity over the course of five seasons. As an undergraduate, a four-year pitcher with the team.

For these reasons and more, I am confident that your students would benefit from my diligent work ethic, friendly demeanor, and professional instructional style.

I am available to interview at your earliest convenience. Your time and consideration are much appreciated.

Sincerely,

Matthew R. Jones

Enclosure

Written By: Laurie Berenson
Font: Tahoma

Jana Elyse Franconia

628 East Church Street
Denver, CO 80207

(303) 935-8672
jefranconia@yahoo.com

March 31, 2006

Ms. Ruth Frazier
Green Valley Elementary School
400 Jericho Street
Denver, CO 80249

Dear Ms. Frazier:

I am an Elementary School Teacher with five years of experience and a strong desire to grow as a professional educator. After earning my Bachelor's degree from Flagler College in Florida, I moved to Colorado so that I could be a part of the International Baccalaureate—Primary Years Program at Liberty Magnet Elementary School. My days at Liberty have been tremendously rewarding, but I am now ready and eager to consider opportunities at innovative schools in the Denver area.

My teaching methodologies focus on hands-on, investigative, and collaborative activities. These strategies engage my students, encouraging them to learn and apply key concepts. I have also found that lessons with these components allow me to provide differentiated instruction. In addition to applying my current knowledge to the classroom, I am continually expanding my teaching strategies and currently earning a Master of Arts in Curriculum and Instruction at the University of Denver.

I have heard great things about Green Valley Elementary School including its excellence in student performance, teacher collaboration, and parental involvement. My teaching approach and credentials should make me a great match for your school. I would like to speak with you about openings for the 2006/2007 school year. If you have questions, please call me at 935-8672 or e-mail me at jefranconia@yahoo.com. I will contact you soon to arrange a meeting and look forward to speaking with you.

Sincerely,

Jana Elyse Franconia

Enclosure

Written By: Julie Rains
Font: Bookman Old Style

NORA BENET

97 Crestville Court ◆ Easton, PA 18040 ◆ (215) 730-0500 ◆ benet@aol.com

October 7, 2006

James Johnson, Ed. D., Principal
Elmerton School District
11 Main Street
Easton, PA 18042

Dear Dr. Johnson:

As a well-regarded elementary school teacher who is passionate about creating positive educational experiences for students, I believe I offer expertise that would make me a welcome and valuable addition to your teaching staff. With strong lesson planning and classroom management skills, a talent for engaging and enthusing students, and the proven ability to tailor activities to meet a broad range of student needs, I would like to consider the possibility of putting my knowledge and experience to work for you.

As you can see from my enclosed resume, my background includes an array of instructional experiences. Most recently, I served as a substitute teacher in the Kingwood Township School District, where I was highly sought after for my dedication and willingness to actively participate in the presentation of daily lessons. I also have more than seven years of full-time teaching experience, most notably at the Tenth Street School in Newark where I spent four years teaching grades 4 through 6.

As a teacher, I pride myself on my creativity and adaptability in the classroom and my determination to do everything I can to help students succeed. I am pleased to say that my efforts have paid off considerably. For example, I have been successful in substantially raising mathematics test scores in an inner-city school, bringing math and science teams from that same school to district-wide competitions, and helping students develop mastery in mathematics, reading, writing, and study skills.

Among my other strengths, you will find that I am someone who always seeks to expand my skills and who enjoys bringing new knowledge into the classroom. I also enjoy being actively involved in education and have a strong record in leadership and service. Dedicated to my students and passionate about helping them to succeed, I believe I exude a sense of warmth and caring that students readily respond to. With these skills and my solid instructional foundation, I am confident that I will prove to be an asset to your school.

I would be pleased to have the opportunity to discuss your needs and how my capabilities can meet them. Please feel free to contact me at the address and phone number listed above to arrange an interview. I look forward to speaking with you soon.

Thank you for your consideration.

Sincerely,

Nora Benet

Enclosure

Written By: Carol Altomare
Font: Georgia

Sharon T. Grassi

2772 Alberta Place, Lawrenceville, NJ 08648
609-771-5555 Home ▪ 609-201-7777 Cell ▪ sharonT@comcast.net

May 14, 2006

Ms. Delores Atherton
Secretary to the Superintendent
Board of Education
1665 Lawrenceville Road
Lawrenceville, NJ 08648

Dear Ms. Atherton:

It's that time again! Spring is here and your office will probably be receiving many inquiries from applicants interested in teaching in your district. You may be asking yourself, "What makes this person (Sharon) stand out from the crowd?" In one word – plenty!

Please take a moment to review my resume (enclosed). Like many teaching applicants, I am certified in New Jersey as an Elementary Education Teacher (K-5). However, with 25 months of elementary and middle-school teaching experience, coupled with a Master's Degree in Elementary Education, I am most decidedly unlike many teaching applicants. Here are a few more facts that set me apart from the crowd:

⇒ **Increased Student Learning in Math.** Designed and delivered skill-building activity for basic math that improved second-grade students' test results by 50%.

⇒ **Improved Students' Writing Skills.** Dramatically improved second-graders' writing skills by introducing a 5-step writing process, modeling effective writing strategies, and sharing my passion for writing. Student portfolios and stories now encompass advanced concepts such as story logic and progression, along with improved grammar, punctuation, and sentence structure.

⇒ **Developed Students' Social Skills.** Encouraged positive interactions, self-respect and respect for others, sharing and generosity, awareness of others' needs, and good manners with current class of second-grade students. They are now recognized by teachers, staff, administrators, parents, and other students as "role-model" students for the entire school.

⇒ **Built Students' Self-Confidence.** Used creative opportunities, such as role-plays, choreographed dance routines, and short plays to get students involved in self-esteem building activities (some of these before the entire student body). Recognition by their peers and others has led to remarkable student transformations and eagerly anticipated planning for upcoming events.

All of this was accomplished during my first year as a full-time teacher (2005-2006 school year)!

If you have an elementary-level teaching position available for someone who gets solid instructional results by taking initiative, promoting students' creativity and confidence, and engaging the FUN factor, then we should meet. I would be delighted to speak with you at your convenience. Thank you for your consideration.

Sincerely,

Sharon T. Grassi

Enclosure: Resume

Written By: Susan Guameri
Font: Tahoma

ESTRELLA RODRIGUEZ
5830 Chavez Avenue • Chino, California 91710
909 921-5678 • erodriguez@resumesos.com

August 10, 2006

Dr. Linda Travis
Director of Human Resources
Los Angeles Community College District
10128 Wilshire Boulevard
Los Angeles, CA 90038

RE: EOP&S Full-Time Counselor

To the Selection Committee:

What an exciting opportunity you are offering! Currently, I am a part-time Counselor and Adjunct Faculty member at Citrus Community College and would love to be considered for a full-time counseling/teaching position. The value I bring to Citrus Community College is as a well-rounded EOP&S Counselor/Educator with more than **10 years of experience in financial aid**.

My passion lies in assisting students to succeed no matter what their academic, socioeconomic, cultural, or ethnic backgrounds. I possess great empathy for the students and can easily relate to them as I was a first-generation, college-bound Hispanic student. I am living proof of what can be accomplished and this serves as great encouragement to students who are academically unprepared. To them, I represent the bridge that closes the gap.

What I would like to contribute to Los Angeles Pierce College is the concept of Learning Communities in which I already volunteer as an instructor and facilitator. An enthusiastic, high-energy educator with a proven track record in fostering academic learning and enhancing student creativity, I believe in making learning as much fun as possible. As such, I have taught **Career, Education, and College Planning** courses that were linked with English, Math, Communications, and Learning Assistance courses along with other counseling faculty. The result was acknowledgment for **raising the bar** in elevating students' standards and **igniting their curiosity**.

As my accompanying resume and letters of recommendation show, I always have the student's best interest at heart. An effective listener and counselor, I am continuously seeking avenues to facilitate a student's college and career success.

An excellent fit exists between your requirements and my background. To be part of the Los Angeles Pierce College community would be an honor, and I look forward to the opportunity to discuss my experience in greater detail. In the interim, thank you for your consideration, attention, and forthcoming response.

Sincerely,

Estrella Rodriguez

Enclosure

Written By: Myriam-Rose Kohn
Font: Arial

Oscar Brown

5415 N Clark Street
Chicago, IL 60604
(773) 907-8660
oscarbrown@acme.com

November 22, 2006

Ms. Mary Ellen Masters
Executive Director, Hiring Committee
Chicago School District Headquarters
11 Main Street
Chicago, IL 60601

Dear Ms. Masters:

Your posting for Director of Student Support Services is most interesting. The enclosed resume outlines my experience and achievements, and I am happy to provide references or further information at your request.

As my resume indicates, I have served in leadership roles on both the building and district level. Working closely with the Principal of Jackson Elementary School (Winslow, Illinois), I have been involved in all aspects of building management. One result of our partnership has been a teacher enrichment workshop that led to improved reading scores. At schools in Winslow and Ellington, I have been responsible for curriculum and discipline. My approach to discipline involves more than simple punishment. Bringing students, parents, and teachers together, I want all parties to agree on what responsible behavior is and to accept that improper behavior has consequences.

Recently, I have had the opportunity to supplement my graduate studies by working with the Winslow District Superintendent in areas that include curriculum, personnel, purchasing, and budgeting. My duties included analyzing a proposed budget, assessing purchasing options, and recommending changes. The Superintendent taught me how to consider all options before making any decision. His action – clear and resolute – provided me with a great example of how to be a leader. I am confident that this combination of attitude, skill, and experience will make me a valuable member of your leadership team.

This summary cannot fully communicate my potential contribution to your district and its students. I would appreciate the opportunity to speak with you personally and answer your questions.

Thank you for your consideration.

Sincerely,

Oscar Brown

Enclosure

Written By: Clay Cerny
Font: Georgia

JOSEPH BLOOMBERG

8756 Choice Drive
Sterling Heights, MI 48312

bloombergjb@aol.com
586-555-7726

March 11, 2006

John R. Sebastian, Ed.D.
Hiring Committee
Cincinnati Public School System
9000 Reed Boulevard
Cincinnati, OH 43242

Dear Dr. Sebastian:

Having made the decision to relocate my family to Cincinnati, I've found your advertisement for an Elementary School Principal position on the Ohio Association of School Administrators' website. This letter is to introduce myself as a candidate for that opportunity.

With over 14 years of experience as an administrator and educator, I believe my qualifications ideally match your requirements. As a Principal of a rural elementary school, I have the experience necessary to lead, supervise, and evaluate the instructional program for your school. My achievements range from successfully bridging the gap between low-income and high-income students, to rebuilding both the school building and hopes of students and staff. Highlights of my qualifications include:

- Built by hand, with the help of parent/student volunteers, a new computer lab, library, resource facility, and athletic stadium after an arson fire destroyed the school.
- Achieved the highest rating among 13 schools in the district, having the highest State test scores in the county for seven years in a row.
- Created an enthusiastic learning approach through empowering faculty with support and positive reinforcement.
- Partnered with United States Forest Service and Michigan State Parks to author funding grants that governed two outdoor schools.
- Collaborated with and trained staff on introducing a new "character-teaching" curriculum and its implementation through electives.

Having the opportunity to actually teach children is an extremely humbling experience. Having the opportunity to govern the procedures, processes, and performances of staff and students is just as challenging, but even more rewarding.

The enclosed resume briefly outlines my experience and accomplishments. With family in Ohio, I am planning to relocate to the Cincinnati area, and can begin work immediately. If it appears that my qualifications meet your current needs, I can be available for an interview at your convenience. I look forward to it!

Sincerely,

Joseph Bloomberg

Enclosure

Written By: Erin Kennedy
Font: Times New Roman

GEORGE R. DEMER, ED.D.

6749 Shipley * Virginia Beach, VA 23865
410-338-9845 (h) * demer@aol.com

May 20, 2006

Office of Human Resources
Community Colleges of Virginia
205 N. Baines Blvd.
P.O. Box 6489
Richmond, VA 23860

RE: District Director of Athletics, Physical Education, and Recreation

Dear Human Resources Director:

I am interested in applying for the position of District Director of Athletics, Physical Education and Recreation for the Community Colleges of Virginia to provide your students and the colleges with the greatest opportunities to flourish in athletics. Over the years, I have effectively grown the wrestling department at Rogers College into a winning organization, well-recognized and respected in the sports community. Moreover, my experience is a unique combination of education, coaching, business, and administration.

I am an enthusiastic University Associate Professor, Sports Coach, and Business Owner, offering my expertise in planning, organizing, and administering sports departments. I meet or exceed your requirements with a mix of education and experience for the position of District Director of Athletics, Physical Education, and Recreation:

Your Requirements	My Qualifications
Master's Degree	Ph.D. in Sport, Leisure, and Exercise Science, Concentration in Educational Sport Psychology. M.S. in Physical Education, Concentration in Sport Psychology.
5+ years of experience in teaching and administrative functions including fiscal and budget management	15 years of combined experience as an instructor/teacher, head wrestling coach, and administrator for business, an athletic department, and Graduate Independent Studies. Manage multiple operational budgets and control fiscal management for sports and business organizations.

May 20, 2006
Office of Human Resources
Page Two

Excellent communicator	Coach, instruct, and mentor students from varied socioeconomic, cultural, and religious backgrounds; communicate athletic, recreational, PE, and intramural policies, goals, and obligations to staff, students/athletes, parents, and the community, including coaches as the President of the Division VIII National Coaches Association.
Contracting	Pursue, negotiate, and administer contracts for various services: busses, facilities, food, and equipment.
Vision, Values, and Goals for the CCS	Fifteen years of experience developing visions for sports teams and sports departments—to create the best possible learning and athletic environments for students and staff.

Enclosed please find the completed application package for the position of District Director of Athletics, Physical Education, and Recreation:

- Signed Application Form
- Letter of Application
- Detailed Resume
- Transcripts

I would welcome the opportunity to speak with your interview team to further describe how I can fulfill your requirements as the District Director of Athletics, Physical Education, and Recreation. Please refer to the enclosed resume and application package for more detailed information regarding my career history and contributions.

I look forward to hearing from your office regarding the next step in the interview process with your college system. Please contact me for additional information.

Thank you for your time and consideration.

Sincerely,

George R. Demer, Ed.D.

Enclosures

Written By: Diane Burns
Font: Book Antiqua

MATTHEW M. GRUNERT
mmgrunert@excite.com
2265 Reynolds Run Drive
Atlanta, GA 30302
404.555.9825

August 19, 2006

National Action Council for Minorities in Engineering
President & Chief Executive Officer Search
1978 Washington Boulevard, Suite 404
Alexandria, VA 22001

Dear Sir/Madam:

I am currently employed as the Director of Educational Initiatives—Corporate University Relations for DEC-NET Computers. In this position for the past five years I have orchestrated a number of programs nationwide to facilitate minority access to educational, training and career opportunities in engineering, science and technology. The scope of my experience is directly in line with the search requirements for the President/CEO of NACME, and I have enclosed my resume, executive profile and references for your review. Additionally, I have completed several key initiatives that I would like to bring to your attention:

- Forged industry-leading partnerships with major educational institutions nationwide to provide technological expertise in advancing their technology infrastructures and student educational opportunities. Currently working on programs with the University of Dallas, University of Nevada, University of Northern Idaho, the State Departments of Education in Georgia and Alabama, and several other institutions.

- Negotiated public/private partnerships to fund and develop emerging technologies (e.g., data mining, virtual learning, global learning, computer modeling/simulation, speech recognition, web-based ventures).

- Led development and funding for DEC-NET's Ph.D. Fellowship in Science, Engineering and Mathematics for Under-represented Minorities and Women.

- Developed and funded several educational grant programs targeted exclusively to African-American, Latino and other minority groups.

- Pioneered innovative technology-based educational opportunities for university and school administrators, educators and students.

- Researched and prepared benchmark analysis of DEC-NET's performance in minority recruitment as compared to other major industry players.

- Created a legal system and business process to stimulate DEC-NET professionals to engage in productive partnerships and interactions with minority universities.

In each and every project we undertake, we are committed to not only increasing educational opportunities, but promoting increased student retention rates, improved academic performance, cultural diversity in the workplace and lifelong career decision-making. And we have succeeded. To date, these initiatives have provided new and enriched educational opportunities for more than 2000 students across the country.

National Action Council for Minorities in Engineering
President & Chief Executive Officer Search
Page Two

Just as critical, my team and I have positioned our organization as a sought-after resource and the preferred method of action throughout DEC-NET and with our customers to recruit and develop a diverse workforce with a special focus on under-represented minorities. Collateral responsibilities have included:

- Steering Committee Team Leader—People with Disabilities in Technology.

- Peer Reviewer—National Science Foundation's Centers for Excellence in Science and Technology. Presented DEC-NET program to representatives of 13 minority-serving institutions.

- Guest Speaker—The Association of Computer & Information Science at Minority Institutions' annual meeting. Presented to 200 minority students interested in science, engineering and mathematics from universities nationwide.

- Senior Advisor—Model Institutions of Technological Excellence. Industry partner to six minority-serving institutions to increase the pipeline of well-trained minorities pursuing careers in mathematics, science and engineering.

Complementing all of this experience are my strengths in strategic planning, organizational leadership, team building, project management, finance and law. Further, I have extensive experience managing relationships with Boards of Directors and other top-level executives. I am an independent thinker and decision-maker, creative in my program and project management efforts, and successful in building solid business systems and infrastructures. What's more, I thoroughly enjoy working with the academic community and know what it takes to win their support and cooperation.

Be advised that my job search is confidential. I am not actively in the market, but am intrigued by the opportunity with NACME and look forward to interviewing with you. Please let me know if you would like any additional information. Thank you.

Sincerely,

Matthew M. Grunert

Enclosure

Written By: Wendy Enelow
Font: Tahoma

Chapter 16

▶ Cover Letters for

Technology, Science, and Engineering Careers

Your cover letter presents an excellent opportunity to show prospective employers and recruiters how the skills and accomplishments documented on your resume relate to their specific hiring needs. Each industry and profession presents unique cover letter writing and design challenges. If you are interested in pursuing a career in technology, science, or engineering, be certain to include highlights of these important success factors in your cover letters:

Success Factor #1

Technology, science, and engineering careers all require knowledge of technical equipment, computer systems and software, and much more. Be sure to mention relevant technical knowledge (for example, scientific/laboratory equipment, computer software and hardware, operating systems, and networks) to clearly communicate your qualifications and technical competencies.

Success Factor #2

Document any research papers, studies, or patents in which you have participated. Elaborate on projects relevant to the targeted position to demonstrate your keen interest in the subject matter.

Success Factor #3

Highlight projects on which you have worked and discuss how your participation contributed to the success of those projects (for example, under budget, ahead of schedule, exceeded customer expectations, or upgraded organizational capabilities).

ℝ Success Factor #4

Showcase all of your *extra* professional activities, which may include public speaking, professional affiliations, publications, or teaching/training. If any of these are directly relevant to the opening you're targeting, highlight those in even more detail.

Keywords and Keyword Phrases

Keywords and keyword phrases are critical components of every successful job seeker's cover letter. By using just one or two words, you're able to communicate a wealth of information about your skills, qualifications, and experience. What's more, keywords are the basis for scanning technology and are therefore critical to every job seeker's campaign in today's electronic-based job search market.

Following are the top 20 technology, science, and engineering keywords, some of which may reflect your skills and some of which may not be appropriate for you at this time. Use these words as the foundation for developing your own list of keywords on the Professional Keyword List form in Appendix B.

Top 20 Keywords

Applications Development	Project Planning & Management
Capital Projects	Prototype Development & Testing
E-Commerce	Research & Experimentation
Engineering Design	Scientific Methodologies
Fault Isolation & Analysis	Systems Engineering
Information Services Management	Technical Writing
Information Technology	Technology Transfer
Multimedia Technology Integration	User Training & Support
Network Design & Technology	VOIP Technology
Performance Optimization	Website Design & Management

Following are some excellent examples of cover letters for technology, science, and engineering careers.

Stella Gordon

12 Miami Road
Fort Lauderdale, FL 33090
315-555-8276
Stella2g@comcast.net

August 16, 2006

Mr. T. Rogers
Manager, Summer Student Program
Liberty Hydro
123 Main Street Avenue, 8th Floor
Miami, FL 33090

Re: Summer Student—Engineering

Dear Mr. Rogers:

Are you looking for a dedicated, focused, and successful summer student committed to excelling in the areas of Mechanical Engineering and / or Applied Sciences?

As a student at King University, I am pursuing a Bachelor of Engineering and Applied Sciences degree. My goals are to find an opportunity that will allow me to demonstrate my base knowledge of concepts and theories, and to explore how they are applied in the day-to-day management of an organization.

I approach all of my projects and work with discipline and organization. As a summer student with Liberty Hydro, I would strive to effectively contribute to your departmental goals and objectives. King's Mechanical Engineering Department and my professors have acknowledged my academic and leadership achievements for excellence in my studies, volunteerism, and peer mentoring.

Thank you for your time and consideration. I am excited about the opportunity to work at Liberty Hydro and believe that my education, enthusiasm, and willingness to learn new things will make me an effective member of your team.

Sincerely,

Stella Gordon

[Resume enclosed]

Written By: Denyse Cowling
Font: Tahoma

THOMAS S. STROMBERG

3489 East Main Street
Mainstream, IL 60107

tss3489@yahoo.com

Home (678) 992-2776
Office (678) 786-4532

March 11, 2006

John A. Clements
Director of Technology Recruitment
AAA Recruiters, Inc.
22 Main Ledge Road
Chicago, IL 60637

Re: Technology Management Opportunities

Dear Mr. Clements:

With a PMI Certification from George Washington University and extensive practical program management and system integration experience, I am currently seeking a challenging and rewarding opportunity in which I can direct teams of technical professionals in achieving project deliverables. I welcome a discussion about any current search assignments you have for a candidate with my qualifications and experience.

For the past 12 years, I have been a dedicated and reliable employee of USA Corporation, with the past five years encompassing management of a wide variety of technical projects. Having established a reputation for outstanding project planning and implementation, I consistently deliver projects on time and always surpass user expectations.

The value I bring to an organization includes:

- Motivating leadership skills with the ability to foster cooperation and maximum productivity in matrix team environments.

- Outstanding planning abilities and meticulous attention to details to ensure project success.

- Resourceful problem-solving skills with foresight in anticipating potential risks.

After you have reviewed my attached resume, please contact me so that we can discuss any appropriate search assignments. Please note that I am open to relocation and anticipate a compensation package in excess of $75,000 annually. Thank you.

Sincerely,

Thomas S. Stromberg

Enclosure

Written By: Rosemary Fish Justen
Font: Times

3986 Trails Court
Columbia, MD 21054

BRETT REYNOLDS

410-398-3985
Brett_Rey@yahoo.com

April 20, 2006

Marc Byron, Human Resources Director
Raytheon
2398 James Road, Suite 123
Baltimore, MD 21205

RE: Systems Engineer

Dear Mr. Byron:

I am currently enrolled at the University of Baltimore to attain a Master's Degree in Systems Engineering, which will complement my Bachelor's Degree in Electrical Engineering and my experience as an Associate Engineer/Research Engineer.

In the past year, I was called to active duty to lead troops in the Middle East, boosting my leadership and communication skills. Please refer to the enclosed resume to review highlights of my Systems Engineering experience.

I meet the requirements you posted for the position of Systems Engineer:

- ☐ Worked on a number of design projects to create solutions related to processes.

- ☐ Served on a number of teams, as a team player or team leader. Managed contractor processes and provided excellent client relations.

- ☐ Technical knowledge of E3, SM, RF, EV, TOC, and M&S lifecycle.

- ☐ Management experience in the U.S. military (reserves).

- ☐ SECRET Clearance (required for your company).

I will contact your office in a few days to see if there is a convenient time to schedule an appointment to meet and further discuss this employment opportunity with your firm. I look forward to providing value and innovation to your projects and project teams.

Sincerely,

Brett Reynolds

Enclosure: Resume

Written By: Diane Burns
Font: Tahoma

LOUISE MIELZEWSKI

1221 Beaver Creek Road
Crayton, AL 33090-8877

Phone: 601.555.9088
millslou@datastar.net

May 24, 2006

David Wright
Technology Talent, Ltd.
11 Martinsburg Parkway
Building 22, Suite 202
Birmingham, AL 33982-1009

Dear Mr. Wright:

I am writing and forwarding my resume in anticipation that you may be interested in a candidate with more than **10 years of experience in information technology, software design and applications development**. Highlights of my career that may be of particular interest to you and your client companies include:

- Pioneering innovative, next-generation GPS and GIS applications.

- Evaluating organizational and operating needs to determine appropriate technologies.

- Designing, testing, and implementing new software and new applications for a broad range of engineering, technical, business, administrative, analysis, and reporting needs.

- Training and supervising less experienced technical and design teams.

- Developing new uses and applications for existing technologies.

- Improving performance, productivity, and efficiency of operations through technological enhancement.

I am most proud of a particular IT project I managed—the development of the only tidal projection software in the U.S. Navy. This was a major initiative that delivered a significant improvement in the Navy's ability to predict adverse tidal impact on land masses worldwide and, in turn, prevent catastrophic damage to people and property. Another notable project I orchestrated was the design of the back-end system for retail POS technology now in use by 11 out of 20 of the top retail firms in the country.

Currently, I am confidentially exploring new professional opportunities and would welcome a personal interview at your earliest convenience. I am open to relocation and anticipate a base salary at a minimum of $75,000, along with a strong portfolio of benefits. Thank you for your time and consideration. I'll follow up with you next week.

Sincerely,

Louise Mielzewski

Enclosure

Written By: Wendy Enelow
Font: Verdana

JOSE M. VASQUEZ

17855 Hollywood Blvd.   415-555-8433
Hollywood, CA 92371   jvasquez@hotmail.com

June 1, 2006

Martin Splicer
Macy's Department Stores
100 Macy Run Road
Dallas, TX 77090

Dear Mr. Splicer:

To remain competitive in today's global Internet marketplace, you need to have a clear vision, technical direction and strategy to take your business to its next level of operational, Internet market, and financial performance. Additionally, you need savvy and innovative Web developers who have already created front ends that have increased interest and additional revenue and traffic to the site.

My value to Macy's lies in the foundation of my experience in e-commerce: building out, testing sites, and maintaining sites. What sets me apart from others is my core understanding of front-end Web development, usability testing, search engine optimization, and e-mail marketing campaigns. Along with these, other highlights include:

- Revitalized a lackluster Internet wine retailer through site optimization, strong e-mail campaigns, and a front-end facelift, increasing sales up to 10% within 3 weeks.

- Created a wildly successful new testing method for application servers at ABC Computer Systems that is now a benchmark for testing new systems.

- Drove widget.com's ranking on Google to #1 after being in the #2 slot for years.

- Authored a hardware review that was published in *PC Computing* magazine.

While my core competencies lie in front-end Web development and site management, perhaps the greatest strength I offer can be found in my ability to drive change throughout an organization. I'm very successful at convincing management and staff alike of the corporate value to be gained through speedy resolutions to search engine optimization issues uncovered during testing. With dedicated training and motivation, I've built high-performance sites that meet customer requirements and standards.

Further, having taken 2 years off to travel through South America, Europe, and the United States, I was able to brush up on my Portuguese and Spanish, an asset when working with international accounts.

Confident that I would add immense value to Macy's, I would welcome the opportunity to discuss opportunities to join your Web development team where insights in designing and executing new quality strategies will result in significant top- and bottom-line growth. To that end, I have taken the liberty of enclosing a copy of my resume, and will phone next week to schedule an interview. Thank you.

Sincerely,

Jose Vasquez

Enclosure

Written By: Erin Kennedy
Font: Arial

SEAN P. O'CONNOR

74477 Rosewood Lane · Pleasant Lake, MI 49272 · 517-555-9606 · soconnor@hotmail.com

August 10, 2006

Joan Allen
Recruiter
Simmons Laboratories, Inc.
1000 Bellpointe Boulevard
Detroit, MI 49280

Dear Ms. Allen:

If your organization could benefit from a strong leader with proven achievements streamlining business processes, maintaining quality control, and governing production and testing in a lab environment, we should talk. I bring 18+ years of lab management experience in the science and technology industry.

The core of my expertise stems from an analytical perspective—concentration testing, flaw-to-background testing, sensitivity testing, and durability testing, while bringing together individual strengths and harnessing collective energies to build a highly process-focused, yet technology-driven lab.

As a seasoned leader, I know what it takes to manage several employees, direct logistics and procurement, and create value through continually monitoring quality performance. I also understand the necessity of having a solid team backed up by sound operational processes to drive daily employee performance. Evidence of my contributions can be seen through my success in:

- Managing the daily operations of a lab that manufactures non-destructive testing materials as dictated by military and society specifications.
- Overseeing several departments including research and development, purchasing, government contracts, safety and training while maintaining a fully operational facility.
- Continual monitoring of employee performances with a deep commitment to process and productivity improvement.
- Recognition as the only company to receive the ISO 9001:2000 certification within 9 months.

With my degrees in the science field, I am eager to transition into a senior-level laboratory management position with your company. Aware of the caliber and reputation Simmons holds in the marketplace, I would welcome the opportunity to meet with you, discuss your needs, and further demonstrate the value I offer as a Laboratory Manager or Director.

Thank you for your time and consideration. I look forward to the first of many positive communications.

Sincerely,

Sean P. O'Connor

Enclosure

Written By: Erin Kennedy
Font: Tahoma

GREG R. WILLIAMSON

grw@msn.com

1112 Ryeson Road   Madison, Virginia 22090   703-555-7761

July 27, 2006

George Appleton
Technology Recruiters of America, Inc.
11 Grover Street, Suite 1100
Charlottesville, VA 22087

Dear Mr. Appleton:

After a four-year tenure with Channel Media, orchestrating the development of advanced website and web content management technologies, I am ready to move on to new professional opportunities. As such, I am contacting you to see if one of your client companies may be interested in a candidate with my unique set of qualifications.

I can be of value to your clients in several capacities:

- **IT Operating Executive** managing complex internal IT organizations. As *Manager of Information Systems* for Peabody Software International, I built and led the entire technology organization as the company grew 400% in just two years.

- **Technology Product Manager** orchestrating the development, market launch, market positioning, sales and lifecycle of advanced technology products, services and solutions. As part of Xerox's Center for Technology Excellence, I facilitated the delivery of advanced networking solutions for major corporations nationwide (e.g., *AT&T, Merrill Lynch, New York Mercantile Exchange*).

- **Professional Services Leader** creating and directing teams selling integrated technology solutions. As *Vice President of Professional Services* for Exceleration, I built the company's first-ever professional services organization, which grew to be the #1 revenue stream in the organization.

In summary, building the strength, performance, operating capabilities and profitability of IT organizations is my expertise. By combining a keen strategic approach with strong technical qualifications, I have been successful in identifying and capitalizing on opportunities that have positively impacted the bottom line of each and every company with which I have been employed.

Now, at this point in my career, I am ready for a new challenge and look forward to speaking with you about any current search assignments for an IT executive with my qualifications. Please note that I am open to relocation and anticipate a salary well into the six figures.

Thank you.

Sincerely,

Greg R. Williamson

Enclosure

Written By: Wendy Enelow
Font: Arial

EUGENE FEDEROV
722 Walnut Grove • Manlius, New York 13077
315-234-4567 (H) / 315-674-0987 (C)
efederov@email.net

August 15, 2006

Mr. William Dorman
Chief Technology Officer
First Choice Telecommunications
1234 Telephone Road
East Syracuse, NY 13055

Dear Mr. Dorman:

With a 13-year track record working for Verizon in the development, implementation, and maintenance of customer relationship management systems and applications, I have knowledge and expertise that can be a valuable asset to First Choice Telecommunications. Attached for your review is a current resume outlining my background and qualifications.

Some capabilities that I can bring to a Web Development or Database Administrator role include:

- *Functioning as a subject matter expert for the HEAT trouble-ticketing system, which has been a key component of customer service operations for Verizon's upstate New York operations.*

- *Developing and administering Web-based tools and applications that facilitate efficient and effective reporting and problem resolution for internal users, and that provide value-added support for external customers.*

- *Implementing, modifying, and maintaining complex Customer Relationship Management (CRM) platforms, including in-depth expertise with HEAT and Clarify.*

- *Using a variety of web development and graphics tools, including Dreamweaver, XML, HTML, ASP, .NET, Cold Fusion, Adobe PhotoShop, and Adobe Illustrator.*

- *Administering current operating systems, including Windows Server (2000, 2003), MS SQL Server, Windows (XP, NT), Linux, and others.*

- *Managing data migration and user transition between platforms, which has included developing applications and facilitating user training.*

I am confident that my knowledge and expertise would allow me to significantly contribute to your IT operations. I would welcome an opportunity to discuss my qualifications with you in person, and encourage you to contact me to arrange an interview.

Thank you for your time and consideration. I look forward to speaking with you soon.

Sincerely,

Eugene Federov

Enclosure

Written By: Arnie Boldt
Font: Times New Roman

LILLIAN A. ARMSTRONG

909 Lucy Lane   Phone: 303.555.8263
Denver, CO 30309   lillarmstrong@aol.com

September 1, 2006

Grayson Arthur
Managing Director
Elevant Technologies, Inc.
700 Miller Boulevard
Denver, CO 30311

Dear Mr. Arthur:

Beginning my career as one of the first female engineers ever hired by Sprint, I progressed rapidly through a series of responsible technical, product development, marketing and sales management positions with Sprint, Lucent and Quasant (an early stage telecommunications venture acquired by Sprint). And, to each organization, I delivered strong and sustainable financial results:

- With Lucent for seven years, I closed a $25+ million contract with Dell and created the company's national account model. I then restored the Kodak relationship and negotiated a $20 million contract for telecommunications support throughout the Far East.

- With Quasant Telecommunications, I delivered a 122% increase in corporate sales in just one year as I raised $35 million to support product development and market expansion. The latter demonstrates the tremendous value and impact of my sales abilities, negotiating with investors and financiers to "sell" something that did not even yet exist.

- During my 14-year tenure with Sprint, I excelled. I sold their first-ever $100 million satellite contract, created a global technical sales support organization and delivered up to 200% of quota within just six months. The experience with Sprint was extraordinary.

Not only is my personal sales performance extremely strong, I am equally effective in recruiting, training and mentoring other sales professionals. I am able to develop a clear strategy, build consensus across diverse functional organizations, and drive sales teams to surpass the best of expectations. Further, my successes in building and managing relationships with top decision-makers of major corporate accounts have been vital to my performance.

I would welcome the chance to speak with you about senior sales and marketing leadership positions with your organization, and thank you for your consideration. I guarantee there has never been a sales situation or challenge that I was not able to meet and conquer.

Sincerely,

Lillian A. Armstrong

Enclosure

Written By: Wendy Enelow
Font: Bookman Old Style

DENNIS L. DAYTON

124 Elm Grove Road   (606) 555-2763
Duluth, MN 57382   dld2244@msn.com

December 11, 2006

Ms. Delores Jamerson
Director of Technical Recruiting
MARSH Technology, Inc.
4709 Delray Boulevard
Chicago, IL 60609

Dear Ms. Jamerson:

I am a Microsoft Certified Systems Engineer (MCSE) with 15 years of experience in Information Systems & Technology. My expertise spans two entirely different functions within the IT arena:

- *Systems Operations*. For 12 years, I managed all IT operations for the Emergency Medical Services Division of Laurel County in Minnesota. During that time, I directed several system upgrades to transition into a state-of-the-art Windows environment.

- *Systems Design & Installation*. For the past four years, I have managed an entrepreneurial venture with sole responsibility for the sale of technology consulting services and the design/delivery of customized technologies to meet a broad range of business applications. Most significantly, I facilitated over 1000 system and device upgrades, built and installed NT systems and networks, and supported 2000+ customers.

My technical proficiency is extensive and is summarized at the top of my resume. Additional information that may be of interest to you includes:

- *Outstanding customer relations skills*. I am able to quickly build and maintain positive working relationships with my customers, responding quickly to their technology support needs, and providing them with technical expertise to manage their work functions.

- *Entrepreneurial spirit and drive*. I thrive in challenging and fast-paced environments, relying on myself to make decisions, solve problems and move projects forward. I am an independent thinker, constantly ready to accept new challenges and new opportunities.

- *Staff training and leadership*. I have extensive experience in training, supervising and mentoring teams of technology professionals.

I would welcome the opportunity for a personal interview and thank you for your consideration. I guarantee you'll be impressed with the quality and depth of my technical expertise.

Sincerely,

Dennis L. Dayton

Enclosure

Written By: Wendy Enelow
Font: Verdana

LEWIS TURNER, JR.

2324 Lucy Boulevard
Smithtown, PA 19093

Phone: 601.555.0287
lewturner@datastar.net

June 10, 2006

Dawn Mumphy
Head of Recruiting Department
Oceanic Research Center, Inc.
100 Dade Mill Run
Miami, FL 33092

Dear Ms. Mumphy:

For the past 12 years, I have advanced through a series of increasingly responsible scientific and engineering positions with the Coast Guard Oceanographic Office. The opportunities have been tremendous, allowing me to work across a broad range of disciplines and providing me with outstanding qualifications in:

- Planning and independently conducting scientific research and experimentation, from initial planning through experimental design, data collection, analysis, synthesis and reporting.

- Managing oceanographic, seismic, geologic, electronic, and systems engineering projects.

- Coordinating project planning, staffing and performance management, including direct supervisory responsibility for up to 20 engineers, scientists and technologists.

- Developing advanced IT, software and applications as noted on the enclosed resume, with particular emphasis on digital, imaging and signal-processing technologies.

- Controlling $4 million in scientific, engineering and technology assets.

In addition, I have extensive technical/scientific writing and public presentation experience.

Currently, I am confidentially exploring new professional opportunities and would welcome a personal interview at your earliest convenience. Thank you.

Sincerely,

Lewis Turner, Jr.

Enclosure

Written By: Wendy Enelow
Font: Tahoma

Appendix A

▶ **Cover Letter Writing Worksheet**

Use this worksheet as a guide for gathering the critical information you will need to develop each of your cover letters. In fact, we suggest you make copies of this form so that you can use it each and every time you're preparing a cover letter.

Who You Are Applying To:

NAME: _____ TITLE: _____

COMPANY: _____

ADDRESS: _____

_____

CITY: _____ STATE: _____ ZIP: _____

FAX #: _____ E-MAIL: _____

Type of Letter:

[ ]   Company Ad-Response Letter

[ ]   Recruiter Ad-Response Letter

[ ]   Company Cold-Call Letter

[ ]   Recruiter Cold-Call Letter

[ ]   Referral Letter (Referral: _____)

POSITION: _____ JOB # _____

Related Educational Credentials or Licenses:

_____

_____

_____

Critical Information To Include:

EMPLOYER'S #1 KEY REQUIREMENT (or need identified from your research):

_____

_____

_____

YOUR SKILLS/ACCOMPLISHMENTS THAT MATCH REQUIREMENT #1:

_____

_____

_____

EMPLOYER'S #2 KEY REQUIREMENT (or need identified from your research):

_____

_____

_____

YOUR SKILLS/ACCOMPLISHMENTS THAT MATCH REQUIREMENT #2:

_____

_____

_____

_____

EMPLOYER'S #3 KEY REQUIREMENT (or need identified from your research):

_____

_____

_____

YOUR SKILLS/ACCOMPLISHMENTS THAT MATCH REQUIREMENT #3:

_____

_____

_____

_____

EMPLOYER'S #4 KEY REQUIREMENT (or need identified from your research):

_____

_____

_____

_____

YOUR SKILLS/ACCOMPLISHMENTS THAT MATCH REQUIREMENT #4:

_____

_____

_____

_____

EMPLOYER'S #5 KEY REQUIREMENT (or need identified from your research):

_____

_____

_____

_____

YOUR SKILLS/ACCOMPLISHMENTS THAT MATCH REQUIREMENT #5:

_____

_____

_____

_____

(Use additional sheets, if necessary, to capture more of your skills and accomplishments.)

Appendix B

▶ **Professional Keyword List**

Each cover letter example chapter in this book (Chapters 5–16) has a list of keywords relating to the particular career field or profession covered in that chapter.

Use this form to highlight all the keywords and keyword phrases that accurately reflect *your* skills, qualifications, and experience.

_____

_____

_____

_____

_____

_____

_____

_____

_____

_____

Appendix C

▶ **List of Contributors**

The following professional resume writers have contributed their *best* cover letters to this publication. All have years of experience in professional resume and cover letter writing; many have earned distinguishing professional credentials, which include:

Bcomm Bachelors in Communications (Canada)

CARW Certified Advanced Resume Writer

CCM Credentialed Career Master

CCMC Certified Career Management Coach

CCTJ Certified Career Transition Jumpmaster

CDP Career Development Practitioner

CEIC Certified Employment Interview Consultant

CEIP Certified Employment Interview Professional

CERW Certified Expert Resume Writer

CIC Certified Interview Coach

CIS Certified Interview Strategist

CJCTC Certified Job & Career Transition Coach

CJST Certified Job Search Trainer

CLTMC Certified Leadership & Talent Management Coach

CMP Certified Management Professional

CPBS Certified Personal Brand Strategist

CPC Certified Personnel Consultant

CPCC Certified Professional Career Coach

CPRW Certified Professional Resume Writer

CTMS Certified Transition Management Seminars

CTSB Certified Targeted Small Business

CWDP Certified Workforce Development Professional

FJSTC Certified Federal Job Search Trainer & Counselor

IJCTC International Job & Career Transition Coach

JCTC Job & Career Transition Coach

MA Master of Arts

MBA Master of Business Administration

MCDP Master Career Development Professional

MS Master of Science

NCCC Nationally Certified Career Coach

NCRW Nationally Certified Resume Writer

RPR Registered Professional Recruiter

Carol Altomare, CPRW
World Class Resumes, Flemington, N.J.
caa@worldclassresumes.com
www.worldclassresumes.com
(908) 237-1883

Paul Bennett, BComm, CPRW
TARGET Career Services,
    Vancouver, BC, Canada
paul@targetcareerservices.com
www.targetcareerservices.com
(888) 782-7438 / (604) 876-9980

Laurie Berenson, CPRW
Sterling Career Concepts, LLC, Park
    Ridge, N.J.
laurie@sterlingcareerconcepts.com
www.SterlingCareerConcepts.com
(201) 573-8282

Anne Brunelle, Career Transitions
    Coach
Making Changes, Toronto, ON, Canada
info@makingchanges.ca
www.makingchanges.ca
(647) 224-8287

Diane Burns, CCMC, CPCC,
    CLTMC, CPRW, FJSTC, IJCTC,
    CEIP
Career Marketing Techniques, Boise,
    Idaho
diane@polishedresumes.com
www.polishedresumes.com
(208) 323-9636

Clay Cerny, Ph.D.
AAA Targeted Writing & Coaching,
    Chicago, Ill.
claycerny2@msn.com
(773) 907-8660

Denyse Cowling, CIS, CPC, RPR
Career Intelligence, Inc., Burlington,
    ON, Canada
dcowlings@cogeco.ca
www.careerintelligence.ca
(866) 909-0128

John Femia, BS, CPRW
Custom Resume & Writing Service,
    Altamont, N.Y.
customresume1@aol.com
www.customresumewriting.com
(518) 872-1305

Gail Frank, NCRW, CPRW, JCTC,
CEIP
Frankly Speaking: Resumes That
Work, Tampa, Fla.
gailfrank@post.harvard.edu
www.callfranklyspeaking.com
(813) 926-1353

Louise Garver, MA, CMP, CPRW,
CEIP, MCDP, JCTC
Career Directions LLC, Enfield, Conn.
LouiseGarver@cox.net
www.careerdirectionsllc.com
(860) 623-9476

Jill Grindle, CPRW
Resume Inkstincts, Agawam, Mass.
j.grindle@resumeinkstincts.com
www.resumeinkstincts.com
(413) 789-6046

Susan Guarneri, NCCC, CCMC,
CPBS, CERW, CCTJ, CPRW
Guarneri Associates, Three Lakes, Wis.
Resumagic@aol.com
www.resume-magic.com
(866) 881-4055

Michele J. Haffner, CCMC, CPRW,
JCTC
Advanced Resume Services, Glendale, Wis.
mhaffner@wi.rr.com
www.resumeservices.com
(888) 586-2258

Loretta Heck
All Word Services, Prospect Heights, Ill.
siegfried@ameritech.net
(847) 215-7517

Susan Hoopes, CJST, CJCTC, CWDP
Cuyahoga Valley Career Center,
Brecksville, Ohio
susan.hoopes@cvcc.k12.oh.us
www.cvccworks.com
(440) 746-8260

Rosemary Fish Justen, CPRW, CEIP
Creative Communication Services, Inc.,
Schaumburg, Ill.
rosemary@CCSResumes.com
www.ccsresumes.com
(847) 490-8686

Erin Kennedy, CPRW
Professional Resume Services,
Lapeer, Mich.
ekennedy@proreswriters.com
www.proreswriters.com
(206) 339-2876

Myriam-Rose Kohn, CPBS, CCM,
CCMC, IJCTC, CPRW, CEIP
Jeda Enterprises, Valencia, Calif.
myriam-rose@jedaenterprises.com
www.jedaenterprises.com
(661) 253-0801

Brian Leeson, MS
Vector Consultants Pty Ltd,
Echunga, South Australia, Australia
vector@adelaide.on.net
www.vectorconsultants.com.au
+61 8 8388 8183

Linda Matias, JCTC, CIC, NCRW
CareerStrides, Long Island, N.Y.
linda@careerstrides.com
www.careerstrides.com
(631) 387-1894

Melanie Noonan
Peripheral Pro, LLC, West Paterson, N.J.
PeriPro1@aol.com
(973) 785-3011

Don Orlando, MBA, CPRW, JCTC,
CCM, CCMC
The McLean Group,
Montgomery, Ala.
yourcareercoach@charterinternet.com
(334) 264-2020

Julie Rains, CPRW
Executive Correspondents,Clemmons,
    N.C.
jr@workingtolive.com
www.workingtolive.com
(336) 712-2390

Michelle Mastruserio Reitz, CPRW
Printed Pages, Cincinnati, Ohio
michelle@printedpages.com
www.printedpages.com
(513) 598-9100

Christine Robinson
Lima, N.Y.
CreativesMarketing@rochester.rr.com
www.CreativesMarketing.com
(585) 624-4232

Jennifer Rushton, CARW, CEIC,
    Keraijen Certified Resume Writer
Sydney, NSW, Australia
info@keraijen.com.au
www.keraijen.com.au
+ 61 2 9994 8050

Barbara Safani, MA, CERW, NCRW,
    CPRW, CCM
Career Solvers, New York, N.Y.
info@careersolvers.com
www.careersolvers.com
(866) 333-1800

Janice M. Shepherd, CPRW, JCTC, CEIP
Write On Career Keys, Bellingham, Wash.
janice@writeoncareerkeys.com
www.writeoncareerkeys.com
(360) 738-7958

Billie Ruth Sucher, MS, CTMS,
    CTSB, JCTC
Billie Ruth Sucher & Associates,
    Urbandale, Iowa
billie@billiesucher.com
www.billiesucher.com
(515) 276-0061

Edward Turilli, MA, CPRW
AccuWriter Resume, Writing &
    Career Services, Bonita Springs, Fla.
edtur@comcast.net
(239) 948-7741
North Kingstown, R.I.
edtur@cox.net
www.resumes4-u.com
(401) 268-3020

James Walker, MS
Serco, Inc., Fort Riley, Kans.
jwalker8199@yahoo.com
(785) 239-2278

Daisy Wright, CDP
The Wright Career Solution,
    Brampton, ON, Canada
daisy@thewrightcareer.com
www.thewrightcareer.com
(905) 840-7039

*I*ndex

About the Authors

▶ Arnold G. Boldt

After experiencing his own "downsizing" in 1994, Arnie Boldt explored a number of options before partnering with his wife, Gail Smith Boldt, to form Arnold-Smith Associates, which has helped thousands of job seekers who have found themselves in transition. Since then, he has honed his skills to become recognized as one of the premier resume writers in the country, contributing to more than 30 different books by eight different authors, including numerous titles by *No-Nonsense Resumes* co-author, Wendy Enelow.

In 2004, he was nominated for two prestigious TORI Awards (presented by Career Directors International) in the categories of Best Creative Resume and Best Cover Letter. He has spoken on resume-related topics to groups in the healthcare and manufacturing fields, as well as delivering presentations geared to the older worker and to executives in transition.

Mr. Boldt holds a Bachelor's degree in Technical Communications from Clarkson University and is a Certified Professional Resume Writer and Job & Career Transition Coach. He prides himself on his experience working with the broadest array of clients, ranging from tradespeople and new graduates to corporate executives. A lifelong resident of upstate New York, he makes his home with his wife and two Chihuahuas in a suburb of Rochester.

▶ Wendy S. Enelow

Wendy Enelow is a well-known and well-respected authority in resume writing and career coaching, and has been in private practice for more than 25 years. To date, she has guided more than 5,000 professional, management, and executive clients to achieve their career goals by providing them with best-in-class resumes, cover letters, and job search strategies. In addition, she has authored more than 20 books on resume and cover letter writing, job searching, key words, interviewing, and more.

Ms. Enelow is a frequently requested speaker at national conferences and workshops including the International Career Development Conference, Career Masters Institute Annual Professional Conference, National Employment Counseling Association Annual Conference, President's National Hire Veterans Committee, Professional Association of Resume Writers Annual Conference, Venture for Enterprising Women, and many more. In addition, she has been interviewed by major media outlets nationwide and has more than 100 articles published on various Internet sites.

Ms. Enelow holds a Bachelor's degree in Psychology from the University of Maryland. She is a Credentialed Career Master, Master Resume Writer, Job and Career Transition Coach, and Certified Professional Resume Writer. Ms. Enelow currently resides with her husband and pet menagerie in southwestern Virginia.